Action Research

Since its first publication, *Action Research: Principles and practice* has become a key text in its field. This new updated edition clearly describes and explains the practices of action research and its underlying values, and introduces important new ideas, including that:

- all professionals should be reflective practitioners;
- they should produce their personal theories of practice to show how they are holding themselves accountable for their educational influences in learning;
- the stories they produce should become a new people's history of action research, with potential for influencing new futures.

This new edition has expanded in scope, to contribute to diverse fields including professional development across the sectors and the disciplines. It considers the current field, including its problems as well as its considerable hopes and prospects for new thinking and practices. Now fully updated, this book contains:

- a wealth of case study material;
- new chapters on the educational significance of action research;
- an overview of methodological and ethical discussion.

The book is a valuable addition to the literature on research methods in education, nursing and healthcare, and professional education, and contributes to contemporary debates about the generation and dissemination of knowledge and its potential influence for wider social and environmental contexts.

Practitioners across the professions who are planning action research in their own work settings will find this book a helpful introduction to the subject while those studying on higher degree courses will find it an indispensable resource.

Jean McNiff is Professor of Educational Research at York St John University, UK. She also holds visiting professorial positions at Beijing Normal University and Ningxia Teachers University, People's Republic of China; the University of Tromsø, Norway; and the Nelson Mandela Metropolitan University, South Africa. She has written widely on action research in education.

Action Research

Principles and practice

3rd edition

Jean McNiff

Routledge
Taylor & Francis Group

LONDON AND NEW YORK

First published 1988
Second edition published 2002
This third edition published 2013
by Routledge
2 Park Square, Milton Park, Abingdon, Oxon OX14 4RN

Simultaneously published in the USA and Canada
by Routledge
711 Third Avenue, New York, NY 10017

Routledge is an imprint of the Taylor & Francis Group, an informa business

British Library Cataloguing in Publication Data
A catalogue record for this book is available from the British Library

Library of Congress Cataloging in Publication Data
McNiff, Jean.
Action research : principles and practice / Jean McNiff. -- Third edition.
  pages cm
  ISBN 978-0-415-53525-0 (hardback) -- ISBN 978-0-415-53526-7
  (paperback) -- ISBN 978-0-203-11275-5 (ebook) (print) 1. Action
  research in education. 2. Action research--Methodology. I. Title.
  LB1028.24.M398 2013   370.72--dc23
  2012033779

ISBN: 978–0–415–53525–0 (hbk)
ISBN: 978–0–415–53526–7 (pbk)
ISBN: 978–0–203–11275–5 (ebk)

Typeset in Bembo and Gill Sans
by Bookcraft Ltd, Stroud, Gloucestershire
Printed and bound by CPI Group (UK) Ltd, Croydon, CR0 4YY

MIX
Paper from
responsible sources
FSC® C013604
www.fsc.org

Printed and bound by CPI Group (UK) Ltd, Croydon, CR0 4YY

Contents

List of figures

List of contributors

I wish to thank the following people for contributing case study material to the book.

Mark Aldrich lives and works in Newtown, Connecticut, US. He is the librarian at a maximum security prison and is enrolled at City University of New York in the School of Professional Studies, Applied Theatre Department. He writes plays and poetry, and illustrates his own book series (see http://www.marcusartproductions.com).

Alison Joy Barton is from Liverpool, England. She works at the University of Central Lancashire. She is especially interested in traditional baking and bread-making.

Pip Bruce Ferguson lives in Hamilton, New Zealand. She works part-time at the University of Waikato and part-time in consultancy. She enjoys her involvement with family, church, reading and music.

Ingunn Skjesol Bulling is from Namdalseid, Norway. She works at the Nord-Trøndelag University College. She loves good food, music and being out in the open countryside with her family.

Vicci Carroll is from Durham, UK. She teaches Beauty Therapy at New College Durham while also studying for her Foundation Degree in Training and Work Based Learning at Sunderland University. Her main interest is having fun with her two sons. She hopes to draw on her own experiences in compulsory and post-compulsory education to help her promote education for all.

Linda Clifford, a New Zealander, works as the Secondary School Deputy Principal at Deira International School, Dubai. She particularly enjoys travel, meeting new people and educational research.

Linda Darbey has a Master's in Education from Trinity College Dublin, and is currently working as a Guidance Programme Coordinator in the National Centre for Guidance in Education (NCGE), Ireland. Her role in the NCGE is to coordinate the development, implementation and review of the NCGE guidance programme for guidance counsellors working in second-level schools.

Eric Deakins is an associate professor of value chain management at the University of Waikato Management School, who happens to be passionate about mentoring practitioner researchers. When not motorcycling through the beautiful New Zealand countryside, he designs organisations to be more enjoyable, professional and personally fulfilling.

Odd Edvardsen is an associate professor and a nursing educator at the University of Tromsø, Norway. His main interest has been the practical training of nursing students both in the practical field and in the Faculty of Health Sciences. He has also been engaged in international trauma care education and anti-imperialistic solidarity activities for many years.

Timothy Golden is originally from Edina, Minnesota, US. He earned a BA in Communication Studies and an MA in Counseling, both from the University of San Diego. Timothy is now a National Certified Counsellor in the United States, and his specialisation is school counselling.

Geraldine Hayes is from Dublin, Ireland and is a lecturer at St Patrick's College Drumcondra (a college of Dublin City University). She has extensive teaching experience in both Ireland and the US. She currently teaches in the area of special educational needs (SEN), where her main area is autism spectrum disorders (ASD). Her research interests include literacy for children with SEN, educational provision for children with ASD, and the delivery of online distance learning.

Peter Hyde is from Cork, Ireland. He worked as a guidance counsellor for a number of years and is currently Deputy Principal in Deerpark Christian Brothers School, Cork. He is married and has three teenage children. He is interested in, among other things, theology, spirituality, music and what it means to be a leader in a Catholic school in modern-day Ireland.

Maria James is a senior lecturer in Religious Education and Masters at St Mary's University College, Twickenham, UK. She was the first to be awarded the status of Teaching Fellow within the School of Education. She is passionate about all teachers realising their great potential for transformational learning.

Rita Jentoft is an Associate Professor and teacher of occupational therapists at the University of Tromsø, an Arctic city in the north of Norway. She is interested in how technology can enhance learning and practical knowledge in both clinical practice and education. Her leisure interests are yoga, winter sports and machine-knitting.

Jonathan Libag is from Binalonan, Pangasinan, the Philippines. He is a Research Scholar at the Oxford Centre for Mission Studies (OCMS), UK, and works with Asia Seed Project Inc. and Tribes and Nations Outreach. He is also currently associated with the organisation called Turning Point Development Programs working among the Kankana-ey and Ibaloi Tribes. He is especially interested in diving, beach-surfing and island-hopping, and loves trekking to the Himalayas and cruising on the Ganges.

Thérèse McPhillips is from Dublin, Ireland and is a lecturer at St Patrick's College Drumcondra (a college of Dublin City University), where she specialises in literacy education. She is particularly interested in teaching approaches and methodologies to support reading among children who have reading difficulties, and in collaborative research in the areas of literacy and inclusive classrooms.

Ana Naidoo is a Professor at the University of Pretoria, South Africa, where she was involved in teaching and teacher education from 1977 to the beginning of 2012. She then moved into the position of Deputy Director in the Department of Education Innovation, where she began to focus on the academic development of students, especially in their first year of study. Her passion is to ensure that students overcome their challenges and succeed.

Bente Norbye is an Associate Professor at the University of Tromsø, Norway. Since 1990 she has been responsible for decentralised nursing studies for nursing students living and studying in rural surroundings. She is leader of a research group in education in the Department of Health and Care Sciences. She hopes to develop health-care education involving health-care professionals as practice-based research.

Julia O'Brien's peripatetic life encompassed careers as a copy-editor, juggler and woodcarver before she settled in Lewes (UK) and began writing poetry. She has an MA in Creative Writing & Personal Development from the University of Sussex.

Alex Pandolfo is from Manchester, UK, and is an educational consultant. He is especially interested in continually developing practices to support social and economic inclusion.

Julie Pearson lives and works in London, UK. She is a Senior Lecturer at St Mary's University College, where she enjoys learning alongside those she teaches on the primary undergraduate, postgraduate and Master's courses. While she continues to work on her doctoral studies, Julie enjoys her important 'relaxing time' with her family and friends.

Martyn Rawson is a Scot living in Germany, working for the University of Plymouth International Masters Programme, and is a teacher in a Steiner Waldorf school. He is currently completing a professional doctorate in education on the theme of salutogenic education and teacher reflection.

Jane Renowden is a senior lecturer at St Mary's University College in Twickenham, UK. She teaches undergraduate, postgraduate and Master's-level teaching students as a member of the professional studies team. Jane has developed an interest in teacher accountability since undertaking her Master's and doctoral studies, and she hopes to use this as a platform for working with teachers in schools.

Margaret Riel teaches action research in an online programme in learning technologies at Pepperdine University, Malibu, California, US. She also organises learning circles (http://www.onlinelearningcircles.org), a structure for collaboration that connects children and adults in global projects. Innovative collaborative tech-tools on the web are her favourite toys.

Ruth Seabright lives in New Zealand with her wonderful husband Keith, her two beautiful sons, Darby and Bailey, and far too many pets to mention. She is passionate about her family, the environment, psychology and platforms that inspire resilient, inclusive, sustainable ways of living such as TimeBanking, Permaculture and the Virtues Project.

Alex Sinclair is from Hampton, UK. He works at St Mary's University College, Twickenham. He notes his interests as growing vegetables at his allotment, baking bread and exercising – and stresses that the latter is not just something for his CV.

Iris Stokes is from Seattle, Washington, US, and is Academic Coordinator at La Casa de los Niños de Yucatán, in Mexico. She enjoys dance, cycling and costume design.

Anne-Lise Thoresen is a midwife educator at the University of Tromsø, Norway. She works with midwifery students on their theoretical studies, and also with midwives who mentor the students in clinical practice settings. She works collaboratively on international projects, and sees action research as a means of creating learning strategies built on dialogue and teamwork.

Hjördís Thorgeirsdóttir is from Iceland. She is acting headteacher in Sund College in Reykjavik. She likes travelling and learning about different cultures.

Gabriella van Breda is originally from South Africa and now resides in the US. She is the executive director of World Impact Network and also a licensed minister with the International Church of the Foursquare Gospel. She is currently completing her research thesis at the Oxford Centre for Mission Studies.

Anne Marie Villumsen is a lecturer at VIA University College, Department of Social Work, Denmark, and also a doctoral candidate at Aarhus University, Department of Psychology, Business and Social Sciences.

Jill Wickham is a Senior Lecturer in Physiotherapy at York St John University, England. She is passionate about physiotherapy education and about how she can continually evaluate and improve her own practice to enhance students' learning journeys.

Lesley Wood is a Research Professor in the Faculty of Education Sciences at North West University, Potchefstroom, South Africa. She is particularly interested in researching the transformative potential of action research to enhance social justice and improve the quality of life of all stakeholders in education.

Eric Yuan is from Zunyi, China. He is currently doing his PhD at the Chinese University of Hong Kong. His research interests include language teachers' professional learning and identity construction.

Sólveig Zophoníasdóttir is from Akureyri, Iceland, and works at the University of Akureyri. She is especially interested in outdoor activities, photography, information technology and having fun with her family.

Acknowledgements

I wish to thank the following people for reading the manuscript, in whole or in part, and their insightful comments that have helped strengthen the book: Maria James, Clare McCluskey, Margaret Meredith, Julie Pearson, Peter Raymond, Jane Renowden, Margaret Riel, Alex Sinclair, Jill Wickham; and especially ... Julian Stern, Dean of Faculty of Education and Theology, York St John University: for scholarly conversations and critical friendship; Philip Mudd, my editor at Routledge Education: for his ongoing support and kindness in the writing of this book; and Peter McDonnell, cherished travelling companion: for lots of laughter.

The eyes of the Lord keep watch over knowledge
Proverbs 22.12

Introduction

A good deal has happened since the publication of the first edition of this book in 1988 and the second edition in 2002. The world of action research has changed, and so has my thinking.

In 1988, when the book was first published, action research was still struggling for legitimacy. This remained the case until about the late 1990s. Many people still positioned action research as a powerful form of learning, especially professional learning, but would not accept it as a methodology for knowledge creation and theory generation. Some, especially in higher education, refused to think of practice-based learning and its outcomes as 'real' research, or to entertain the idea that practitioner-researchers could generate theory.

Since those days, however, because of the hard work, determination and collaborative work of many people, action research has become fully recognised, and today countless people everywhere speak about doing action research, or something like it. In 2009 Susan Noffke commented in *The Sage Handbook of Educational Action Research* on the 'remarkable growth in the acceptance of action research' during the last decade (Noffke and Somekh 2009: 12). The acceptance today takes many forms, for example: the inclusion of action research on work-based professional development courses and higher education accredited degree courses; its international take-up; its spread across the professions and sectors; the beginnings of interdisciplinary dialogues; publications in textbooks and scholarly journals; and many other areas. This remarkable spread and range of action research are also demonstrated in the stories and case studies in this book. Reading the work of action researchers from around the world is like being part of a global conversation, where people ask questions about what they are doing, why they are doing it and what they hope to achieve. It is just wonderful.

Yet not everything is wonderful, and the field is not without its difficulties. If action research has arrived, questions arise about how long it will last, for all movements and initiatives change their shapes and patterns in some way (Kuhn 1996). The question for action research is whether this will happen sooner rather than later, for dangers threaten from within the field as well as from without; so perhaps the action research community needs to research itself critically, and check whether this is not just another Celtic Tiger boom that may end up as a bust.

In this Introduction, therefore, I would like to explore the following:

- what I see as changes in the external world in the last decade that have influenced the field, the gains that action research has made, and possible hopes and prospects;
- some of the changes in my own thinking, and some thoughts about potential dangers and threats to action research;
- how these issues might be addressed.

The chapter is organised under the following headings:

- Gains, hopes and prospects
- Dangers and threats
- Back to first principles
- Action research and a third cognitive revolution
- Organisation of the ideas in the book

Gains, hopes and prospects

Here are what I see as some of the most important gains, hopes and prospects.

Global epistemological shifts

Because of the social and scholarly activism of millions of people, including action researchers, a global epistemological shift has been taking place in recent decades in relation to what counts as knowledge, how it is produced, where, and who by. Key ideas have appeared in the literatures, including these.

Gibbons *et al.* (1994) identify what they call 'Mode 1' and 'Mode 2' kinds of knowledge. 'Mode 1' refers to dominant conceptual, abstract forms of knowing, and 'Mode 2' to practical knowledge. Like Schön (1983, 1995), they make the case that practice-based practical knowledge is relevant to everyday lives and should be awarded status equal to that of Mode 1 forms, contrary to the dominant view that positions Mode 1 forms as superior to Mode 2.

The shift has also happened because of the recognition that knowledge is socially developed. Brown and Duguid (2000), for example, speak about the social nature of knowledge creation, recognising, like Lave and Wenger (1991), that knowledge is always situated within the groups of people who create it, although its uses for wider influence are potentially infinite; and Wenger speaks about communities of practice (1999), emphasising that knowledge is a collective endeavour among individuals who share a practice.

This recognition of the value of Mode 2 forms of knowledge has inspired its take-up by continuing and higher education in terms of new forms of courses for a range of professions and disciplines, including professional doctorates linking professional development and practice-based knowledge production. Action research has become a preferred methodology for many of these courses, on the understanding that practitioners need to build an evidence base to show the validity of what they are doing as competent researchers.

The new scholarship

Similarly, and symptomatic of the epistemological shift, Boyer (1990) proposed a new focus for continuing and higher education faculty because, given the high status and prioritising of Mode 1 conceptual forms of research and theory, practical attention to teaching and learning matters was being overlooked. He proposed four separate but integrated forms of enquiry:

- The scholarship of discovery, similar to traditional forms of research, with the aim of advancing propositional knowledge.
- The scholarship of integration that brings together knowledge from across disciplines.
- The scholarship of application that involves community service.
- The scholarship of teaching that involves the systematic study of teaching practices.

These ideas have had wide take-up internationally, across the sectors although mainly by continuing and higher education. However, different perspectives are evident. Some people study teaching as a topic, while others like to study their own teaching. In addition, the field has been confined mainly to the profession of teaching, usually mainstream, and needs to be extended to a broader view that sees teaching as what we all do when working with learners, including nurses, physiotherapists, bankers and shopkeepers.

Schön had laid the groundwork for the new scholarship in his (1983) *The Reflective Practitioner*, and in 1995 he developed the idea of a new epistemology for the new scholarship, i.e. new ways of knowing and coming to know. A favourite analogy is his story about the topology of professional landscapes – but things are changing here too.

Levelling out of the topology of professional landscapes

In 1983 and 1995 Schön presented a caricature of the topology of professional landscapes and their characteristic epistemologies. There was, he said, a hard high ground that favoured technical rationality, and a swampy lowlands that valued intuitive, practical forms. The high ground tended to be the home of institutions, and was peopled mainly by elitist intelligentsia from the corporate and formal education worlds; Chomsky often refers to these as a 'high priesthood'. These intelligentsias are much occupied with generating abstract theories about issues that, while valuable in themselves, often have little to do with everyday living. Because of the prestigious social positioning of the theorists, their abstract forms of theory would become seen as dominant. Practitioners, on the other hand, said Schön, dealt with issues of everyday significance, yet, because practitioners were not seen as legitimate knowers, either by the high priesthood or by themselves (because 'ordinary' people are systematically taught through the formal education system to devalue their own contributions), their form of theorising tended to be regarded as practical problem-solving rather than proper research.

The situation was topsy-turvy to the realities of everyday living. Precisely those issues of everyday living that occupy practitioners were trivialised, along with the status of the practitioners as knowledge workers and theory generators, while abstract theorising continued to maintain institutional legitimacy through the creation of the grand theories that the institution favours. Furthermore, the situation would become one where the grand theorising turns into grand narratives, and the voices of everyday people and their local narratives become distorted and made silent.

Schön, along with Boyer and others, calls for a reappraisal of what counts as legitimate scholarship, research and theorising. Research that celebrates important issues of everyday living should be given as much priority as traditional forms – often more perhaps, for practical, practice-based research is a key means of contributing to holistic and relational forms of cultural, social and intellectual progress. The practical theories of practitioners are the most powerful and appropriate forms for dealing with contemporary social issues; and these are located in and generated from everyday practices, inspired by tacit intuitive forms of knowledge as much as by cognitive forms. This, says Schön, all comes down to action research, a way of researching one's practice and generating personal theories of practice that shows the processes of self-monitoring, evaluation of practice, purposeful action to improve the practice for social benefit, and a commitment to making the process public for moral and social accountability.

However, the situation remains problematic, because, while the topology of *professional* landscapes may be levelling out, and while many continuing and higher education practitioners would position themselves as workplace-based practitioners, the topology of *epistemological* landscapes still needs attention. Many people still automatically position academics as qualified researchers who generate theory out of their expert knowledge, but also still tend to perceive practitioners as not clever enough to generate theory. The situation in many instances is still that practitioners are largely expected to implement academics' theories, and that professional researchers will observe practitioners as they do so and generate theory about them. It is not so much a matter of who does the research in terms of gathering and interpreting data as of who is seen as competent and authorised to generate the theory, and who makes decisions about these things. Anyone can call themselves a researcher, but not everyone can call themselves a theorist. Somehow, 'theory' and 'evidence' are seen as more prestigious than 'practice' and 'data'.

Academics do action research

However, the levelling-out that is going on can be seen by the fact that many people working in formal academic settings also do action research. Whereas 20 years ago it would have been unusual for academics to study their practices, these days it is becoming normal and, in some cases, expected. A range of dissertations and theses from academic staffs may be seen on websites such those by Diana Ayling (http://tlcommunityunitec.ning.com/), Pip Bruce Ferguson (http://tlcommunityunitec.ning.com/) and Bob Dick (www.aral.com.au/). There are many more. My own website (www.jeanmcniff.com/) contains some of the dissertations and theses of people whose master's and doctoral studies I have supported (see examples later), some of whom have gone on to work in continuing and higher education or hold senior positions in schools, colleges, hospitals and businesses.

As well as such websites, accounts from academics are also available in documentary, book and journal article form: such accounts from higher education people I support include those from colleagues in St Mary's University College, UK; York St John University, UK; the University of Tromsø, Norway; the University of Limerick, Ireland; the Nelson Mandela Metropolitan University, South Africa; and elsewhere. Stories from these and other colleagues also appear in this book. Significant features are that the academics in question regard their practice not as simply communicating subject matters, but also as accepting pedagogical and epistemic responsibility for their work; and not only about teaching, but more about inspiring a mindset towards life and lifelong learning by practitioners across the professions.

Note: following common practice, I use the term 'academics' to refer to people officially in the Academy, i.e. in continuing and higher education settings. I use the term 'practitioners' to refer to people working in workplace settings such as offices and shops. I use the terms only to denote their different work settings and different roles and responsibilities in relation to learning and supporting learning. I do not, however, see any difference between 'academics' as workplace practitioners and 'practitioners' as academics when they are doing academic work, or between their capacity for knowledge creation or critical engagement. I do see all as intellectuals who are able to think for themselves and make their contribution to the wider field of knowledge and personal and social wellbeing through realising their humanity in relation with others.

Dangers and threats

There are, however, considerable dangers around, and these constitute potential threats to the integrity and even the continuation of action research. First I present some of the dangers as I see them, and then I outline how these could constitute threats.

Dangers

Loose words

The term 'action research' is now everywhere, as is 'reflective practice'. You hear it in mainstream literatures and international educational research association meetings. Special departments are set up in universities for practitioner research and/or action research, and accredited courses arranged. However, when something becomes popular, it tends to be taken for granted, or used so much that it gets misused and loses meaning. Therefore, instead of maintaining that research must generate theory of some kind, 'action research' is often domesticated into 'telling stories'. More than one book on the market accepts only practitioners' descriptions of their work as legitimate research, and this becomes a teenager form of action research, rather than showing the need for mature and thoughtful explanations and an articulation of the significance of explanatory frameworks.

Fragmentation of the field through tribalism

There is an increasing tendency to compartmentalise action research, sometimes as idiosyncratic movements, with the perhaps inevitable consequences of territorialism. Researchers declare their allegiance to this or that brand of research only, and refuse to talk with others. Sometimes it becomes more about themselves and what they identify as their grand theories, and practitioners become the means for promoting the self-interests of the grand theorists. So you can find movements called variously 'Participative Action Research', 'Practitioner Action Research', 'Organisational Action Research', 'Living Theory Action Research', 'Collaborative Action Research', 'Contextual Action Research', 'Radical Action Research' 'Self Study', 'Autoethnography' – and so on and so forth; and they all come with capital letters, and become common nouns, things in themselves, and sometimes lose touch with the voices of people in the streets and workplaces, which is what action research should be all about.

A desire for narrow linguistic definitions and lock-step approaches

I am concerned about some trends that appear to be turning action research into a set of techniques, or require the execution of a specific set of steps or actions. This turns it into an oppressive technology that denies the humani-tarian and egalitarian ideologies that inspired the action research movement in the first place. Such practices, I think, are part of a wider tendency to box in ideas and define concepts so that they can become manageable and may be spoken about without necessarily showing how the ideas are generated from existing action and inform further action. I recall having a lively debate with a colleague who insisted that we were born thinking in terms of boxes. The aims of my work are to (1) deconstruct the idea of boxes, and (2) deconstruct the idea that we should think in boxes. I love ideas such as those communi-cated by Mitroff and Linstone (1995), about unbounded thinking; but this means that we need to see thinking as free, emergent and unfolding, rather than boxed in and tidy.

The continuing search for certain knowledge

Many people working in the field still seem to expect to get answers by doing action research. Often still using the methods of the social sciences, themselves derived from the methods of the physical sciences, people ask, 'If I do x, what will happen?', expecting the answer to be, 'y will.' Any answer from real-life experiences should be something of the kind, 'Who knows? Anything could happen.' Experience teaches that it is important to let go of the need for certainty, for there is no such thing; no one has any idea what will happen in the next moment. The only thing anyone can be certain of is life itself, which is unpredictable, surprising, creative and self-transforming. An implicate order underpins everything (Bohm 1983), and this order is generative and transformational. This also is the nature of practice, as part of life (McNiff 2000). Life and practice are evolutionary and move towards life-affirming and life-renewing forms.

This way of thinking (logic) goes beyond the propositional Aristotelian logic beloved of many theorists of education, such as Pring (2000). Propositional logic attempts to eliminate contradiction from human enquiry, whereas transformational logics embrace the idea that human living is full of contra-dictions that need to be understood and lived with rather than resolved, and that experience can provide the grounds for new beginnings.

This capacity for confidence in uncertainty needs to become part of learning and professional development contexts. Personally, I have learned that I cannot be certain of anything; that I do not know best; that I am not responsible for how people think or what they learn. My work instead is to encourage people to have confidence in their own capacity for independent thinking, to play with ideas, to challenge me and to resist all efforts to bring their thinking to closure. My job is to support them in becoming aware of how they learn and use their knowledge to contribute to improving their work with others.

Manufacturing identity or creating it?

These concerns travel to ideas about how identity may be manufactured by others. In *Orientalism* (1995), Edward Said explains how 'Orientalism' is a concept created by Western intellectuals, and how social categories are themselves fabricated. The same practice of colonisation is today visible in the world of action research. Dominant theories of education are still manufactured mainly by intellectuals in higher education settings. And some of these use their positioning in a careless and frequently self-serving manner (see Lilla 2001). The responsibility of intellectuals, in my view, is to support others in creating their own identities with critical discernment, and to have the confidence and capacity to do so.

An ego-centred, researcher-centred focus on the 'I'

A good deal of work exists that focuses on the 'I' as the centre of the enquiry, from an ego-centred, researcher-centred perspective (this links with resisting the idea of action research as a problem-based approach, outlined on page 35). I have contributed to these literatures. However, my thinking has changed over time, and I no longer see the 'I' in isolation, nor as the centre, as used to be the case, and not necessarily as a 'we'. Although I thought and wrote about 'we', the image was of a collective of 'I's working together.

I do not see things like this now. I see the 'I' always as in relation; 'I' am always already in relation with others, with the environment and with my God. The 'I' of the research is concerned about contributing to the wellbeing of others in the relationship and developing the kinds of dialogical relationship that will let this happen. Collaborative working therefore becomes more than a 'we'; it is 'I in dialogical relation with others, and others in dialogical relation with me and others', the development of dialogical community, as John Macmurray (1957, 1961) says (see also McIntosh 2011). We are speaking about relationships among individuals who recognise themselves as always already in relation, and not about individualities. Julia Kristeva also develops ideas of this kind:

> Each person has the right to become as singular as possible and to develop the maximum creativity for him or herself. And at the same time, without stopping this creativity, we should try to build bridges and interfaces – that is, to foster sharing. ... It is not a question of creating a community in the image of the past; it is a question of creating a new community on the basis of sharing singularity.
>
> Kristeva 2002: 162; from an interview with John Lechte

I also like what Said says, in his conversations with the musician Daniel Barenboim (Barenboim and Said 2004). He says (p. 11):

One of the striking things about the kind of work you [Barenboim] do is that you act as interpreter, as a performer – an artist concerned not so much with the articulation of the self, but rather with the articulation of other selves. … There is more of a concentration today [on oneself], on the affirmation of identity, on the need for roots, on the values of one's culture and one's sense of belonging. It's become quite rare to project one's self outward, to have a broader perspective.

He also (p. 5) speaks about:

the sense that identity is a set of currents, flowing currents, rather than a fixed place or a stable set of objects …

This has been a mind-changing understanding about how I think about myself, and has had consequences for what I do and how I do it.

Potential threats

The kinds of dangers I am speaking about may actually be perceived as threats, as follows.

As noted, action research is now accepted by universities, governments and policy-makers because of social and academic activism. But this is where there is a danger of the potential abuse of the original philosophy. The ideas of personal involvement and commitment to practice fit well with shifts in international government policies about the need for highly skilled and knowledgeable workforces, and for schools and colleges to 'turn out' people with employable skills and knowledge.

This in turn fits with a new emphasis on work-based learning for a new knowledge-creating society (Hargreaves 2003; Nonaka and Takeuchi 1995), and it has potential implications for current drives towards the internationalisation of business and education that sees knowledge as a purchasable commodity. This focus on productivity factors out the original emancipatory and collaborative intent of action research (Carr and Kemmis 2005), and plays right into the hands of those same agencies whose interests it serves to have practitioners doing action research, provided it is of the right kind, where action research is perceived as implementing interventions to be used to change situations and societies, with anticipated outcomes.

It could be seen, therefore, that official agencies permit action research because it suits their agendas of command and control and achieving outcomes. This understanding began to dawn from experience in the 1990s. An example was when I was working in Northern Ireland while introducing action research for teachers in the then new curriculum initiative Education for Mutual Understanding, as part of the peace process. One of the teachers in a group I was working with was furious with me, and said, 'This is the implementation of government policy through the back door.' She was not right, but I could see her point. Isaiah Berlin would also have seen her point, because he speaks about the enemies of peace as those who wish to impose it (Berlin 2002).

I also recall how I was a member of a panel at an international research association meeting, and was asked whether I thought that action research should have specific outcomes. My response was 'No, other than learning.' The response of various others was yes: there should be an identifiable outcome otherwise you could not say that the action research had been successful. This kind of thinking later influenced a high-profile UK initiative, in which teachers could receive funding to do action research in their classrooms on condition that learners achieved designated outcomes. I do not think we should be thinking about 'success' in such terms. I think action research should be a process of helping other people to think for themselves and to realise their humanity in doing so. This, if there is any success, is it; for the world turns because it thinks for itself, as part of the natural order, and not because people tell it to.

So this is where it all gets tricky. Action research is now open to the same core challenge that has consistently bedevilled the social sciences, which is their assumption that one person may do research on another and speak on their behalf. One person gathers data, generates evidence and provides explanations for what another person is doing and saying. This assumption is rooted in a deeper assumption that runs right though history and the history of ideas: that it is permissible for one person to do things to another, and that everyone will agree to it. It can be seen in some forms of health care (not all), for example, as a technical rational medical model where patients are 'done to' by doctors and nurses, but don't get the opportunity, don't even get invited, to do things for themselves. The assumption is, 'I'm a doctor (or an expert of some kind); trust me. I know what is best for you.' This assumption travels to a range of settings, including the politics of nation states, where one group assumes that it is permissible to invade another's land for their own purposes; and higher education expansionism, where it is assumed that one group may export their knowledge to another, without due regard for local customs or indigenous epistemologies (see McNiff 2011).

The same assumption is everywhere visible in action research, and raises questions about its sustainability; for invasion never did anything to win over the hearts and minds of those whose country has been invaded, but usually succeeds rather in inspiring them to find ways of getting rid of the invader, while availing of the most appropriate goods that the invader has to offer. Many people working in these forms of action research seem to have lost sight of a key guiding principle, that social change happens when people think for themselves and mobilise themselves for action (the impulse that inspired Kurt Lewin's work: see page 56). Many books on action research (including my own earlier ones) use the language of 'we implement change', and some speak of 'we change people' (I hope I never said this). There is an overwhelming assumption that it is permissible to do action research on other people (Reason and Rowan 1981), to regard action research as a 'tool' to be used to achieve desired outcomes, and to observe others doing action research and theorise and report on what they are doing.

I think this is awful. Perhaps it is because of working in problematic contexts over the years, especially with people who have been done to all their lives, that I have come to see the potential disaster in this view. No one can, or has the right to, change another person. No one can, or has the right to, do things to that person without invitation. People think for themselves; we all have rights. It is the responsibility of one to act with respect for the rights of the other; this means all of us, so rights and responsibilities become mutually reciprocal. Unless we think seriously about these things we will continue killing one another, and in an accelerated fashion, given the advanced state of our knowledge and technology.

Action research, if it is anything, is about finding ways to encourage change, but the word 'change' must be said from the premise that 'I change me' not 'I change you': sustainable change happens from within. The telos of action research must be to honour the other, and to find ways of encouraging the other to think and speak for themselves. For this there must be certain conditions, the primary one of which is freedom, as Sen (1999) says, for people are always in community, so each person needs to be in free and equal relation to the other. Freedom becomes both means and ends of the process.

So how do I justify these ideas? To do so, I go back to first principles, to the idea of human nature and the conditions for its realisation, and how action research can enable us to realise this human nature that constitutes our humanity. I also relate human nature to the implicate natural order (Chapter 12).

Back to first principles

My starting point is to try to clarify my understanding of what it means to be human. The ideas expressed here are my present best thinking. No doubt they will develop over time and through conversation.

On human nature

I draw first on the thinking of many authors, including Chomsky, and the debate on human nature between him and Foucault (Chomsky and Foucault 2006). Working with empirical evidence, he concludes that a major dilemma for linguistic theory is to account for:

> the gap between the really quite small quantity of data [in the form of speech acts] ... that's presented to the child, and the very highly

articulated, highly systematic, profoundly organized resulting knowledge that he [sic] somehow derives from these data.

p. 3

Elsewhere, in his (1986) *Knowledge of Language*, he has identified this as 'Plato's problem', i.e. how to account for the amazingly rich capacity for language that even a young child develops in spite of a relatively small stimulus of the language they hear. Chomsky concludes that 'the individual himself contributes a good deal, an overwhelming part in fact' (Chomsky and Foucault 2006: 3); in other words, they exercise their innate capacity for an unlimited number of original creative acts. Chomsky says, 'this collection, this mass of schematisms, innate organizing principles, which guides our social and intellectual and individual behaviour, that's what I mean to refer to by the concept of human nature' (pp. 4–5). He assumes also that 'something of the same sort' may be relevant in 'other domains of human cognition and behaviour' (p. 4).

I agree, and I am interested in these other domains. I agree that people, pathology aside, have certain innate capacities, including for an unlimited number of creative acts in any area of their lives (although their individual physical or mental make-up may prevent the realisation of those capacities). It is part of our genetic inheritance to be curious, to make choices, to be creative, to think for ourselves; and a key distinguishing feature is that we also have language, which we can adapt for any situation, and use to reflect on our thinking. This contributes to the capacity for meta-cognition, which we use to help us make moral choices according to our chosen values system.

Yet we are born of another, and live and die in relation with others, and so must understand ourselves as in relation with others. The capacity for relationships is also innate, and links with needs (Maslow 1998). I would argue that a profound need and part of our human make-up is the need to be with others, for attachment, spiritual relationship and a sense of belonging (Gray 1995b). There is plenty of empirical evidence to show this: Piaget's (1932) ideas about theory of mind (more precisely, theories of other people's minds), when children come to appreciate that others are in the relationship and have their own perceptions; and in other areas of the animal world (Ridley 1997) and the natural world (Abrams 2011). Human nature is about loving and being loved, about realising our creative capacity for engagement in life through productive work and loving relationships (Fromm 1995), through spiritual connectedness with humans and non-humans and with the living planet.

These and other ideas are significant for action research. Hannah Arendt speaks of the individual's 'natality', the idea that one's birth holds the promise of a new beginning, so we are thereby 'prompted into action' (Arendt 1958: 177). The idea of new beginnings is also explored by authors such as Vico (1999), Bergson (1998) and Said (1997), that there are no endings in life because each ending constitutes a new beginning, relating to Habermas's idea (1975) that it is our nature to learn, and in processes of social evolution we cannot *not* learn (see Chapter 4 in this book). It is therefore our responsibility to use our place on earth well, as well as our capacity for learning anew, and to explain how and why we do so (Chapter 11).

Other key theorists have influenced my thinking about human nature, and why this must be a main starting point for action research. Speaking about the social and moral world, Berlin says that there is no one overarching guiding principle or value that helps people make choices between competing values and courses of action (Berlin 1997; see also Gray 1995a; Ignatieff 1998). His standpoint is that it is part of our human condition, perhaps our nature, to recognise that we have to embrace contradictory values, given that we live in situations of great diversity. This idea would have been helpful to people like Al Capone, who maintained throughout his life that he was a regular businessman, providing a service for people by selling them what they needed, and also providing a stable social structure through his control of the gangs of Chicago (MacDonald 1999). Eliot Ness may not have agreed with him, and they obviously had different values about the worth of other people, but both had strong values around the need for order.

However, realising Berlin's ideas about the contested basis of individual and social living carries obvious personal and political consequences. Enabling human capacities to flourish means providing the conditions of freedom in which it may flourish, as well as dialogical spaces that are always kept open for new thinking (Friedman 2002; Rorty 2006). At a personal level it means exercising one's choice for freedom and critical thinking, and not opting for a life of quietude; at a political level it means not allowing oneself to be persuaded not to think. This is not always allowed, either by oneself or by others. The idea of human nature as an unstoppable original creative act with evolutionary potential has considerable significance for wider political science, in respect of the potentials for individual and collective agency in deciding what kind of social order should be established, and how a social order may help or hinder the development of the natural order. The significance is intensified when linked with the idea that we are in a constant process of development, always learning, always curious and creative, and always exercising our originality of mind in making choices about what we learn and what we do with this knowledge. The idea that in processes of learning and development 'the individual himself contributes a good deal, an overwhelming part in fact', may lead some rulers to review the state of their war chests (Chomsky and Foucault 2006: 3).

I have tried to communicate these ideas visually on several occasions – see page 66 of this book – and can now articulate their significance in light of engaging with authors who have been consistent influences, including: Von Bertalanffy's (1968) ideas about living systems theory; Bateson's (1972) ideas about ecological approaches to learning and systems of influence; chaos and complexity theory (Lewin 1993; Waldrop 1992), which are premised on specific principles, including spontaneity, emergence, self-organisation, unpredictability and self-renewal; Capra's (1996) and Wheatley's (1992) ideas about the interconnected nature of relationships, and Argyris and Schön's (1995) ideas about the dynamic nature of organisational learning. This may be seen as an ecological approach, and I have called it this occasionally. However, I am conscious how the words 'ecological' and 'environmental' tend quickly to become linked only with issues of planetary wellbeing and sustainability, so I tend to use the language of relationships. These relationships are between thinking and practice, individuals and groups, people and the planet, and all in a process of generative transformational relation.

Furthermore, practices may be seen as both topic and process, and, most importantly, relationships become the topics. This becomes a key new feature for this book; for the emphasis throughout is on the nature of relationships, between knowledge and practice, and between people and the living world. For if practice communicates what we know, then research enables us to say that we know what we know, to articulate its significance for future knowing, and to explain the relationship between knowing and action. The focus on an ecological approach to living systems is especially important, because a breakdown or lack of growth in one part of the system will have implications for the entire system, which is especially relevant when speaking about the cognitive and affective aspects of mind that go towards the constitution of human nature, and its realisation as a means of showing the transformation of values into virtues.

This links directly with action research, for if action research is about personal and social change in the interests of social equality, recognition of diversity, and appreciation of the problematics of social living (James *et al.* 2012; Zuber-Skerritt 2012), with implications for contributing to the natural order, then the change must be undertaken by the individual themselves, always already in relation with others, and the process begins first in their own thinking and then transforms into their involvement in their social, political, cultural and environmental worlds.

If these are the conditions, then, for the realisation of our humanity, what do those processes for their realisation look like?

On processes of development and the natural order

Since a very young age, I have been fascinated by (but until the 1980s lacked the language to describe) ideas about immanence and generative transformational processes, the idea that every phenomenon or thing has within itself its own latent potential for self-renewal and self-organisation (two of the vital indicators of life). Even rocks have this potential, as part of a living planet. I came to this intuitive understanding when, as a child of four or five, I watched a snowflake settle on the outside windowpane. It was perfect in its symmetry, each part holding the other parts within itself and the whole containing all its parts, so it became more than the sum of its parts.

I later learned the language of fractals and complexity theory. In undergraduate German studies I learned from Spinoza how these patterns are representative of both the natural order and the ethical nature of the natural order; and from Goethe (who was also deeply influenced by Spinoza: see Bertoft 1996) about how the relationships of life may be understood in these terms. From postgraduate studies in linguistics I learned from Chomsky (1965) about the relationships between conceptualisations of language and its manifestations in speech; and later still from Krashen (1981) and others that language and its uses need also to be located within social interactions. This strengthened the idea of generative transformational systems (Chomsky 1965), the idea that each level of a system is embedded within, and transforms into, higher levels: thus concepts may transform into practices, acorns may transform into oak trees, and individuals may transform into communities, given the right conditions. I have always found thrilling the images of the patterns that connect (Bateson 1972), although I see them, like Capra (1996) as dynamic and multidimensional, changing through time and space, offering universal theoretical structures for the fluid and chaotic processes of life itself.

Furthermore, these images of physical and spiritual connectedness and transformation have developed into ideas about the generative transformational dynamics of influence. One person's ideas may influence the entire world, a people's entire history, as demonstrated by figures such as Gandhi, Stalin and Jesus. For me, the idea of the generative transformational nature of influence in one's own and others' thinking lies at the heart of action research, as well as ideas about what kinds of influence matter, and why; for the nature of the influence of Stalin or Al Capone may not have been the same as the influence of Gandhi or Eliot Ness. These ideas incorporate other ideas, about the need for dialogical mindsets, seeing oneself in relation with others and the universe, insisting for others and oneself on the conditions of freedom that will enable these processes to flow in an untrammelled and self-organising fashion.

Action research and a third cognitive revolution

In his *Powers and Prospects*, Chomsky (1996b) speaks about the first and second cognitive revolutions. The first cognitive revolution took place during the seventeenth century, during the Galilean revolution, with the onset of 'the mechanical philosophy'. People were creating automata, and came to see the world as part of a giant machine. The Cartesians argued that everything in the world, except humans, should be regarded as complex machines. This provided the basis for philosophical-scientific thinking, and a fertile ground for the later emergence of structuralism and behaviourism. The second cognitive revolution took place, he says, in the early to mid-twentieth century with the rise of computers, where attention shifted from the study of behaviour to the properties of mind that entered into thought and action (see also Gardner 1987).

I am suggesting here that we have entered a third cognitive revolution, where attention is shifting yet again, from a study of properties of mind to a study of embodied minds and their interactions, especially through the mediation of Web 2.0 technologies, the move from abstract theorising to embodied communicative action, where the responsibility for the enquiry has also shifted from external researchers to persons themselves. Theory is no longer seen only as communicated symbolically to represent thought, but as enacted through the lives of people who recognise themselves as in relation with one another for personal and social purposes. Thus the locus of power has also shifted. These ideas are explored further in Chapter 11.

So, how do all these ideas enter into this new edition? Here is an outline of how the ideas are organised.

Organisation of the ideas in the book

The book is written as five parts:

Part I What do we know? The principles of action research

Chapters 1–4: These chapters deal with the philosophical frameworks of action research and ask 'What is the nature of action research? What are its origins?' Chapter 1 sets out what we need to know in terms of good research practice; Chapter 2 deals with issues of linking theory and practice; Chapter 3 gives a brief history of action research; and Chapter 4 links these ideas with personal and social development.

Part II What do we do with our knowledge? The practices of action research

Chapters 5–7: These chapters focus on practical issues and ask 'What is involved in doing action research? How do we create knowledge?' Chapter 5 contains information on how to do action research; Chapter 6 gives examples of putting action plans into action and gives advice about monitoring practice and data-gathering; and Chapter 7 outlines some practical 'dos' and 'don'ts' of doing action research.

Part III How do we share our knowledge? Writing up and making public

Chapters 8–10: These chapters focus on sharing and communicating action research and ask 'How do we show that our knowledge is valuable? How do we test and communicate its value?' Chapter 8 focuses on generating evidence to make knowledge claims, and testing their validity; Chapter 9 gives advice on writing as a means of communicating those claims; and Chapter 10 discusses how to judge the quality of knowledge claims as they are communicated through your action, research and writing.

Part IV How do we use our knowledge? Action research for good order

Chapter 11 and 12: These chapters discuss the significance and implications of doing action research and ask 'How do we use our knowledge? What do we use it for?' Chapter 11 is about the uses of action research, and how these may contribute to personal and social development; Chapter 12 discusses how the development of good social orders can contribute to the creation of good ecological orders, and to the maintenance of the natural order, for the benefit of all.

Part V Hopes and prospects

Chapter 13 offers some ideas about where action research may be going, and gives examples of the kind of work that may move it in the direction of explaining what might count as universal values.

The book is written from several perspectives.

From a focused perspective, it may be seen as a straightforward guide to doing action research: how and why to do it, how to make judgements about its quality and explain the significance of what one is doing, and how to disseminate the findings. It is a 'how to do' book, framed within the conceptual issues discussed here.

From a wider perspective, it is a report of the action research I have engaged in since 1988. It sets out what I have learnt, how my learning has developed and what I hope to learn in future, so it becomes my report on knowledge (see Lyotard 1984). I have learnt about action research through doing action research.

From a wider perspective still, it is a critical reflection on my own practice as an action researcher and a writer who is presenting ideas for other people's consideration. Writing as a practice carries considerable responsibility; for writers have to be honest with their readers, alert the reader to the language they are using, and try not to use language to cover up the hidden messages they are persuading their readers to assimilate. This is especially important if the message is supposed to be educational, which involves being self-critical. It is especially important if dialogue also becomes a key criterion and organising framework, because it then becomes a case of using language to reflect on itself, to ensure that the language is dialogical and to make visible the underlying logic of critical dialogue that it allegedly espouses.

I hope to show how, through studying my practice as a professional educator, a researcher and a writer, it may be possible to explicate the transformational relationships between the following:

- How I can encourage others and myself to explain how we hold ourselves accountable for the development of good order in our practices.
- How this personal accountability can contribute to the development of good social orders through education, in the sense of exercising our educational influences in learning to enable others to do the same. Furthermore, 'education' is not meant in the narrow sense as only to do with the profession of teaching, but as about exercising the kind of influence in people's thinking, and one's own, that will enable us to realise our humanity, which includes realising the capacity for thinking critically about what we are doing and saying, and how we are relating to one another (Kemmis 2009).
- How such improved personal and social orders may help or hinder the development of the environmental order, as a realisation of natural order.

Thus a focus on the individual-in-relation may transform into the social, which in turn may transform into the global. While a focus may remain on each or any aspect, all aspects may be seen as parts of a focus on the wider whole, where the whole becomes more than the sum of its parts.

I hope therefore to show how, over the years, I have undertaken focused research projects within the broader research project of working to contribute to a global order that is a realisation of the natural order, and how I have come to reconceptualise the nature of action research as a problematic process of coming to know and demonstrating epistemological accountability rather than as a pathway to right knowledge. I have come to see that there are no happy endings or 'end of' statements in action research, only new and more interesting (and probably more problematic) questions that form the beginning of new enquiries, always holding the spaces open for the emergence of new possibilities as new realities.

So I am asking, 'What have I learned? What do I know now? How have I come to know it? How do I test the validity of my knowledge? How do I explain its significance, and who is it significant for? How do I share my knowledge? What will I use my knowledge for?' These questions act as organising principles throughout; they are the kinds of questions used in any action enquiry.

A key aspect of the enquiry is an understanding of the importance of critiquing the assumptions that underlie my own ideas and practices. This would not have been the case when I wrote the first edition, and was only partly the case for the second. By this edition, I think I have become more critical, and I try to influence others also to become critical, because criticism would seem essential for generating non-coercive knowledge in the creation of good order (Said 1991: 28).

Today, I think I understand my practice and its contexts better than I did before, as a professional educator, a scholar and a writer; this book, I hope, provides evidence to ground this claim. However, I continue to ask questions about what I am doing and how and why I am doing it. These questions lie at the heart of the book because I want to know better what counts as good, and how to justify what I am doing and the values I hold, in relation to all the practices of my living; and how and why we may claim some values as virtues, and what entitles us to do so (Chapters 11 and 12).

Action research should never be perceived as only about actions, but also as about thinking, and how a particular form of thinking informs a particular form of action. So, like Elliott (2007), I believe that action research should be appreciated as a kind of practical philosophy, and even practical theology, inspired by an enduring sense of awe and wonder as we ask questions about what we should do and why we should do it; and it is also about psychology, and ethics, an ever-present awareness that we need to understand what we are doing in order to do it well, and to think critically about which standards we are prepared to use that enable us to say this with justification. It moves from rights to responsibilities, from a main focus on improving practice from the researcher's perspective to an equally important focus of making judgements about the improved practice from other participants' perspectives.

There is the old saying that you should always let caged birds fly free. If they come back to you, it is because they want to be with you. If they don't, they never did. It is the same with people. People make up their own minds; as participants in one another's lives we can advise but we cannot tell. We need to remember this, as action researchers and as ordinary people, for it is only by recognising the right of, and creating the conditions for, each person to accept the responsibility of their own decisions that the world will ever be a happier and more productive place.

Please contact me at jeanmcniff@mac.com, or at www.jeanmcniff.com. I will respond.

Jean McNiff
Dorset, June 2012

A note about case studies

All the case studies in this book are from people I have worked with or met while working, or communicated with through email. Their names appear on pages viii–xii. Most of the texts are edited with permission. The full versions are at http://www.jeanmcniff.com/action_research_principles_and_practice/.

Part I

What do we know?

The principles of action research

This Part introduces ideas relevant to action research and the field of educational research in general. It gives an outline of the main philosophical traditions that inform the field, and contains the following:

Chapter 1: 'What do we know? The principles of action research'. This chapter outlines some of the core principles of action research, and some of the implications they may have for everyday practices.

Chapter 2: 'How do we come to know? Linking theory and practice'. This chapter deals with issues about how knowledge is created and its relationship with practice. It deals with interrelationships between different typologies in the literatures, specifically those to do with knowledge, human interests and methodologies.

Chapter 3: 'Who has influenced our thinking? Key theorists in action research'. Here we consider some key theorists in the field of action research, and possible new directions for the field.

Chapter 4: 'What do we need to know? Exercising educational influence'. The chapter focuses on issues of educational influence, and how this may be exercised for specific purposes.

You can of course do action research without knowing these foundational issues. However, they may help your thinking by providing theoretical and conceptual frameworks. They are essential if you are doing action research study for accreditation.

In Part II we consider how these ideas may be put to use in a practical way.

Chapter 1

What do we know?
The principles of action research

Action research is a name given to a particular way of looking at your practice to check whether it is as you feel it should be. You may be checking it as part of your critical reflection on your practice, or perhaps in response to a professional development review. If you feel that your practice is satisfactory, you will be able to explain how and why you believe this to be the case, and produce authenticated evidence to ground your claims that you are doing well. If you feel your practice needs attention in some way, you will be able to take action to improve it, and produce evidence to show how the practice has improved. You can show the relationship between your learning and your actions in the world: you explain how you have learnt to improve your practice.

Because action research is done by you, the practitioner, it is often referred to as practitioner research, or practice-led or practice-based research. It is a form of on-the-job research, undertaken by people in any context, regardless of their status, position, age or previous experience. It involves you thinking carefully about what you are doing, so it becomes critical self-reflective practice.

Critical self-reflection is central. In some social science forms of research, researchers tend to do research on other people. They observe other people and ask, 'How do I describe and explain what they are doing?' In many forms of action research, action researchers prefer to do research on themselves, in company with other people who are doing the same. They observe themselves and ask, 'How do I/we describe and explain what I am/we are doing?' No distinction is made between researchers and practitioners (although some people who wish to maintain their status as a 'professional' researcher like to keep the distinction). Traditionalist social science researchers tend to enquire into other people's lives and use them as data to demonstrate the validity of the researcher's theories (and, to be fair, some action researchers also do this). Generally speaking, action researchers prefer to enquire into their own lives, and speak with other people as colleagues. Action research therefore becomes an enquiry by the self into the self, with others acting as co-researchers and critical learning partners. Therefore, although you think for yourself and explain how you hold yourself personally accountable for what you are doing, you recognise that you are always in relation with other people, always situated in a real-life social, political, economic and historical context.

Action research involves learning in and through action and reflection, and is conducted in a variety of contexts. Today, you can do action research in the social and caring sciences; in education, nursing and health care; in artistic and creative practices; in organisational, management and business studies; and in virtually any other discipline or area. You can find action research programmes on workplace professional education courses and higher degree studies, as well as in international relations, peace studies and disaster management programmes. Recommendations are made everywhere for learning programmes and professional continuing education courses to use an action research approach.

The case studies in this book show some of this variety and range. Because action research is always to do with improving learning, and improving learning is always to do with education and personal and professional growth, many people regard action research as a powerful form of educational research. This means that learning across all disciplines needs to be seen as a form of educational research: it is as important to be aware of the process of learning as much as the process of developing subject knowledge.

However, it important to remember that there is no such 'thing' as 'action research'. It is a form of words that refers to people becoming aware of and making public their processes of learning with others, and explaining how this informs their practices. Furthermore, no one can learn on behalf of anyone else; we all have to learn for ourselves. Often, however, people write about action research as if it were a 'thing', a self-contained area to be studied, separate from themselves. I am doing this right now, in that I am speaking about an object called 'action research' but not doing anything other than talk about it. Many people speak like this all the time, as if action research were something abstract, a set of procedures to be applied to practice, rather than a living experience. This perspective tends to distort the underpinning values of action researchers such as autonomy, independent thinking and accountability. So when we speak and write about action research, it is important to remember that we are speaking about the real-life experiences of real-life people. The meaning of action research is in the way people learn to negotiate ways of living together and explaining how they do so, emphasising the problematics as much as the successes.

Yet while there might be no such thing as action research, there are people who are action researchers. They might not always call themselves by that name, but if they wished to give their work a theoretical framework, or some underpinning organising principles, they could well call these 'action research'. When people first encounter the idea of action research, they often say, 'This is what I do in any case', and to a certain extent they are right (see Part II, about what else needs to be done to turn practice into research).

The idea of action research refers to the theoretical framework and organising principles that guide practice, as well as its procedures, which is why it comes under the broad heading of 'practice-based research'. Action research is not a thing in itself; the term always implies a process of people interacting together and learning with and from one another in order to understand their practices and situations, and to take purposeful action to improve them.

Action researchers share certain sets of beliefs, commitments and hopes. What they do (action research) is a set of practices that demonstrates those beliefs, commitments and hopes in practice. They undertake research to help them learn how to exercise their individual and collective educational agency, which they use to contribute to improved human, non-human and environmental wellbeing. Lawrence Stenhouse wrote in 1983 that 'research is systematic enquiry made public'. I added in 2002 (McNiff 2002) 'with social intent', and I am now expanding this to 'with social and environmental intent'. I see the task of social formations as contributing to the wellbeing of all forms of life.

Questions therefore arise about what action researchers do, and how and why they do it. These are questions to do with how we view ourselves (ontology), how we come to know (epistemology), how we do things (methodology) and what we hope to achieve (socio-political intent). These aspects are always interrelated and mutually reciprocal, as now explained.

Aspects of research

Action research (and, for that matter, all kinds of research) is more than just doing activities. Remember that the term 'action research' contains two words: 'action' and 'research'.

- The 'action' of action research refers to what you do.
- The 'research' of action research refers to how you find out about what you do.

The action part of action research involves you thinking carefully about the circumstances you are in, how you got here and why the situation is as it is, i.e. your social, political and historical contexts. It also involves you thinking carefully about whether your perceptions of the situation are accurate, or whether perhaps you need to revise them in light of what you have discovered about the current situation. As a nurse, how can you be reasonably confident that you are giving the best care to patients? What might they or other people say if you asked them? This is where the research part comes in.

The research part of action research involves data-gathering, reflection on the action shown through the data, generating evidence from the data, and making claims to knowledge based on conclusions drawn from authenticated evidence. When you produce your report, it is not enough only to offer descriptions of activities, i.e. to say what you are doing. You also need to give explanations for the activities, that is, to say why you are doing it (your reasons) and what you hope to achieve (your purposes). Reasons and purposes are grounded in values. If you claim that you have helped others become more confident through initiating self-help groups, the values that inform your work would include the idea that people should feel respected and speak for themselves. When people demonstrate their confidence, such as asking a question in public, you could claim that you had helped them and perhaps fulfilled your values. You are not saying that you caused this to happen; you are saying that you were in there somewhere and, even perhaps in small part, influenced their learning.

Case study: Ingunn Skjesol Bulling, Norway

An abiding research interest is what makes us able to learn and change, and how I can help others do this in ways that are right for them. This interest informs my work with health-care workers who support children who need help in handling their daily lives, and with professional colleagues. We work together in writing and creating theories that have implications for the people we work with and for ourselves. For me, an interesting aspect of doing action research is that the understandings that emerge through the process can often be quite different from the expectations you had in the beginning. But I continue to try.

This idea of showing how you are trying to live your values in your practice is at the heart of debates about demonstrating and judging quality and validity in action research. It includes issues relating to:

- identifying and articulating your values, i.e. what gives meaning to your life and practices;
- whether you really are living and practising in the direction of your values, and how you test the validity of what you are saying when you claim that you are;
- how you justify those values as they emerge in your practice; this involves interrogating your values and seeing whether they are the right ones for you and your situation; as well as whether your values are shared by others in, say, culturally diverse settings;
- how you judge quality of practice and research in relation to whether you have helped yourself and other people to come to think for yourselves and develop critical perspectives on what you are doing and saying.

If you wish to engage fully with these issues it is helpful to know some key terms, as follows:

Ontology – the way we view ourselves, a theory of being. You ask, 'Who do I think I am?' How you think about yourself influences how you see other people, and how you position yourself in the research.

Epistemology – a theory of knowledge (what is known), including a theory of knowledge acquisition and creation (how it comes to be known). You ask, 'What do I know and how do I come to know it?' The idea of what you know and how you come to know it includes ideas about logic, i.e. how you think. Some people think in linear and analytical ways, while others think in dialogical and relational ways. There are many kinds of logic or ways of thinking, contrary to the dominant idea that there is only one kind, which is rational and one-dimensional.

Methodology – how we do things: do we see action research as the application of a fixed set of steps, or perhaps as a journey where we find things out as we go?

Socio-political intent – purposeful action is always intentional; your research needs to be understood in relation to what you intend to do and how you intend to do it. A main aim of action research is to generate knowledge that can lead to improved understanding and experience for social and environmental benefit. For example, Howard Zinn (2005b) says that educators need to get involved with real-life issues, otherwise they may position themselves as intellectuals without getting involved in the real world.

These issues have implications for action researchers, because key questions arise:

- What do action researchers believe in? – ontological issues
- How do action researchers come to know? – epistemological issues (which includes how they think, and their forms of logic)
- How do action researchers act? – methodological issues
- What are the implications of our knowledge for socio-political and environmental issues?
- How do action researchers use their knowledge for social and environmental wellbeing?

The chapter engages primarily with the first three issues. Matters regarding socio-political and environmental implications are dealt with in Chapters 11 and 12.

What do action researchers believe in? – ontological issues

Action researchers believe that all people are equal and should enjoy the same rights and entitlements. They are able to exercise their capacity for creativity of mind to create their own identities and allow other people to create theirs. They try to find ways of accommodating different values perspectives, which can be difficult when values differ. They try to find ways of living together in spite of possible differences, and see things from the other's perspective; this involves recognising and suspending their own preconceptions.

Creating what they feel are good societies involves their personal commitment to action. This means having the courage to speak and act in ways that are often contested. They know that if they abandon the vision of a better society in light of the troubles of the present one, they may settle into stasis and possibly give up. However, if they try to do something, just one positive life-enhancing action, there is hope of improvement, no matter how small.

Action researchers accept the responsibility of ensuring that their own lives are in order before they make judgements about other people's. This means honestly critiquing their practice, recognising what is good and building on strengths, as well as understanding what needs attention and taking action to improve it. It involves commitment to the idea that learning will transform into purposeful personal and community action for social benefit, with potential implications for non-human and environmental benefit.

They often express these ontological commitments in the language of values, communicating ideas about truth, social justice, compassionate ways of living and respect for diverse and seemingly alien forms of life. They aim to understand these issues in order to influence the transformation of forces of oppression into forces for liberation.

Ontological assumptions also influence how we position ourselves in the research. We can adopt an outsider or an insider perspective, or various points in between. Researcher positionality is a major consideration in deciding which approach to take. It is linked with Buber's (1937) idea about whether you see others as an object, an 'It', or as a person with whom you have a close relationship, a 'Thou'; do you have an 'I–It' or an 'I–Thou' relationship with them? As a nurse, do you speak about 'the fractured femur in bed 32', or as 'Mrs Smith in bed 32'? How do you see your patients or clients in relation to you?

These ideas are especially relevant for a fragmented and hurried world where connectedness with others is in danger (see for example Gray 1995b; Putnam 2000; Sennett 2011). The ideas are relevant for living and working with racial and religious understanding (Sacks 2007). The values of action research make it a pertinent methodology for our time.

How do action researchers come to know?
Epistemological issues

Epistemology is the name given to the study of what we know and how we come to know it. Traditional scientific and social scientific researchers tend to see knowledge as a free-standing unit, to be found 'out there' in books and databases. Knowledge therefore becomes separated from the people who create it.

Case study: Jonathan Libag, the Philippines

During the American colonization of the Philippines in 1900–46, Evangelicals/ Protestants, or what are often called 'born again Christians', created a radical movement extending to all provinces, municipalities and even *barangays* (small villages). My action research focuses on observing and evaluating how they live while responding to their calling through preaching the Gospel and helping the poor and needy.

I work with a non-profit/faith-based (Christian) organisation as a consultant and lecturer on basic sustainable agriculture. I come into contact with many individual pastors, especially in rural settings, and some institutions such as orphanages and Bible schools (in the Philippines and other parts of Asia). Most suffer from limited income, which prevents them from extending help to others. Using a participatory action research methodology, I support them in finding ways of enhancing their incomes and improving their capacities.

Action researchers see knowledge as something they do, a living process. People generate their own knowledge from their experiences of living and learning. Knowledge is never static or complete; it is in a constant state of development as new understandings emerge. This view of knowledge regards reality as a process of emergence, surprising and unpredictable. There are no fixed answers, because answers become obsolete in a constantly changing present, and any answers immediately transform into new questions. Life is a process of asking questions to reveal new potentialities. Action researchers ask questions of the kind, 'I wonder what would happen if … ?' They aim to disturb fixed ways of knowing through deliberately troubling ideas (Butler 1999); this can cause epistemological trouble when one system of ideas comes into conflict with another – essential, however, for seeing things in new ways.

Learning is seen as rooted in experience (Winter 1989). It involves reflecting on practice (a process of critical discernment), deciding whether this practice is in line with your espoused values, and deciding on future action. If you consider your practice good, how can you develop it to deal with an uncertain future? If you consider it less than good, how can you improve it?

Some theorists believe that learning happens only in critical episodes, or in official settings such as classrooms. Yes, but learning also happens in our moment-to-moment living. We learn to walk, catch a ball, avoid difficulties and respond to our feelings. Chomsky (1986) says we are born with the capacity for an unlimited number of original acts of creation; and Mary Catherine Bateson (1994) says we learn a good deal peripherally, without conscious intent. Polanyi maintains (1958) that we know more than we know we know or can say. Drawing on Chomsky's early ideas of generative transformational processes (1965), knowledge can be understood as emerging from the deep levels of tacit knowing to explicit consciousness. This process enables us to make new connections and reconfigure existing knowledge into new forms.

A main idea is to appreciate that sure knowledge is not complete knowledge. We can never really know, which has implications for our practices. In the same way as Habermas (1975) says we cannot *not* learn in processes of social evolution (see p. 13), so Berry (2000) says we cannot *not* act: 'we *have* to act on the basis of what we know, and what we know is incomplete. What we have come to know so far is demonstrably incomplete, since we keep on learning more ... ' (Berry 2000: 10). The question then becomes how to continue without knowing where we are going or what the next step will be. Knowing, as Macdonald (1995) says, involves an act of faith; it is a prayerful act. From an action research perspective, it becomes a question of how to act in faith, to show how we are faithful to others and ourselves.

Case study: Alex Pandolfo, UK

I have set up action research groups in colleges across the country to explore ways of developing non-databased assessment tasks, with an emphasis on basic pedagogical skills in workplaces. All participants record their findings for their continuing professional development (CPD) and publications. I am developing new forms of presentation for action research accounts that show inclusional practices and the importance of action research for our daily teaching.

Many of our teacher training programmes tend to put action research modules at the end of the course, which means that practitioners have to 'find' issues in their practice that they have changed. We now encourage trainee teachers to view the full teacher training programme qualification as a range of action research opportunities.

The aim is to establish that action research is about explaining what we do as professionals who wish to make productive changes. This would also provide evidence of formative learning/assessment for agencies such as Ofsted for the proposed wider interpretation of observing learning.

How do action researchers act? Methodological issues

Action researchers regard learning and experience as processes that enable individuals and groups to negotiate choices about who they are and how they are together. They do not aim for consensus or harmony, but try to create spaces of understanding for negotiating differences.

Therefore, reflection on action, an idea popularised by Schön (1983, 1995) becomes a core assumption. However, this makes sense only when practice is seen as in relation with others, a process of dialogue and encounter (Buber 2002), which may also be understood as a form of spirituality (not necessarily to do with religious belief, although it can be). Capra *et al.* (1992) believe that relation means belonging. We are all connected in deep ways, and, because we are made of the same stuff as the stars (Feynman 1999), we are also connected with the whole of creation. We belong to one another and therefore to the universe.

These ideas have implications for how people understand their practices and make judgements about them. In traditional social science methodologies, practice tends to be seen as separate from practitioners, something they observe and comment on. For example, they might imagine work as in a building or office. I used to think like this. Work was something I did, separate from me. These days I understand my work as embodied in myself, in relationship with other people. The focus of the work is to find ways of developing creative and healthy opportunities for all, for learning and growth. When action researchers reflect on their practices, they are reflecting on their relationships with others, and the experience enables them to embrace life more fully.

Such ideas form the basis of Berry's *Life is a Miracle* (2000). He draws on Shakespeare's *King Lear*, a play he says is about kindness, and tells how the old Earl of Gloucester is devastated because he has been blinded and has also driven away his loyal son, Edgar. In utter despair, Gloucester wishes to give up on life and tries to commit suicide – on Berry's interpretation, out of the hubris that he can control his life by taking it – but Edgar saves him, and so returns him to the pain of engaging with ordinary living. 'Thy life's a miracle', says Edgar. 'Speak yet again' (IV, vi, 55). Similarly, our relationships have potential influence for helping us find our way out of despair or non-commitment, or to develop strategies to choose whether to give up on life or engage with it (Frankl 1984). Most importantly, our relationships help us make wise choices, and hold ourselves accountable for them. 'Speak yet again'; change your mind as necessary, and don't let anyone tell you that you can't.

These ideas also have implications for how we judge the quality of our practices and research. If we are in relation with other people, what we do influences them, and what they do influences us. We have to judge reciprocally what we do, and how we investigate these relationships. 'Practice' therefore cannot be judged only in terms of 'Have I influenced someone's learning?' or 'Have I improved my practices?' (as I wrote in 2002), but also by 'How do others judge my involvement and influence? Do they feel I have helped them to engage more fully in life?' And also, 'How have I/we learned with and from the other? What do we do with our learning?' And even more complex, 'How do I/we justify what I/we have done and the values that inspired our practices?' These questions need to be at the heart of practice-based research, to help us explain how we hold ourselves accountable for our choices.

Some implications

These ontological, epistemological and methodological considerations have implications for social and political practices. Key issues arise:

- Challenging the dominant epistemology
- Challenging the dominant form of theory
- E-theories and I-theories of practice.

Challenging the dominant epistemology

The purpose of research is generally understood as creating new knowledge that will contribute to new theory. 'Theory' may be understood broadly as 'descriptions and explanations of how something works and why it works like this'. We all have millions of theories about how and why the world works, and we bring these with us wherever we go. However, it is not enough just to say, 'I have created new knowledge and what I am saying is correct'. Someone is bound to say, 'How do I know? Show me why I should believe you.' It is then your responsibility to explain to the other person why they should believe you. This involves explaining the methodology you have engaged in when producing the new knowledge, which involves gathering data, generating evidence, producing theory and making judgements about its quality and usefulness.

There are different forms of theory, including propositional, abstract forms, and living, dynamic forms (contrary to the dominant social sciences view, which says there is only one kind). Most social science research sees theory as an abstract body of knowledge that informs practice, a theory-into-practice model (which is seen as the dominant form). In traditional education and training contexts, it is expected that people will listen, take notes, and not ask questions: a control and command form of relationship. Some researchers produce conceptual models that work in practice provided people are obedient and do what the model says they should do. If people exercise their independence of mind and spirit, and disagree with the model itself, or with the fact that they are expected to agree with abstract models and theories, they are often seen as nuisances and dissidents.

Traditional positivist views of research and theory dominate much institutional thinking and practice. Recent movements such as action research have challenged traditional views. These challenges are naturally unwelcome to dominant elites, who then use a range of control strategies to silence the critique, including ridicule and marginalisation, what Lyotard (1984) calls intellectual terrorism. The most characteristic response is to pretend that critique does not exist. Chomsky (2000a) explains how terms such as 'dissident', 'radical' and 'troublemaker' are used to silence people who raise questions.

There is nothing radical or unorthodox about people wanting to have a say in their own lives, however, so when a critical mass of resistance builds up, other measures are needed. Foucault (1991) developed ideas about how those in power keep people compliant, such as the exercise of disciplinary power and governance, by which people are persuaded to be obedient and to believe that obedience was actually their idea. It is important to build our intellectual resources to combat such propaganda, and not let harassment or fear of being labelled as reactionary stand in the way of realising a vision for what could be a better way of life.

Challenging the dominant form of theory

The issue becomes the legitimacy of forms of theory, as well as who is entitled to generate theory, and how the theory is judged: 'who decides what knowledge is, and who knows what needs to be decided' (Lyotard 1984: 9). Ball (1990: 17), drawing on Foucault's ideas, says that it is not only about 'what can be said and thought but also about who can speak, when, where and with what authority. Discourses embody meaning and social relationship; they constitute both subjectivity and power relations.' The issue then extends to not only what should be judged as worthwhile theory, but also who should be judged a worthwhile person. It also becomes a matter of whether people are allowed to speak for themselves. Marx famously said, 'They cannot represent themselves; they must be represented' (1987: 124). All this raises questions about how others treat us and how we treat them, and what kind of society we wish to create.

In 1965, and focusing on linguistic analysis, Chomsky explained that research can operate at three levels of adequacy: observational, descriptive and explanatory. In a sense, all research begins with observation, and most research offers descriptions of events. In 1960s linguistics, the dominant research methodology was behaviourist. The aim was to study a particular language, gather instances of its significant features, and provide descriptions of the language under study (Lyons 1970). The same tendency is still visible today across the social sciences, business and management, nursing and health care and educational research. Everywhere there are descriptions of how things work, or ought to work, and what needs to be done to make them work like this. These are inert theoretical models. They work in principle, but often there is no live evidence to show that they work in practice. They need to move towards levels of explanatory adequacy, to show the realities of practice. These ideas are echoed in Schön's (1995) views about the need to move from observations and descriptions of action towards explanations for action. The focus then shifts to showing the reasons and intentions of the person that inform the behaviour.

The issue remains therefore, whose research is it? Some views of action research say it is enough for an external researcher to observe, describe and explain the actions of others who are doing action research. This view generates an interpretive view of action research (see Chapter 3). However, this could be seen as a distortion of the values of action research, including democracy and respect for others as critical thinkers. A dynamic form of theory means that the locus of responsibility and the ownership of the theory shift from the 'external' researcher to the practitioner-researchers themselves, as they give explanations for their own actions in terms of their values and hopes.

E-theories and I-theories

Chomsky (1986) also developed the idea of E-language and I-language. The emphasis in traditional American linguistics in the 1970s and 80s was still on the sound and word structure of sentences, where a language could be understood 'as a collection (or system) of actions or behaviours of some sort' (p. 20). Chomsky referred to this as 'externalized language' (E-language). An 'internalized language' (I-language), on the other hand, is 'some element of the mind of the person who knows the language acquired by the learner, and used by the speaker-hearer' (p. 22). In his *New Horizons in the Study of Language and Mind* (2000b), Chomsky developed the concept of I-conceptual and I-belief systems, a concept that revolves around the internalised nature of beliefs and ideas. This indicates a shift from descriptions of language or theory generation as an external body of study, towards an explanation for how language or theory generation informs the way a person creates and justifies their own version of reality.

This is a most important concept that I have used to refer to different forms of theory and ways of coming to know (McNiff 1993). An E-theory exists as a form of theory external to its creator and generated from the study of people as external objects. This is a propositional form of theory, used widely in social scientific analysis, behaviourist in orientation, and synchronic – that is, analysing something at a fixed point in time and place, without acknowledgement of outside influences or its transformation through history.

An I-theory is a dynamic, transformational form of theory, a property of an individual's belief system, and is diachronic, that is, understood as transforming through time. This view may be helpful for understanding different forms of theory throughout broad areas of human enquiry, including educational research. In this book, I take the view that action research leads to the generation of I-theories of knowledge, already located within the practitioner's tacit forms of knowing, that emerge in practice as personal forms of explanations for what is done and what is known. These theories are linked with other I-belief systems, including values and relationships. The way the theories manifest as living practices is congruent with the belief system of the knower.

These ideas may be linked with the idea of living theories, developed from original work by Ilyenkov by Jack Whitehead (see Whitehead 1989, 1999), where he takes the view that the descriptions and explanations offered by practitioners for their practices may be termed their 'living educational theories'. Engaging with such an approach means, as Whitehead says, placing the 'living I' at the centre of the enquiry and recognising ourselves potentially as living contradictions when our values are denied in our practices. We might believe we are working in an effective and morally committed manner, but then find from other people's and our own self-evaluations that we are denying much of what we believe in.

However, while acknowledging the usefulness of these ideas, I do not see action research as about problem-identification or problem-solving, but as about realising human potential. This means thinking about how we are positioned in relation with others and accepting the responsibility for accounting for our own practices. In work contexts, it means accounting for our professionalism. It is our responsibility to realise our capacities for creative living for one another's benefit. We offer descriptions and explanations for our work by producing professional narratives that show how the work influenced the quality of life for others. We gather data about our practices and produce evidence to show that our claims are well grounded. Those with whom we work state that they have benefited (or not), and those with whom they are working testify that they are benefiting (or not).

So it is possible to trace lines of influence from ourselves to others with whom we might have no personal contact, but with whose lives we can claim to have been in contact, albeit at a remove. There are, as Bakhtin (1986) says, voices in everything. I am alone as I write but I am influenced by the voices in texts I have read and seminars I have attended, as well as voices in the supermarket and at the airport. You are listening to my voice as you read, and responding, and in turn others will hear your voice and respond. How do we ensure that we are speaking well, and using our influence for others' benefit? In some instances, the lines of influence are too complex, and it is impossible to know the extent of our influence. Consequently, in all contexts, whether its effects are visible or not, we need to try to ensure that our influence leads to life-enhancing growth for all.

Descriptive E-approaches cannot do this. Processes of social change begin with the processes of personal change: 'change can only come about when the individuals who belong to a particular organization [or social formation] can see the point in changing' (Rizvi 1989: 227). The idea of 'change' is not an abstraction: change is us. It is we who change, and so we change our social situations. It is pointless to produce abstract models of social change and expect other people to apply them to their own circumstances or locate themselves within the models. I think Popper (2002) is right when he critiques Marx's ideas about the existence of concrete laws of history. Bourdieu (1990) is also right when he explains how the model supposed to represent the reality can become the reality instead of the reality itself (see p. 63).

I once attended a workshop where a well-known educational researcher presented his five-point model for professional education, which included the need for critical reflection. He invited comment, so I observed that while I thought his model was lovely, it did not represent the realities of my life. Furthermore, his model demonstrated the same issues he was critiquing, i.e. the lack of critique. This is an issue right through the disciplines-oriented social sciences. Said (1991: 28) observes:

> On the one hand, 'the disciplines' are institutions more than they are activities; on the other hand, they regulate and normalise what they study (which in a sense they have also created) far more readily than they analyze themselves or reflect on what they do.

I am not saying that models are not important. They are important, but they do not substitute for real life. It is not enough for an external observer to prescribe another person's actions and then present a model or an account of those actions as if to give a full explanation of their reality. The practice is also ethically questionable. I am saying that people need to offer their own explanations for practice in the form of their dynamically transformational I-theories that are always already in a process of evolution. The whole evolutionary process is integrated within the life of the person who is telling the story.

These issues are important for future developments. Action researchers need to show their collective intent to live in the direction of the values that inform their work and not be content to stay at the level of abstract analysis, in the same way as you have to be in the water to learn how to swim, and not lecture people about the value of dialogue. Action researchers cannot afford to be armchair philosophers if they wish to maintain their integrity.

So, what do we know? What have we learnt so far?

We know that research processes may be analysed in terms of a researcher's ontological, epistemological, methodological, socio-political and environmental commitments, and how these may come together to inform how they theorise their work. We also know how to rationalise decisions about which kinds of theory are most appropriate for doing so. What we now need to do is:

- explain our choices in relation to how we understand good quality practice and research;
- explain how and why we understand 'good' in this way, and how we make judgements about what we believe is good;
- produce a systematic body of evidence-based case study knowledge containing stories that explain how we are doing so. Some of this material appears in this book.

Case study: Anne Marie Villumsen, Denmark

In Denmark, approximately 90 per cent of all children aged three to five attend childcare on a daily basis. However, some childcare personnel sometimes experience difficulties in identifying children at risk and in initiating multidisciplinary collaboration. Traditionally, challenges have existed in collaboration between childcare and social service personnel, and little research has been conducted into such collaboration and its potentials to change the developmental pathways of children at risk. My research focuses on helping childcare and social care personnel develop more meaningful collaborative approaches.

However, in multidisciplinary collaboration there can be a tendency to exclude the child's parents, so parents' extensive knowledge of their own children is disregarded and they can feel alienated. I am therefore trying to develop collaborative relationships between all parties in order to create better opportunities for the children.

If we can do this, we can move action research from its currently dominant surface-level focus on methods and practices to the deeper levels of moral accountability, so that we can explain why we do what we do, and therefore contribute to the explanatory power of our work as research-active professionals and morally committed citizens.

Having discussed some of what we know, we now turn to ideas about how we come to know, and begin to focus on linking theory and practice.

Chapter 2

How do we come to know?
Linking theory and practice

This chapter deals with issues about how knowledge is created and its relationship with practice. It is therefore also about the relationship between the researcher and their own knowledge, and with others in the research who are also creating knowledge, and with whom they make up a knowledge-creating community. Making these issues explicit involves thinking about the underpinning values and logics of practice, and how these are embedded within and inform new practices and encourage a view of practice as research-informed and evidence-based.

Educational research, including action research, is always socially, culturally, historically and politically situated, undertaken by a real person or persons, within a particular context, for a particular purpose. Research does not just happen. It has an overall design, which enables the researcher to plan in a systematic way to:

- identify a research issue;
- formulate a research question;
- explain why the issue is important;
- monitor practice and gather data to show what the situation is like;
- take action;
- continue to gather data and generate evidence;
- state the findings so far and make a provisional claim;
- test the validity of the claim;
- explain the significance of the research;
- decide on potential future action … which may provide the basis for a new investigation … and so on.

However, as soon as topics such as 'new knowledge' and 'more appropriate theories' are voiced, politics enters, because what counts as knowledge and theory are often contested by different researchers and theorists working in their particular contexts and with their own values base and purposes. Research and theory form tightly interpenetrated areas of influence, including social purpose, justice, power, politics and personal identity.

When speaking about educational research in general, and action research in particular, it is important to remember that the conversation is being conducted in a cultural, historical and socio-political context.

Here I outline some of the main aspects relevant to the emergence of action research, and suggest why the work is often contested. This involves a constellation of considerations, including values, logics and ideologies. If the action of action research is the visible part of the iceberg, these aspects are silent below-the-surface influences. So here I explore why, for others and myself, a main task is to investigate what might be the most appropriate way of knowing and coming to know (epistemology) that takes these considerations into account, and possibly influences developments towards more dialogical and ecologically aware communities of educational enquiry.

The ideas are organised in terms of established typologies, and their relevance for action research, as follows:

- Typologies of knowledge
- Typologies of human interests
- Typologies of research
- The relevance of these ideas for action research.

There are everywhere overlaps and similarities. In addition, while different people may look at things differently, no one way is 'better' or 'worse' than others: they are different, each appropriate for different contexts and purposes, in the same way as a bicycle and a racing car are both vehicles but each is used for a different purpose.

There is also debate about whether action research is a paradigm, a methodology or a method:

- *A paradigm* (see Kuhn 1996) refers to a set of ideas about the world that is held by a particular community, for example a democratic or autocratic worldview. In research, it becomes a set of attitudes and ideas that inform the research.
- *A methodology* is a way of conducting research. Your choice of methodology is informed by your attitudes, reasons and purposes. Examples of methodologies are ethnography, case study research and appreciative enquiry.
- *A method* is another word for 'technique', and usually refers to data-gathering and analysis.

A key issue is researcher positionality, i.e. how you position yourself in the research. How do you gather data and about what? Are you inside or outside the action you are investigating? This depends on whether you see the other people in the research as subjects, participants or colleagues, and on the kind of relationships between you. This links with Buber's (1937) idea of 'I–It' and

'I–Thou' relationships (see p. 28). Questions arise: Whose research is it? Who decides on the findings? Who says?

Here are some common typologies in research. Thinking about these issues will help you explain why you have chosen action research as your preferred methodology. Also note that although these typologies are presented separately for analytical purposes, they are interdependent and transformational.

Typologies of knowledge

There are different kinds of knowledge and different ways of coming to know (i.e. different epistemologies). It is widely held that forms of knowledge include 'know that', 'know how' and personal knowledge; while ways of knowing, or forms of logic (thinking) include propositional forms, relational forms, dialectical forms, dialogical forms and others. Which ones you choose depend on your positionality, reflecting your attitudes to and relationships with others.

Forms of knowledge

This section deals with ideas about 'know that', 'know how' and personal knowledge

Know that, also called propositional and technical rational knowledge, refers to knowledge about facts and figures. Knowledge exists 'out there', external to a researcher, whose job is to discover it and pass it on to others who may use it and perhaps exchange it for other goods. This is especially so in post-industrial knowledge-creating societies: 'Knowledge is and will be produced in order to be sold' (Lyotard 1984: 4; see also Hargreaves 2003). A fixed body of knowledge holds truths about the way things are. When people claim, 'I know that this is the case', they need to produce evidence to ground and test the validity of the claim. 'Know that' is linked with the idea of E-theories, and refers to bodies of public knowledge external to the knower. Propositional knowledge is highly valued today for its bargaining power in gaining a competitive edge in results-driven societies.

Know how, also called procedural knowledge, refers to procedures, skills and technical capabilities. 'Know how' is not a fixed body of knowledge external to ourselves but involves practical procedural knowing. 'I know how to do this' refers to actions in the world, and the claim to knowledge can be tested by demonstrating, for example, that you can do mathematics or ride a bike. 'Know how' therefore often becomes linked with skills and competencies, though knowing how to do something does not guarantee that one can do it. Ryle's (1949) *The Concept of Mind* contains an account of 'know that' and 'know how'.

Personal knowledge, also called tacit knowledge (Polanyi 1958, 1967), refers to a subjective, intuitive way of knowing that cannot be rationalised. Often we cannot articulate what we know: we 'just know'; and we tend to know more than we can say. It seems we all have a vast fund of tacit knowledge, possibly developed through experience, possibly part of our genetic inheritance, that enables us to act in a certain way without recourse to external facts or authority. Personal knowledge is linked with the idea of I-theories, and refers to the latent knowledge that is within the individual's mind.

To illustrate, here is a passage from Jo Nesbo's *The Devil's Star* (2006: 241–2). Harry Hole, a detective, and his colleague Øystein are speaking about the difficulties of cracking a code:

> ... Harry held his head in his hands. 'But I hoped you could tell me something about the principles behind cracking codes.'

> 'The codes I cracked were mathematical codes, Harry. With interpersonal codes there's a completely different semantics. For example, I still can't decide what women are actually saying.'

> 'Imagine that this is both. Simple logic and a subtext.'

> 'OK, let's talk about cryptography. Ciphers. To see that you need both logical and what is called analogical thinking. The latter means that you use the subconscious and intuition, in other words, what you don't realise you already know. And then you combine linear thinking with the recognition of patterns. ... If I can put it this way, it is the dimension above letters and numerals. Above language. The answers that don't tell you how, but why. ... It has something in common with religious visions and is more like a gift.'

> 'Let's assume I know why. What happens after that?'

> 'You can take the long road. Going through all the permutations until you die. ... [Or you can go into a trance.] You keep staring at the data until you stop thinking conscious thoughts. ... If your subconscious cracks the code, you'll get there. If it doesn't ... [it'll] crack you.'

This could be one way to develop a high level of understanding and performance in a subject. Musicians, writers and other artists often speak about this kind of experience, when the process almost takes over. Researchers always need to link their ways of knowing with the capacity to reflect on what they are doing and why they are doing it.

Ways of knowing, including forms of thinking or forms of logic

When speaking about ways of knowing, it is common to identify different forms of thinking, or logic, including propositional forms, dialectical forms, relational forms and dialogical forms. Knowing and thinking are interrelated and mutually transformational.

Propositional (or formal or symbolic) forms of logic refer to abstract, analytical ways of thinking and knowing. We view reality and knowledge as objects external to ourselves; we study them and make proposals about how they work, and why they work as they do. This is a conceptual system of knowing, which uses an abstract form of logic: ideas and objects may be represented by symbols – for example, 'if x, then y' – and it regards theories as static models of reality that may be understood intellectually. When we think and express our knowledge in propositional ways, we make positive statements about the way we think about things. Abstract forms abstract from reality; the thinking is abstract, a conceptual exercise. This form of logic, often associated with Aristotle, who wanted to eliminate contradiction from rational thought, initiated what tends to be called the Western intellectual tradition, and is now adopted worldwide as the basis of many of its social, including institutional, practices, especially when these involve assessment exercises.

Dialectical forms of logic refer to the capacity to accept and incorporate contradiction. We view reality as something we are part of, not separate from. Knowing becomes a process of creating new forms out of previous ones, a process of becoming, of coming into being. It works on the principle of question and answer, where one answer generates a new question, so nothing is ever complete or final. This view is part of an ancient tradition, existing long before Plato, who saw contradiction as part of life processes, the need to hold the one and the many together at the same time, and it lies at the heart of relational forms of practices.

Relational forms of logic refer to open, fluid forms of thinking when we recognise ourselves as in relation with our contexts, including the people and objects we are with. This way of knowing is embodied in the knower and their practice: they bring into being that which is already latent within themselves and their relationships. It is also part of many so-called indigenous ways of knowing (Thayer-Bacon 2003).

Dialogical forms of logic emphasise the need for recognising that we are always in relation with other people, and seeing the relationships as forms of coming to know: we come to know and learn in and through community. We keep the conversational space open through maintaining a mindset of 'I in relation with the other'. Self is not seen as the centre, and the idea of 'centre' disappears because there is no identifiable centre. This way of thinking is important for developing communities of practice (Wenger 1999), especially communities of critical enquiry, where you enter into and 'dwell in' the spirit of the community. This has significant implications for communities of action researchers.

Case study: Ana Naidoo, South Africa

Ana Naidoo's paper 'Towards a just world' (Naidoo 2011) includes the following.

At my institution we recently opted for a re-curriculation process for our pre-service teacher education programmes. The aim was to strengthen the discipline knowledge of future teachers in their area of specialisation. The process was grounded in the idea of developing a critical pedagogy.

It was anticipated that I would act as an authority in education and curriculum change and see my work through the lens of an objective 'I'. However, my profession is informed by a subjective 'me'; this 'me' represents my background and informs my worldview and my epistemological base. So the context and content of the 'me' shapes what the 'I' believes in, and the two are mutually inclusive. The expectation for how I would position myself came from a form of thinking resonant with what Buber (1937) calls an 'I–It' relationship, where the 'I' is the subject and 'It' the object. This communicates a sense of detachment, and is seen as the usual way in which we conceive of and analyse a material world.

Buber also speaks of 'I–Thou', a relationship that alludes to a spiritual world, where relationships are built on mutual trust and reciprocal action. I have also added an interim stage, an 'I–me' relationship. This requires me to look at myself, and to generate my transformational theories of practice. This comes naturally to me because my profession focuses on the need for social justice, a pressing need in South Africa. I have also created a further 'I–we' relationship where the 'we' are the academic staff who will be the ultimate bearers of change and then the implementers. 'I–we' may be seen as a transition stage between 'I–It' and 'I–Thou'.

I have come to these understandings partly through interrogating my personal baggage of growing up in a country where the atrocities of the apartheid government were everywhere visible. I cannot help but bring the 'me' into the picture. I was born in the year when the Bantu Education Act (1954) came into force, which affected my entire schooling. Each racial group had a separate education system and we lived in segregated areas. The need to prioritise social justice in teacher education stems from the past.

In South Africa a question that any 50+-year-old person of colour asks any white 50+-year-old person is, 'How can you not have questioned how we were treated in the sixties and seventies?' A common answer is, 'We did not know.'

The Bantu Education Act ensured that school curricula differed for the different racial groups. Most white people, it appears, stayed in blissful ignorance of how others were educated. However, now that the laws have changed, we need to check whether we are still living in blissful ignorance. Teachers will encounter learners from all kinds of backgrounds, and we need to ensure that we are educating them for the future, not the past, through encouraging critical reflection and self-interrogation.

Typologies of human interests

Habermas (1972, 1987), a major theorist in social science, rejected the view that knowledge generation is a neutral activity carried out by an external 'mind' somewhere, resulting in the production of 'pure' knowledge. Instead, he suggested that knowledge is an activity undertaken by a real person who is driven by particular desires and interests. From this perspective, knowledge is always constituted of human interests. Habermas categorised personal-social practices as three broad sets of interests: the technical, the practical and the emancipatory. In 2002 (McNiff 2002), I added a fourth category of relational interests and will elaborate on this shortly. First, here is an outline of Habermas's typologies of human interests.

Technical interests are mainly concerned with controlling the environment through the production of technical-rational knowledge. The aim of knowledge is to support technical and scientific progress. Although this has come to be the dominant epistemology in technologised and knowledge-creating societies (Hargreaves 2003; Nonaka and Takeuchi 1995), it is a quite narrow view that sees knowledge creation as instrumental activity that can be measured, usually quantitatively. Technical rationality is generally seen as the form of knowledge most appropriate for contemporary social and work practices. Thousands of people, including myself, do not hold this view, and suggest that other forms of knowledge are also essential for human wellbeing.

Practical interests focus on understanding, meaning-making and interpretation. Habermas maintains that communicative action goes beyond rational interaction and scientific enquiry, and involves understanding other people and their lifeworlds. Communicative action aims to generate intersubjective agreement, where people come together to share ideas and work towards agreement, even when this is possibly agreement within disagreement, or the other way round. This process, however, can distort the understandings we arrive at, because what we do and think are always subject to wider historical and cultural influences of which we may or may not be aware. It is important, says Habermas, to understand these influences and find ways of working with them.

Emancipatory interests help us to free ourselves from dominating forces that control our thoughts and actions. We learn how to recognise and deal with influences that force us to become the people others wish us to be, and we work consistently to create our own identities. We recognise the politically constituted nature of all our social practices, and work within those frameworks to liberate our thinking in order to take more purposeful action in shaping our lives.

Relational interests is a category I introduced in the 2002 second edition of this book, and enables us to understand the kind of relationships we have with others. This recognition is essential for an understanding of the meaning of action research. It involves recognising that while the focus of the enquiry may be the 'I', the 'I' is always already in relation with others and their environment, so the responsibility of the 'I' is to find ways of contributing to the learning and wellbeing of the other. The 'I' needs to accept responsibility for their actions, recognising that actions always have consequences for others and self. Also it is not about 'we' as a collection of 'I's, but of how each 'I' is in relation with other 'I's. The focus of the enquiry shifts to the relationships among people, more than on the people themselves. These views involve developing new dialogical interests, as follows.

Dialogical interests (a new category) enable all members in a conversation to find ways of keeping the conversational space open. It is not a question of developing the right interactive skills, but more of maintaining a mindset that sees relationships more than things. Dialogue is more an attitude than a way of speaking: 'It goes into the process of thought *behind* the assumptions, not just the assumptions themselves' (Bohm 1996: 9, emphasis in original). This may also be seen as a spiritual interest.

The discussion now moves to types of research, for the type of research we choose is grounded in the types of relationships that the research requires.

Typologies of research

Arising from ideas like these, a three-paradigm approach has become widely accepted (Bassey 1999; Carr and Kemmis 1986; Hitchcock and Hughes 1995; McNiff 2000). In research contexts, a paradigm is taken to mean a set of ideas and approaches, mental models that influence the development of particular intellectual and social frameworks. The main research paradigms were taken as the empirical, the interpretive and the critical-theoretic, and these may reflect the categories of technical, practical and emancipatory interests. These paradigms may in turn contain their own subsets. Here I am suggesting that this separatist three-paradigm approach appears to be becoming embedded within a broader, more ecological and holistic approach that emphasises the relational nature of people and their contexts, as well as the gradual epistemological shift through the legitimisation of work-based knowledge and the personal knowledge in which it is embedded.

The three usually accepted paradigms are as follows.

Empirical research

Empirical research is rooted in the Newtonian–Cartesian (from Descartes) worldview. In this view, the natural world can be understood as a set of interrelated parts, and one part causes certain effects in the others. Phenomena are seen as if they are pieces of machinery, which act in a predetermined manner, with predictable outcomes (see Davies 1992). Descartes said that mind and body were separate entities. This view gave rise to a philosophy of dualism, that is, that things could be understood in terms of binary opposites:

either–or rather than both–and. The worldview was one of fragmentation, isolation and alienation (Dawkins 2006). In historical accounts of research, the idea of 'empirical' as an objective methodology often changed to 'empiricist', with overtones of control and domination, particularly when the metaphors and methods of the physical sciences, in which scientists studied rocks and trees, were transferred to the social sciences, where they now studied people. Like machine parts, people are assumed to occupy particular places that they should keep to maintain the equilibrium of an established order.

Early empiricists believed that only objects 'out there' were worthy of study. Anything which could not be seen, heard, felt or tasted was not real, so 'imaginary' phenomena such as hopes, intentions and experiences should not be taken seriously. Studying reality involved a careful process of experimentation, usually involving control and experimental groups. The aim was to show how variables could be manipulated to predict and control behaviour in terms of cause and effect; data were subject to quantitative analysis and evidence in terms of established categories of analysis. The validity of empirical research came to be judged in terms of traditional criteria such as replicability, generalisability and objectivity. If an experiment were repeated in a new situation, would it follow a specified method exactly, and could its results be generalised to other situations? Would it be sufficiently objective as to avoid contamination by the researcher's own values and situatedness? If these criteria were not met, the research and its theory might be rejected as invalid.

This view travelled extensively throughout human enquiry and is still highly regarded, rightly so, especially in the world of science and technology. It is important to know that the food we are eating has been properly prepared, and that the car will stop when we apply the brakes. Scientific and technological advances have contributed enormously to human wellbeing.

However, in social contexts, the machine analogy breaks down. It works provided people are prepared to behave in ways approved by the researchers. If, however, people challenge those power relationships and act according to their own choices, trouble usually breaks out.

Some critical implications for action research

Many contexts in which action research approaches are used, such as professional education, community development and organisational transformation, still traditionally draw on the idea of empirical research, so action research is (mistakenly) placed in the social sciences. This may be because the traditional model for managing learning (usually other people's learning) continues to be a mode of instruction. People are expected to receive information and apply it to their work. The locus of power is in the external researcher or provider who gathers data about the situation and theorises what is happening in the situation. People then become data to be manipulated and spoken about. Boundaries are established in terms of what can and cannot be done. The collegial and humanitarian values base of human living is systematically factored out, to be replaced by values of self-interest, power and control. Participants are discouraged from acting as agents, and are instead required to become skilled technicians whose job is to apply received knowledge generated by so-called 'experts'.

The epistemological basis of empirical research is that theory determines practice – and it is usually the theory of the expert that determines the practitioners' practices. Practitioners are encouraged to fit their practices into a given theory, not to question and not to exercise their own originality of mind and action, a situation that entirely denies the creativity and spontaneity of practice and the self-reflective nature of responsible action. Knowledge is seen as a thing; in the increasing market orientation of today, knowledge is seen as a commodity to be acquired and sold, imported and exported (Donn and Al Manthri 2010), not necessarily a process to be engaged in (although there is considerable critique: see for example Lankshear and Knobel 2011). The relationship between the researcher and other participants in the research process therefore increasingly emerges as one of control and domination where the researcher is seen as the knower and other participants are seen as trainees; and the communication of knowledge is seen as forming a linear pathway from the researcher's head directly into the head of the trainee.

The commodification of learning and its management disregards questions of the kind 'How do I understand my practice?', or why such questions are necessary. 'How do I … ?' forms of questions regard the knowledge base of practice as fluid, developmental, generative and transformational. All people are potential knowers who create their own responses to practice as they study it, and so generate their personal theories of learning. Learning becomes a creative process grounded in relationship, whether with someone who is physically present as in learning settings, or virtual as in a book or video, or with one's own thoughts. The epistemology of practice is one of spontaneity and emergence (Johnson 2001), leading to educational encounters in which each person decides what is the right course of action in relation to the other.

Interpretive research (sometimes called interpretative research)

In empirical research, participants act as data whose personal involvement is factored out; any personal intervention would contaminate and potentially skew the results. Interpretive approaches, however, acknowledge the contributions of practitioners as real-life participants in the research. In some views, their accounts are seen as as valid as those of the researcher-observer's. The question always remains, however – who generates the theory and therefore who owns the research? This question is at the heart of choice of research methodology and never goes away.

The interpretive tradition grew mainly out of sociological enquiry, as the social sciences began to dislodge a worldview of human action as deterministic. It arose initially out of the hermeneutic tradition, the name given originally to the practice of the interpretation of religious texts by Protestant theologians in the seventeenth century (Carr and Kemmis 1986), and which later came to be associated with literature and the arts. From the nineteenth century onwards, more efficient communications and travel opportunities gave rise to an interest in anthropological and naturalistic research: researchers began to study people in their own settings. A number of perspectives developed including phenomenology and ethnomethodology, and debates arose within the movement over whose voices should be heard – the researchers' or those who were being researched. The same dilemma as that found in empiricist approaches became problematic: who had control of the research process and whose theory was being generated? While interpretive research valued the importance of people as actors, the question still remained of who was a researcher, whose voices were heard, and who wrote the script.

During the 1960s and 70s, a new type of ethnographic research arose in education studies, which came to be known, among other names, as illuminative evaluation (Parlett and Hamilton 1976). This gradually evolved as case study research (Bassey 1999; Yin 2008), with its underpinning ideologies that included democratic popular involvement in research processes and the interpretation of its findings (see also Stringer 2007). This view, however, is frequently distorted in much case study research, where the external outsider researcher does research on insiders' practices, reflecting a view critiqued by James (1991) that ordinary people are often believed to be incapable of speaking for themselves. This view tends to be perpetuated by elites who like to keep it this way.

Case study has become a major approach in much social science, including health care, management and business studies, public administration and educational enquiry. Its methods include the systematic collection of objective data and rigorous analysis to arrive at agreed interpretations of the data (Yin 2008). A main technique to ensure analytical rigour is triangulation, which is a strategy involving the cross-checking of findings using three different data sources and comparing one account with another (Cresswell 2007).

Depending on the commitments of the researcher, the data and their interpretation may or may not be made available to participants for their scrutiny and possible reinterpretation (as access to findings has changed considerably in recent years with the introduction of Freedom of Information Acts).

Some critical implications for action research

This interpretive view of the research process and the positioning of the researcher and research participants is potentially little different from that of traditional empirical research. The same power relationships exist in terms of who is regarded as a legitimate knower, whose practice is to be studied, and whose knowledge counts. The external researcher is entitled to regard people as objects of study, and to make statements about their actions and the purposes and intentions that inform these actions. The external researcher speaks on behalf of other people. The form of theory remains conceptual; the researcher generates a theory about an external situation.

When these assumptions are brought to action research, as they frequently are, the contradictions become clear. On the one hand, researchers produce high-sounding rhetoric about democracy and the rights of people to be involved in decision-making, whereas, on the other, they systematically rule people out of the decision-making process. There is a clear assumption that it is acceptable for researchers to watch other people doing their action research, and advise on what they should do and how they should do it.

The contradictions continue in the form of a power relationship that positions the researcher as external to the situation, but still able to interpret the situation and make judgements and offer explanations about other people, without consulting them; and also with the researcher advising people what to do without necessarily taking their own advice. It is questionable whether they even see this need. In my view, those positioned as appointed researchers should engage in the same process of critical discernment and informed action that they advise other people to engage in, and take their own advice. Perhaps, however, it is a significant feature of those in authority that they do not see the need to change, and will not change without a challenge. It would appear that some interpretive views rest on a limited conceptualisation of democracy and participation (Zinn 2005b); for some people, models of democracy are to be applied, rather than lived, a process of convenient discrimination rather than moral commitment.

Of note, it is important to distinguish between interpretive approaches and those situations in which experienced researchers support the enquiries of new researchers, as in, for example, the case study on p. 69, where the relationship is one of collaborative learning, not of a take-over; see also Reason and Bradbury's (2008) ideas about second-order action research, p. 55 of this book.

Critical-theoretic approaches

A new swell of critical voices began to be heard from the 1930s onwards. The most coherent were from what later came to be known as the Frankfurt School (Horkheimer, Adorno, Marcuse and later Habermas), who said that then-current methodologies were inadequate for social scientific enquiry because they failed to recognise the historical, cultural and social situatedness of researchers. People could not comment on their experience unless they understood how that experience was shaped by their own situatedness. They could not be free until they realised they were unfree.

A new approach was needed that enabled people to become aware of the historical and cultural forces that had influenced them and their situations. People needed to appreciate the power-constituted nature of their lives, and learn how to challenge. This view came to stand as an ideology critique that enabled people to become aware of their historical and cultural conditioning and find ways to recreate their personal and social realities.

Critical theory developed as a systematic approach to offer both an oppositional response to dominating influences and emancipatory hope. Today, there is a large critical literature in teacher, health and other professional education and organisational studies, and its influence continues to grow – for example, the idea of critical literacies (Lankshear and Knobel 2011), critical pedagogies (McLaren 1995) and critical narrative analysis (Goodson 2012). Other research traditions have emerged from critical theory, or have been strengthened by it: for example, critical feminist research and liberation theology, as well as action research.

Some critical implications for action research

It is well to remember that critical theory works from within the broad context of social science. Although its overall approach is appropriate to educational settings, it does not claim to be educational in Dewey's (1916) view, or in the views expressed in this book, that is, developing relationships that can lead to further growth. The aim of critical theory is to critique, not to initiate or manage change. While critical theorists appear to support action, they tend to remain at the level of rhetoric: their theorising is limited to propositional statements rather than being embodied in their own practices as they engage with changing social processes.

This is the main limitation of critical theory as a theory for social renewal. It stays at the abstract linguistic level of description and propositional explanations. While critical theorists say what ought to be done to right wrongs, they do not show how it can be done or what needs to be done to realise the potentialities of their theories to turn them into living realities. They still cling to the reality of the model. Furthermore, they tend to believe it sufficient to critique other people but not to critique themselves, which leaves them open to challenges of contradictory behaviours.

Critical theory has amazing powers for social renewal, provided critical theorists themselves take the all-important step of showing how their theories work. This would mean transforming abstract theories into concrete action plans, acting in the direction of those plans, and producing accounts of practice to show how they were able to work towards social transformation. Nothing could be simpler, or perhaps more difficult, because this means stepping out from the safe places of abstraction into risky reality, and showing how one is living one's own theory in practice – not easy, but entirely possible, as long as one's commitments provide the courage to do so.

The relevance of these ideas for action research

The ideas discussed here about different conceptual frameworks show how and why action research has become distinctive in human enquiry. Action research is about putting ideas into action, not only talking about them. Adopting a relational stance, which is required in action research, allows you to see how different forms of knowing and different forms of interests are integrated; and also how conceptual categories may be turned into living practices where people offer real-life explanations for what they are doing. For example, a counsellor might know the conceptual theory of counselling ('know that') and be skilled in counselling techniques ('know how'), but would always work on an understanding of the person (personal knowledge). Similarly, health-care workers and judges see the whole person and work with people on a real-life basis. Knowing becomes a real-life practice; the boundaries between theory and practice dissolve and fade away, because theory is lived in practice and practice becomes a form of 'living theory' (Whitehead 1989) – in my interpretation, living the theory in action.

I am not claiming that action research is the only way to move in this direction. Much can be learned from musicians, religious leaders and others. I am claiming, however, that action research, as a practical way of generating one's own theory of living, is a potentially powerful methodology for theories of relationship.

I like the idea expressed in the old Irish saying, '*Is ar scáth a chéile a mhairimid*' – 'We live in the shelter of one another',[1] – similar to the African idea of '*ubuntu*', as 'I find myself in you'. To check that our practices are as we wish them to be, and make claims that we understand and do things better, we have to produce evidence to show how and why things have changed because of our influence. The process of research becomes the practice, and because the process is one of learning, evaluating and acting, it therefore stands as a form of research. The boundaries are dissolved: knowledge, interests and practices are within a life.

There is an example to show how this is being done overleaf.

We now turn to some of the people who have developed the field, and see how they have put ideas into the field that guide people's thinking and practices.

Case study: Lesley Wood, South Africa

The social and economic disparities in South Africa make it morally impera-
tive that educational research contributes to improving the circumstances and
lives of our teachers, learners and the wider community. Working in contexts
where poverty, crime, violence, illness and death are the norm takes its toll on
teachers, and provides little hope for learners of a brighter future. My experience
of working in such environments has convinced me that educational research has
to be aimed at social change, beginning with individuals and groups. Research
thus has to be participative to enable personal and professional transformation.
Action research, based on non-negotiable values such as democracy, equality,
accountability, mutual respect, care and a belief in the potential of others, can
influence epistemological and ontological change that helps people to accept
responsibility for improving their social circumstances. I have evidence from
several projects to support this assertion.

One project involved engaging with school leaders to help them reflect critically
on how they could improve their schools. It was evident that these leaders transformed their thinking and practices through the project, and were more motivated and confident about their ability to lead. The full reports can be accessed at
http://aru.nmmu.ac.za/Projects/Action-Research-for-School-Leaders/.

HIV and AIDS compounds the many social and economic problems in certain
communities in South Africa. Education is severely impacted by the ever-increasing
numbers of children orphaned and rendered vulnerable by the illness and death
of their parents; educators are also personally and professionally affected by the
consequences. It is daunting to work with teachers who feel immobilised by the
severity of the problem and who feel overwhelmed by their personal and professional burdens. Yet engaging these same teachers in action research can help to
restore their hope and mobilise them to start doing something to improve the
situation. The following extract from an interview with a teacher whose project
addressed gender inequality (a major driver of HIV) puts it thus:

> This has been a motivating experience for us and we have grown in terms of
> self-esteem and self-efficacy. The more involved we become in projects like
> this, the more we enjoy our job; therefore we plan to continue with further
> cycles of action research to address gender equity and other problems.

More stories from participating teachers transformed can be accessed at
http://aru.nmmu.ac.za/Writings/.

I have also personally experienced the transformational potential of action
research, looking at my own practice as an academic, researcher and lecturer.
I have learnt that if I wish to influence educational transformation to make it
relevant to the social reality in South Africa today, I need to create knowledge
that can also influence the learning of others. I have learnt that I can engage in a
process of enquiry that changes me at a cognitive level and also at a deep emotive
level. The more I engage, the more passionate I become about creating knowledge to contribute to social change through critically reflecting on whether my
practices and interactions with others mirror my espoused values. This holds

me to be accountable and responsible for my practices (see also http://ejolts.net/node/177/).

There is a burgeoning interest in action research in South Africa, attested to by the increasing numbers of postgraduate theses being produced, the significant membership of virtual networks such as Action Research Africa Network, and the projects being conducted, possibly because the methodologies of action research allow for relevant epistemological and ontological change. The first issue of a new journal, *Educational Research for Social Change* (http://ersc.nmmu.ac.za/) offers insight into what kinds of action enquiry are being conducted in South Africa.

Chapter 3

Who has influenced our thinking?
Key theorists in action research

The world of action research today is wide and diverse. Until the 1990s it would have been possible to read or listen to accounts that could be identified unequivocally as action research. Now, because the action research family has developed so many different perspectives, it is sometimes difficult to see action research as an overall 'movement' or genre with a set of defining principles. Some constants do appear to endure in relation to the nature, origins and uses of action research, but how they are treated is frequently contested. These constants appear to be:

- *The nature of action research*: action research is still seen as about change and improvement, whether personal, social, political or organisational. However, the field remains problematic because different people see 'change' and 'improvement' differently. Action research is also still seen as participative. This, however, depends on how people are positioned in the research: do all participants participate in theory generation, or do 'researchers' see 'practitioners' as data?
- *The origins of action research*: this involves issues about whether 'change' is a property of the individual (whether from ego-centric or relational perspectives), and whether change is carried out intentionally by persons themselves, or whether someone imposes change on them.
- *The uses of action research*: this involves issues about whether action research is a technique or strategy or methodology to be developed as part of change processes, or whether it becomes a tool or technique to be applied to practices in order to change them. Is it a 'change strategy', or a process of change itself?

Engaging with these issues is essential if you wish to contribute to the field. Taking stock of your own ontological and epistemological positioning will help you to communicate how you see action research and why you choose to see it this way. Do you see yourself thinking in closed boxes, and listen to voices that tell you this is normative and to adjust your thinking accordingly? Or do you see yourself as thinking free, seeing the possibilities in everything, and willing to find out what others say and do, so you can learn with and from them? Which literatures do you draw on to develop your understandings? You need to think for yourself, because powerful voices mandate what action research is and is not; and we learn to believe those voices, and opt for one form or another, without considering that there may be more authentic and credible voices to listen to.

Major theorists speak about these things. Noffke and Somekh (2009), for example, organise their ideas about action research into the categories 'professional', 'personal' and 'political':

> This structure reflects Noffke's [1997] scholarly analysis of the very wide range of work undertaken under the broad category of action research since the 1940s, including participatory action research, critical action research, classroom action research, action learning, etc. The categories 'professional', 'personal' and 'political' are fluid with porous boundaries rather than essentialist. They reflect orientations towards action research, which, to a degree that varies between authors, are also open to the other two orientations.
>
> p. 1

Reason and Bradbury (2008) speak about a 'family of approaches':

> We have described action research as a 'family of approaches', a family which sometimes argues and falls out, whose members may at time ignore or wish to dominate others, yet a family which sees itself as different from other researchers, and is certainly willing to pull together in the face of criticism or hostility from supposedly 'objective' ways of doing research.
>
> p. 7

Both sets of authors also emphasise the importance of not dwelling overmuch on differences, and of celebrating commitments to contribute to the social good.

Reason and Bradbury also suggest that accounts may be seen as first-person, second-person and third-person action research, as follows:

- First-person action research occurs when an individual practitioner reflects on their personal practice and offers an account of what they are doing and thinking.
- Second-person action research is when people enquire with others about how they can address issues of mutual concern.
- Third-person action research aims to connect individual researchers with wider communities, whether face to face or virtually at a distance (see Reason and Bradbury 2008: 6).

Comprehensive histories of action research are available from Carr and Kemmis (1986), McKernan (1991), Noffke (1997) and others. Here, I set out a brief history of action research and identify some key theorists who have influenced people's thinking, including mine. Names will inevitably be left out because of lack of space, not a denial of their influence. I also need to emphasise that I do not see history as being about dates and the achievements of famous people. I like Zinn's (2005a) idea that we need a people's history, and I return to this idea in Chapter 12.

Here are some important theorists.

Early influences: the work of John Collier and Kurt Lewin

Susan Noffke (1997a) tells how the work of John Collier, Commissioner of Indian Affairs from 1933 to 1945, might be seen as the first identifiable starting point for action research. Collier was committed to developing 'community' in relation to the education and social contexts of Native Americans; this was to be accomplished through 'the experience of responsible democracy' (Collier 1945: 275). Kurt Lewin, a Jewish refugee from Nazi Germany, shared the same interests, but from the perspective of industrial contexts and how participation in decision-making could lead to enhanced productivity. Collier and Lewin were both aware of the potential of democratic practice for self-determination as well as for social engineering – 're-education' as a way of ensuring compliance and loyalty to the dominant culture.

Some historical accounts (see for example McKernan 1991) locate the development of action research alongside other contemporary developments in education and the social sciences: the widening acceptance of new approaches in ethnography; the Science in Education movement of the nineteenth and early twentieth centuries; the Progressive Education of John Dewey and its practical implementation by people such as Hilda Taba and Stephen Corey, and the Free Schools movement (see Miller 2002); and the Group Dynamics movement in social psychology and human relations training. These trends were significant for the reconstruction of post-war society, in which practitioner research came to be seen as an important factor.

Lewin developed a theory of action research as a spiral of steps involving planning, fact-finding (or reconnaissance) and execution (Lewin 1946), which later came generally to be understood as an action–reflection cycle of planning, acting, observing and reflecting (Figure 3.1). This could in turn be extended into ongoing action–reflection cycles (Figure 3.2).

This model has informed the development of most subsequent models, including my own, although I try to make mine come to life rather than remain an abstract visual on the page (see p. 66).

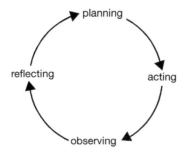

Figure 3.1 Action–reflection cycle

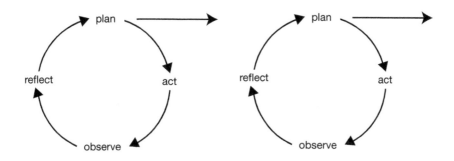

Figure 3.2 Sequences of action–reflection cycles

Case studies

Two case studies appear at the end of this chapter. The first is from Eric Deakins, who reflects on 15 years of action research in New Zealand. He writes a first-person account.

The second is from Thérèse McPhillips and Geraldine Hayes, lecturers in education at St Patrick's College, Drumcondra, Dublin. They were part of a Zambia–Ireland teacher education partnership. They write a second-order account.

Lewin's work was located in industrial and organisational settings, but the relevance of his ideas was also seen for contexts of education, and his ideas were soon taken up in educational research in the USA. In 1953 Stephen Corey's book *Action Research to Improve School Practices* became highly influential. After the initial enthusiasm for the book, however, interest declined and action research began to lose momentum, being replaced by a post-Sputnik Research, Development and Diffusion model, a model much favoured in

1960s USA and Britain, which emphasised the separation of research and practice. The decline of action research is captured in the title of Nevitt Sanford's (1970) paper 'Whatever happened to action research?'

In the late 1960s a new impetus for action research developed in teacher education. An influential paper by J. J. Schwab, 'The practical: A language for the curriculum' (1969), captured the influence on education of an increasingly inward-turning mood in the USA, arising, for example, out of the social unease generated by civil rights movements, protests against the Korean and Vietnam wars, McCarthyism and an increasing focus on technological control. Attention turned again to the potential of localised practitioner research as a form of educational and social change.

By now, work elsewhere was becoming influential.

The work of Lawrence Stenhouse

In Britain, similar trends were evident in the work of Lawrence Stenhouse and the Humanities Curriculum Project. Stenhouse took as central the idea of teacher as researcher. He saw teaching and research as closely related, and called on teachers to reflect critically and systematically on their practices as a form of curriculum theorising. Teachers should be the best judges of their practice, and, by accepting the responsibility for their own work, they could examine how they were influencing educational processes:

> All well-founded curriculum research and development, whether the work of an individual teacher, of a school, of a group working in a teachers' centre or a group working within the co-ordinating framework of a national project, is based on the study of classrooms. It thus rests on the work of teachers.
>
> Stenhouse 1975: 143

Teachers should thereby aim to become extended professionals, a theme developed in the work of Hoyle (1974) and Hoyle and John (1995), which involved:

> The commitment to systematic questioning of one's own teaching as a basis for development; the commitment to and the skills to study one's own teaching; the concern to question and to test theory in practice by the use of those skills.
>
> Stenhouse 1975: 144

Stenhouse saw the responsibility of higher education personnel as supporting the work of teachers. Teachers were not yet encouraged to explain their own epistemological and social commitments in improving their practices. Stenhouse's views were that 'fruitful development in the field of curriculum and teaching depends upon the evolving styles of co-operative research by teachers and using full-time researchers to support the teachers' work' (Stenhouse 1975: 162).

The form of theory, however, remained conceptual, the approach interpretive. Outsider researchers were more powerful than the teachers they worked with when generating theory. It was possible to generate E-theories of practice from observing how the teachers behaved in classrooms, and to evaluate their behaviours in terms of anticipated outcomes. There was, in Stenhouse's time, little mention of teachers producing their personal accounts of practice to check to what extent they were evaluating and theorising their practices in relation to their educational values; this applied as much to the researcher as to the teachers they were supporting.

Stenhouse's work was taken up by John Elliott.

The seminal work of John Elliott

Stenhouse's ideas were extended by John Elliott and his colleagues such as Clem Adelman in the Ford Teaching Project, 1973–6, which was perhaps 'the greatest impetus to the resurgence of contemporary interest in educational action research' (Kemmis 1993: 180):

> This project, initially based at the Centre for Applied Research in Education, University of East Anglia, involved teachers in collaborative action research into their own practices, in particular the area of inquiry/ discovery approaches to learning and teaching (Elliott, 1976–77). Its notion of the 'self-monitoring teacher' was based on Lawrence Stenhouse's (1975) views of the teacher as a researcher and as an 'extended professional'.
>
> Kemmis 1993: 180–1

Elliott has developed these ideas considerably (see for example Elliott 1991, 1998), particularly as they relate to an objectives view and a process view of curriculum, and the social processes involved. His *Reflecting Where the Action Is: The Selected Works of John Elliott* (2007) represents an overview of his work and thinking.

Other researchers gathered around Elliott, including David Hamilton, Stephen Kemmis, Barry MacDonald, Jean Rudduck, Hugh Sockett, Robert Stake and Rob Walker. These people did much to establish action research as an educational tradition (see for example Ebbutt and Elliott 1985; MacDonald and Walker 1976; Rudduck and Hopkins 1985). Some have further developed the field by producing influential models of action research.

Elliott has also been an active supporter of educators across a range of professions. He is well known, for example, for his support of police work, and is currently active in a wide range of international contexts in developing policy to encourage participation in education. Until recently, he was co-ordinator of the Collaborative Action Research Network, and he continues to emphasise the need for a process model in curriculum theorising.

His model of action research (Figure 3.4) is widely used. Like Kemmis, Elliott agrees with the basic action–reflection spiral of cycles, but presents his own critique:

> Although I think Lewin's model is an excellent basis for starting to think about what action research involves, it can … allow those who use it to assume that 'the general idea' can be fixed in advance, that 'recon-naissance' is merely fact-finding, and that 'implementation' is a fairly straightforward process. But I would argue that:
> - The general idea should be allowed to shift.
> - Reconnaissance should involve analysis as well as fact-finding and should constantly recur in the spiral of activities, rather than occur only at the beginning.
> - Implementation of an action step is not always easy, and one should not proceed to evaluate the effects of an action until one has monitored the extent to which it has been implemented.
>
> Elliott 1991: 70

In his 1991 work, Elliott presents Kemmis's interpretation of Lewin's model of action research (Figure 3.3.)

Elliott then goes on to present a new model (Figure 3.4).

The work of John Elliott has inspired others, including Bridget Somekh, James McKernan and Stephen Kemmis.

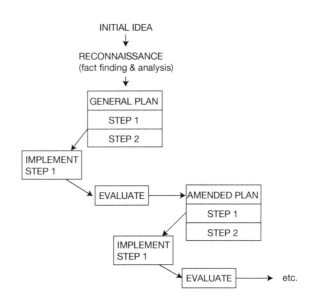

Figure 3.3
Kurt Lewin's model
of action research as
interpreted by Kemmis
(1990)

Source: Elliott 1991: 70

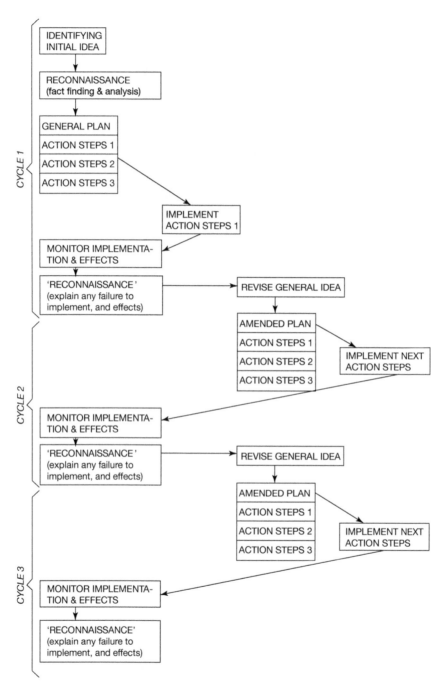

Figure 3.4 A revised version of Lewin's model of action research

Source: Elliott 1991: 71

Bridget Somekh

Bridget Somekh is Emeritus Professor at the Educational and Social Research Institute, Manchester Metropolitan University, and holds a number of other institutional positions. Bridget is well known for her work in ICT, professional education and the management of change (see Somekh 2006; Somekh and Lewin, 2011). She has published influential articles, and is co-editor of the *Handbook of Educational Action Research*, with Susan Noffke (Noffke and Somekh 2009). She was the main co-ordinator of the Collaborative Action Research Network, following John Elliott's retirement, and has herself retired, although like most of us of a similar generation, is now probably busier than ever. In 2010 the journal *Educational Action Research* produced a special issue to celebrate her contribution to education.

James McKernan

The entry for James McKernan at Wikipedia reads as follows:

> McKernan's educational theory emphasizes the teacher as researcher and schools as agencies of cultural reconstruction using action research to improve school practices. His curriculum theory rejects the use of educational objectives determined in advance of instruction in favor of a 'procedural model' of design that elicits the intrinsic values of the educational experience as the aim of the educational encounter, and not a pre-specified outcome. He is an advocate for action research, the idea that research should be conducted by the practitioner who experiences a problem, with a view to improving the quality of action in the problematic situation through reconstructed actions. His theory holds that there is no division of labor between teachers and researchers and that school practices will only be improved by teachers researching their own practices.
>
> Retrieved 24 June 2012 from http://en.wikipedia.org/wiki/
> James_McKernan

He has published several influential works on action research and curriculum, notably his *Curriculum Action Research* (1991) and *Curriculum and Imagination: Process Theory, Pedagogy and Action Research* (2007).

Stephen Kemmis

Kemmis bases his ideas on the original conceptualisations of Lewin and has also been influenced by the critical theory of Jürgen Habermas and others. Consequently, his work is particularly significant in understanding the socially and politically constructed nature of educational practices. Together with Wilf Carr, he has encouraged the use of the term 'educational action research' (see Carr and Kemmis 1986), now the title of the journal *Educational Action Research*. In 2005 Carr and Kemmis celebrated the 20-year success of their *Becoming Critical* (1986), emphasising the need to retain the original emancipatory impulses of action research (Carr and Kemmis 2005).

In recent work (Kemmis 2009; Kemmis and Smith 2007), Kemmis has developed the idea of action research as the 'sayings, doings and relatings' of people, in what he calls 'ecologies of practice', where practitioners focus on developing their practices, their understandings of their practices, and the situations in which they live and work. I would be enormously sympathetic to these approaches since they mirror my own commitments to collaborative working and to appreciating action research as an ecological approach and philosophy for life.

Kemmis's model of action research processes (see Kemmis and McTaggart 1988, and several revised editions since) shows a self-reflective spiral of planning, acting, observing, reflecting and re-planning as the basis for understanding how to take action to improve an educational situation). The diagram shows the principles in action, the movement from one critical phase to another and the way in which progress may be made through systematic steps.

A pause for critical reflection so far

These theorists do not always agree, and offer critique to one another, which helps to move ideas forward. My critique of the ideas presented is about the assumptions that inform all metaphors and models, my own included, that they are potentially prescriptive and are disconnected from real-life practices. I would also be concerned when authors do not offer justification for their choice of approach. I think this needs to be a major focus if the research is to be seen as praxis, i.e. morally committed practice.

In addition, while I recognize that models are examples of what Jenkins calls 'cognitive devices – metaphor and analogy are good examples – which we use to structure and produce our knowledge of the world' (Jenkins 1992: 56), I also appreciate that they often appear as fixed and reified (see below).

Bourdieu (1990) has similar concerns. One concern is that model-makers do not sufficiently emphasise that a model is a metaphor, not a universal 'given'. While a model communicates an idea about how reality works (or should work), there is often slippage between the model and reality. This especially refers to models that are sequential and predictable (as are the models so far presented), and are presented as synopses of events. Bourdieu calls this a 'synoptic illusion' because the model of reality does not necessarily communicate people's experiences of reality. A calendar, for example, does not communicate the reality of a life lived.

Bourdieu wishes, however, for 'a simple generative model which makes it possible to give an account of the logic of practice' (p. 100). Such a model 'generates an infinity of practices adapted to situations that are always different' (p. 101). My own model aims to do this (see p. 66), and aims to communicate dialogical processes with infinite transformational potentials appropriate to the emergent nature, fluidity and unpredictability of practical living and the improvisatory knowledge base that underpins it.

An inherent assumption of propositional models is that practice can be portrayed as linear and sequential, neat and orderly. This frequently is not so. In her (2000) report, Agnes Higgins also makes the point that, 'Action does not proceed in a fixed linear fashion':

> Hence telling the story in a concise and coherent manner without losing sight of the confusion and human dimension that was such a part of the process was a major challenge. Given the open systemic nature of organisations and the diversity of people involved, a variety of issues arose during each cycle that influenced progress and demanded that we return to previous stages.
>
> Higgins 2000: 134

As with many things, we might like to think we can predict and control the future, but reality is different. To return to the need for uncertainty and the inevitability of surprise, while models and other metaphors can indicate how things might go, they should be presented as possibilities, useful heuristics for understanding how one might proceed. Furthermore, if model-makers claim theoretical validity for their models, they need to go beyond speculation and also present stories of their own real-world practices to show how the models worked for them (or did not), and show how their metaphors are grounded in experience.

This all means that you do not have to follow models, for they are not necessarily representative of the realities you experience. See models for what they are: guidelines for how it is hoped things will eventually turn out. To propose that action research models can be imposed on practice is to turn action research into a technology, an oppressive instrument that can potentially distort other people's creative practice. The best thing, perhaps, is for you to create your own, to communicate metaphorically the way you live and learn.

Living approaches, living forms of theory: the work of Jack Whitehead

While Lawrence Stenhouse was working on the Humanities Curriculum Project, and John Elliott and Clem Adelman were developing the Ford Teaching Project in East Anglia, Jack Whitehead at the University of Bath was working with teachers as part of his Schools Council Mixed Ability Exercise in Science. He was studying his own practice of supporting teachers in their science enquiries.

Throughout his project, Whitehead has aimed to develop a form of theory different from traditional propositional forms. Drawing on original ideas from Ilyenkov (1977), he calls this 'living theory'. I have always seen the term as a verb more than noun – i.e. theory is something you do and live (not an unusual idea in the literatures; see also Chomsky's idea of 'I-theories' below) – and I have actively supported it, from my perspective that practitioners live their own theories of practice through the way they conduct the practice and explain how they do so. If 'theory' is about offering descriptions and explanations for a practice, practitioners' explanations for how and why they practise as they do constitute their personal theories of practice, and these theories are dynamic, living and transformational. My support for the idea even extended to my writing a book and putting Jack's name as first author to honour his contributions to the field, although the book you are reading moves beyond the ideas explored there.

However, I have become increasingly concerned that the original idea of 'living theory' (as a practical form of action) seems to have become reified into 'Living Theory' (as a proper noun denoting a movement). This change can be confusing for practitioners. A teacher once asked me at a workshop, 'What is the difference between "living theory" and "action research"?' (this may have been 'Living Theory'). The idea of 'Living Theory' as a reified object presents the theory as something separate from the practice. Once again, 'theory' becomes an object of study rather than a living practice, and the reification of the term potentially denies the very principles and values that inspired it. So since about 2010 I have distanced myself from this form of language.

Since the 1970s Whitehead has aimed to have this form of theory legitimated by the Academy, so the focus of the work has now shifted from legitimation for the form of theory to securing influence at world level.

Ideas about living theories are similar to Chomsky's I-theories, in that both emphasise that practitioners are able to generate their personal theories of practice through studying the practice, which can lead to the evolution of good social orders.

My own work

It will be evident to anyone reading this book that I am indebted to Noam Chomsky's influence in my thinking. Although he is not an action researcher, he is sympathetic to the idea, drawn as it is from the work of, among others, Dewey, in the same way as his thinking has been influenced by Dewey.

I first encountered the ideas of Chomsky when I studied for a Master's degree in applied linguistics. I loved his ideas about the generative transformational nature of language, its acquisition and development that could be embedded within issues concerning the nature, acquisition and development of knowledge. When I began to support practitioners' action enquiries, I also got to grips with his political theories, about the need to respect pluralistic practices and the responsibility of intellectuals to tell the truth and expose lies (Chomsky 1966a). I began to understand my responsibility as an educator to arrange spaces for people to create their mutually negotiated identities. I took heart from his indomitable courage and tenacity.

I first met Noam in 1993. I had boldly sent him a new book and asked if we could meet, and we did. From the wonderfully enriching encounter, I began seriously to re-visit ideas developed during my doctoral studies, and make connections with action research. I had already begun to see that traditional models and forms of theory did not reflect the hurly-burly nature of my professional practice or enable me to explain how and why I was practising as I was. So I developed my own to communicate what I had begun to see as the generative transformational potentials of my thinking and practice (Figure 3.5).

Noam Chomsky and I continue to connect, and I benefit from his kindness and support. I also have to say that I do not necessarily agree with all he writes. I am aware of differences between his ideas and those of, say, Daniel Everett (2012), who produces empirical evidence to show that language use is context- and culturally specific. This does not deny, however, the validity of the ideas from Chomsky that I use in this book, about the innate capacities of all people and the politics of knowledge.

I learned much from studying Chomsky's work about a centuries-long interest in the emergent, generative transformational nature of organic systems. These same ideas appear in the literatures of the new science, complexity and systems theory, including the representations of creative and spontaneous aspects of living, for example through the patterns of fractals. I was and remain interested in how order can evolve from chaos, and how

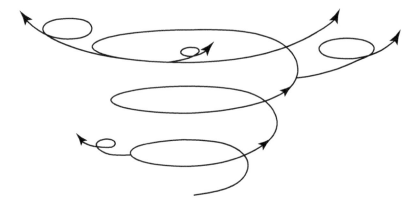

Figure 3.5 A generative transformational evolutionary process

the nature of chaos itself contains a simple implicate order (Bohm 1983) that maintains evolutionary processes (see McNiff 2000; see also Chapter 12).

I have consistently been in awe of how living systems rest on a finite number of components capable of producing an infinite number of novel phenomena. A grammar contains a finite number of elements that may generate an infinite number of original utterances; a fixed number of mathematical principles − adding, multiplying, subtracting, dividing − can produce an infinite number of computations; and a fixed number of facial components − eyes, nose, mouth, ears − can produce an infinite number of human faces. An acorn has the potential to become an oak tree; a drop becomes an ocean. We all have the potential to be more than we are. Who we become depends on who we are now and who we want to be (provided, of course, that politics and power do not distort those potentials). We have the potential to recreate ourselves.

Research has this same capacity. It is the responsibility of those with educational power to ensure that people are able to realise their capacity for self-re-creation, and remove barriers to self-development. I am committed to these ideas, possibly because I have had to re-create myself over the years, and see personal re-creation not as a response to troublesome times, but as an engaged form of living that follows the natural order of things. Each day, each moment, is a new creation.

Therefore I have come to see action research as a spontaneous, self-re-creating system of enquiry. I like the notion of a systematic process of observe, describe, plan, act, reflect, evaluate, modify, but I do not see the process as sequential or necessarily rational. It is possible to begin at one place and end up somewhere unexpected. The visual metaphor in Figure 3.5 represents an iterative spiral of spirals, an exponential developmental process. I have come to see the process as beyond words. While it may be analysed in terms of an action research approach, I do not think it should be so confined. The spirals of action reflection unfold from themselves and fold back again into themselves. They attempt to communicate the idea of a reality that enfolds all its previous manifestations, yet which is constantly unfolding into new versions of itself, constantly in a state of balance within disequilibrium. I am certain of uncertainty; I am balanced within my own disequilibrium. In action research terms, it is possible to address multiple issues while still maintaining a focus on one, a realisation of Plato's idea of holding together the one and the many.

Case studies

Here are two case studies. The first is a first-person story by Eric Deakins. The second is a second-person research account by Thérèse McPhillips and Geraldine Hayes, acting as advisers and supporters of practitioners in Zambia. Both accounts draw on the ideas of the key theorists presented above. They also speak about practices where 'other-centredness' becomes a criterion for explaining how they hold themselves accountable for their work.

Case study: Eric Deakins, New Zealand

First action–reflection cycle

I migrated to New Zealand from the UK in the 1990s, and began working in the Management School at the local university. Because I was working, I deposited my nine-month-old son Jonathon into the infant unit at the Cambridge Child Care Centre. This was a happy experience, and I was soon asked to join the Trust Board of the Centre, and became the chairperson and licensee a year later.

At that time, the early childhood sector was not in good shape, with poorly paid staff suffering from low self-esteem and lack of pride in their profession, although passionate about their work as educators. Parents often viewed them as paid babysitters; and new funding and regulatory systems meant structural difficulties. Our older buildings were dilapidated, and a new private centre nearby represented competition. As Trust chairperson, I needed to steer the organisation appropriately, thereby learning about my own leadership.

As licensee, I was responsible for delivery of the early childhood curriculum, Te Whariki. I was aware that the staff perceived me as 'the man from the management school with the answer', although this was not my self-perception, given my background.

I was raised in a loving working-class family in England, with a strong sense of fairness, hard work and a desire to help the disadvantaged. I left school with few qualifications and joined my first merchant ship bound for West Africa. I later used my seafaring qualifications to enrol for a Bachelor's degree. I joined the University of Waikato having completed my doctorate and an MBA, and held down a number of management positions in the UK and the USA. I now perceived that action research within a childcare organisation could enable staff to create their own futures and feel valued as employees.

I had read Senge's ideas (for example 1990) about expanding people's capacity for critical thinking and organisational learning, and discovered from Learning Organisation Theory how organisations can encourage practitioners' participation and support for whole organisational development. My research therefore explored how effective these theories were for achieving our organisational goals.

I initiated dialogue with staff: dialogue takes a group beyond any single individual's understanding, and requires everyone to interrogate their assumptions and regard one another as colleagues. I also learned to change public perceptions of myself as 'the man with the answer', to encourage mental models to be modified and disagreements to be bridged (although not always resolved). The Centre's commercial viability improved. Within five years new facilities were constructed, and new policies and practices enabled us to develop a competitive edge. We were inundated with applications, and received an unbroken series of excellent Education Review Office audit reports. We hired 22 professional staff, and employees' self-esteem improved markedly.

Second action–reflection cycle

We undertook further cycles of action research, which involved envisioning a new dedicated Teaching Development and Research Centre known as the Pagoda. The Centre would accommodate rigorous action research as part of its teaching and care roles. In August 2006 the new 30-place Pagoda opened its doors to paying customers. Our then Prime Minister, Helen Clark, officially opened the Pagoda in 2007 declaring: 'I haven't seen anything else like this in early childhood education in New Zealand … so exciting. I am so really very, very impressed by what I've seen … '

Third action–reflection cycle

The Pagoda continues to provide opportunities for staff to use action research to improve their practices in extending children's learning. We have received extensive external funding, produced our first peer-reviewed publications, and recently formed alliances with university academics in New Zealand and Germany. Projects have included:

- ICT-effectiveness and human computer interface design for non-literate users;
- sharing children's literacy progress using multimedia;
- using tablet-PC technology for preschool education, with a special focus on female students;
- use of iPads and social networking to ease emotional transitions to school.

Following a visit by Jean McNiff, the Pagoda team now undertake their action enquiries for personal professional development, while still focusing collectively on improving the Centre's processes. As a Centre, we appear to have developed a durable culture, created by and for every member of the organisation.

Case Study: Thérèse McPhillips and Geraldine Hayes, Ireland

This is an account of the Zambia–Ireland Teacher Education Partnership (ZITEP), an initiative of the Ministry of Education Zambia and the Department of Education and Skills (DES), Ireland, sponsored by Irish Aid and DES. The goal of ZITEP is to improve the quality of teacher education and build a partnership between colleges of education in Zambia and Ireland. It has done so over the past three years, and has enabled Irish lecturers to experience teacher education in a context outside their normal experience, and interact with peers from other colleges within Ireland as well as from Zambia. Peer learning and sharing of experiences during this time has consisted of study visits and an exchange of pedagogical skills (DES/Zambia 2012).

The issue of low literacy levels among primary school pupils (SACMEQ 2010) was a concern to Zambian lecturers, despite the introduction of the Primary Reading Programme and teachers' guides (Longman Zambia/Ministry of Education 2001); the research focus became how to raise standards.

The team consisted of two Zambian lecturers in Language and Literacy Education from Charles Lwanga College of Education, Monze, Zambia, and the Director of a Teacher Resource Centre and two lecturers from St Patrick's College, Drumcondra, Dublin. As this was the first experience of action research for the Zambian participants, topics were grounded in their experience. The framework for the study was based on that of a graduate diploma in our own institution, St Patrick's College, Drumcondra.

The focus was to investigate how teachers in Zambia could help Grade Four pupils improve their literacy levels at three selected schools in the Monze district. The participants were teachers of Grade Four pupils who were implementing the Primary Reading Programme, the head teacher in each school, the district education standards officer and the resource centre coordinator. Data were gathered from parents, pupils and teachers about perceptions and levels of achievement, and how these might be improved.

Critical challenges included the distance between our countries and poor access to technology, time constraints and the lack of experience of our Zambian partners in research methods. The Irish lecturers also needed to develop a balanced working partnership while respecting the Zambian partners' sense of self-efficacy.

We on the Irish team saw ourselves as critical friends and research advisors to the project, to help the Zambian teacher-researchers develop reflective and learning capacity. It was important to maintain their autonomy as researchers so they would begin to influence the development of educational policy in their own country, and, as they explained, 'be taken seriously by the Ministry of Education'. Throughout, we encouraged the Zambians to 'think out loud' about research questions. Our persistent 'What do you want to find out?' and 'Why do you think this is so?' helped to explore any contested issues.

The analysis of data was problematic, and extensive input was required from both sides. The Irish team guided the data analysis sessions, conducted with the visiting Zambians in Dublin, ensuring that everyone agreed the meaning and interpretation of the data, although the Zambian researchers contextualised and interpreted the findings. The Zambian team undertook to write up the report in Zambia, with support from Dublin.

We met again for the final time in Lusaka for our end-of-project conference. We presented our findings at the conference, and our Zambian colleagues took responsibility for any culture-specific interpretations of the data.

It was perhaps the experience of the conference that made us Irish appreciate the structural differences between educational systems in Ireland and Zambia, especially the hierarchies of Zambian culture. It was encouraging to participate in the lively discussions that followed our team's presentation of the findings. We Irish stood back and let the Zambian team members take over.

Thinking forward

Feedback from our Zambian partners on the collaborative learning experience has been positive. Our small-scale project has helped to shape our Zambian partners' goals for their future. One is pursuing a qualification at Master's level. The Irish researchers now wish to explore action research as a collaborative methodology with other international institutions, also aiming for their own personal and professional development.

These case studies show how researchers can learn from theories in the literature, as well as create their own personal and professional theories of practice from the experience of doing the practice. These ideas are explored further in Chapter 4, where we address issues of what we need to explore more extensively to contribute to personal and social wellbeing.

Chapter 4

What do we need to know?
Exercising educational influence

This chapter is about what we need to know to use our knowledge for personal, social and environmental betterment, how action research can help in the process, and the kind of mindset necessary.

Action research has potential for human, non-human and environmental betterment. Although the term itself may eventually be superseded or embedded within newer forms of research (it is already linked with narrative inquiry, appreciative inquiry and others), what it stands for is durable. However, the values as well as the knowledge they inspire need to be under constant critical review.

What action research stands for is the realisation of human needs towards autonomy, loving relationships and productive knowledge, as well as the urge towards freedom of thinking and choice, creativity and self-realisation (Carr and Kemmis 1986, 2005) – in other words, a realisation of human nature. The political counterpart of action research is liberal democracy; its spiritual counterpart is a sense of unity between self, others and the cosmos. We are at home in the universe, as Abrams (2011) and Kauffman (1995) say, one with another, and we contribute to its evolution.

These ideas raise questions about the form of theory needed to study, explain and develop processes of personal and social change, for these cannot be investigated using only the externalist theories of the social sciences. The form of theory most appropriate for explaining processes of change is already in the mind of the person; each person is able to say, 'I understand what I am doing and why I am doing it.' These I-theories are embedded in and generated through practice and are in the collective mind of groups of people in dialogical communities of enquiry. Studying our practices and their underpinning assumptions enables us to develop a creative understanding of ourselves and our own processes of learning and growth. When we do action research, we make our thinking different:

> Having made a discovery, I shall never see the world again as before. My eyes have become different; I have made myself into a person seeing and thinking differently. I have crossed a gap, a heuristic gap which lies between problem and discovery.
>
> Polanyi 1958: 143

These themes are developed through this chapter, and through the book. I argue that improving knowledge and learning is the basis for improving practice, and this improvement can happen at personal, social and community levels. Learning can be encouraged through the exercise of influence, but we can influence and be influenced in violent as well as friendly ways. This has significance for how practitioners decide to use their influence.

The chapter is organised as follows:

• the transformational relationships between values, knowledge, practices and the social order;
• the nature and purposes of educational influence;
• the responsibility of practitioner–researchers in exercising their influence.

The transformational relationships between values, knowledge, practices and the social order

As an action researcher, you would aim to show the links between what you value and what you know (your values and knowledge), and how these enter processes of development. Through making these links explicit, you can show how you hold yourself accountable for your practices.

Linking values, knowledge and development

Isaiah Berlin (1997) spoke about the relationships between values, knowledge and development. He held the view that knowledge had to be seen as the property of a knower, and was therefore always incomplete, because the knowers were themselves each a living person and in a process of development. He critiqued traditionalist ideas that believed the following:

• Every question had an answer.
• The answer could be discovered.
• When it was discovered, everyone would agree with it.

In other words, it was held that knowledge was certain, and could be discovered by following designated rules and strategies.

Berlin challenged this view, saying that:

• Some questions have no answer. Think of the awful dilemmas when parents separate and both parties want the children. It is not a question of right and wrong, but of competing rights.
• Sometimes there are no answers to be 'discovered'. How can intractable problems be resolved, such as the competing claims to Jerusalem by Muslims and Jews?

• People seldom agree on answers or solutions. This is perhaps why peace and reconciliation movements are so problematic. Hampshire (2001) says that it is more straightforward to agree on procedures than to agree on matters of substance. My own view is that conflict (critique and challenge) is necessary for creative thinking (if you disagree with this, you are proving the point); but if conflict is necessary, violence in conflict is not.

Popper also spoke about the strong links between what we know and what we do, between knowledge and practice. He argued that the social sciences are inadequate for social transformation because action is informed by knowledge. Because we cannot predict what we shall know, we cannot predict what will happen either: 'if there is such a thing as growing human knowledge, then we cannot anticipate today what we shall know only tomorrow' (2002: xii). The capacity to live with the uncertainty of not knowing what the next moment will bring is basic to action research. It is not about moving towards a given 'end' or 'answer', but about taking the next step into an unknown future and working to make it the best it can be.

Similarly, Sen (1999) holds that freedom is essential for development and has a dual nature:

• The process of development itself is free and untrammelled.
• Freedom is essential for achieving other goals.

Sen focuses on what he calls 'human capabilities', the basic freedoms needed for wellbeing and flourishing – in terms of this book, for the realisation of our human nature. These ideas are also taken up by Chomsky (1996b: 77):

> The ideas expressed in the not very distant past by such outstanding figures as Russell and Dewey are rooted in the Enlightenment and classical liberalism, and retain their evolutionary character: in education, the workplace, and every other sphere of human life. If implemented, they would help clear the way to the free development of human beings whose values are not accumulation and domination, but independence of mind and action, free association on terms of equality, and cooperation to achieve common goals.

Yet while agreeing with Sen and Chomsky, I also acknowledge that different people have different views about freedom, so questions arise about what counts as freedom and wellbeing, and for whom. A good friend in a religious order has explained to me how and why he freely chooses not to be free.

Here I am asking, 'What do we need to know in order to realise the potentials of action research at a personal and collective level? How do we use our knowledge for purposeful action?' I also ask, 'How do we justify what we believe? How does this influence what we do?' Exercising freedom is not trivial, especially when it involves combating forces that suppress personal and collective activism, for this can lead to a struggle for freedom involving personal dissonance (see the case studies below).

Here are some ideas about how action research can stand for the education of individuals, communities and social formations, so that the potentials do transform into influence.

Action research for personal and professional development

As noted, action research is now used everywhere, most often as a form of professional education, across the disciplines and professions, and on professional development courses. A main focus is to help practitioners claim that they understand their practices through their reflection on practice, and can use this learning to improve their practice. An influential document from the *Lancet*, in relation to health workers, says:

> all health professionals in all countries should be educated to mobilise knowledge and to engage in critical reasoning and ethical conduct so that they are competent to participate in patient and population-centred health systems as members of locally responsive and globally connected teams.
>
> Frenk, Chen and Associates 2010: 1924

This, however, raises issues about how practice is judged; for if you say, 'I have improved my practice', people ask, 'How do you judge improvement?' This question is embedded within the deeper question, 'How do you judge good practice?' So judging what counts as quality in practice is equivalent to asking what counts as 'good' in 'good practice'. Saying what is 'good' becomes key. Similarly, when you say that you have improved your practice through research, people ask, 'How do you judge quality in research?' The question is always, 'What counts as "the good" in "good practice" and "good research"?' These questions are dealt with further in Chapter 10.

In addition, claiming that one's practice is good links with explaining how you hold yourself accountable for what you are doing, i.e. demonstrating personal accountability. This is a matter of professional morality, for it emphasises that there are different interpretations of accountability, depending on your perspectives. There is a difference between bureaucratic understandings of 'accountability' and educational understandings. This implies that professionals need to appreciate what counts in demonstrating professional accountability and encourage others to do the same.

Issues of accountability

There is currently a massive emphasis on professional accountability across the professions and in the literatures. In some professions, such as nursing and chiropody, ongoing professional education is compulsory, and professional accreditation is also compulsory for some. However, given the global shifts towards market-driven cultures and results-driven curricula, the idea of 'accountability' has for many come to mean demonstrating expert behaviours, emphasising skills and competences ('know that' and 'know how'). The values base of practice (linked with personal knowledge) is systematically factored out as irrelevant and meaningless. The form of knowledge that counts is technical rationality, knowledge of facts and figures, and how to use them. The purposes and nature of productive work and relationships are rewritten as knowing how to make a profit and gain competitive edge, 'techne' in Aristotelian terms (excellence in skilful making) rather than phronesis (excellence in wise practice).

Today, all kinds of personal and social practices are being technologised. Knowledge has become a commodity and the process of knowledge production a for-profit business (see Gibbons *et al.* 1994 for an overview of modes of knowledge production). However, in the rush towards excellence (whatever that means), we need to stop and ask 'Excellence for what? Knowledge for whom?' We need to ask, like Mary Midgley (1991), 'What is knowledge for? Who needs to know? Why?'

Practitioners ask these questions as they study their practices. They undertake rigorous evaluation processes to ensure the validity of their claims when they say, 'I am good at my job', not out of arrogance but out of a sense of personal accountability to the other (Harland and Pickering 2011). This has implications for which criteria are important in testing the validity of knowledge claims (Chapter 8), and acts as a form of critical professionalism in which practitioners' acceptance of responsibility to others becomes acceptance of their responsibility to truth. There is something untruthful about drives towards marketisation in which humanity is reduced to a technology and relationships are embittered by competition (although the truth of institutional power is real enough). It is somehow unfaithfulness to the idea of being true to our human nature.

The case studies in this chapter are from colleagues who are senior lecturers at St Mary's University College, Twickenham, UK. We worked together initially on a Master's programme of study, and now all four are engaged in their doctoral studies.

When action research is turned into a technology, it becomes a set of techniques to be applied to practice rather than a way of life that constitutes practice. This means, however, that doing action research can lead to improvement of what many may see as evil practices as well as good. There is nothing at a procedural level to stop practitioners from asking, 'How can

I become a more effective terrorist?' (or gangster in the case of Al Capone). This is made possible when people follow prescriptive models that emphasise procedures without acknowledging the reasons and intentions that inform practice. Even when the reasons and intentions are emphasised, there is still no barrier to asking, 'How do I improve my practices as a terrorist?' Terrorists have values the same as philanthropists. Taylor (2011) explains how so-called 'terrorists' can hold values that enable them to see themselves as law-abiding citizens or freedom fighters. Perhaps it depends on which side of the peace wall you are standing.

Case study: Jane Renowden, UK

Here is an extract from Jane's draft PhD thesis (Renowden 2012).

Action research has become so much more than just the way I choose to conduct my doctoral research. At a time when I had many questions about my practice, when I made the transition between primary teaching practice and higher education, I was able to put myself and my actions at the centre of my enquiry.

In my thesis, I write that action research has been like a bridge over which I have travelled from the 'then' of my practice as a teacher to the 'now' of my practice as a teacher educator. The methodology has gone beyond being a structure and a type of discourse to being a way of viewing the world that has begun to inform how I choose to conduct my life. As I strive to hold myself educationally to account for what I do, action research as an educational process has enabled me to use one way of doing something to understand another. I have learnt to understand what I am doing and improve it as I engage in doctoral research, and in doing so I am learning to hold myself to account for what I do. The two processes have become inter-dependent. I am conducting a self-study enquiry because I want to be accountable for what I do, using my values as standards of judgement. I am being accountable because I am engaging in action research and offering it up for the critique of my peers. The two are becoming one and the same educational process.

There are no ready answers. Perhaps action research is undertaken by people who appreciate the need for mutually reciprocal relationships of accountability; who are of a critical inclination, and are concerned about issues of social justice for all and participative living. This is already a reality, as shown in the case studies in this book as well as by the global networks of practitioners who explain how they are influencing social systems. How then to strengthen these networks and persuade others who see action research as a form of technical application to develop the kind of knowledge that will contribute towards sustainable social orders?

Several practical steps are important: first, the production of case studies to show the development of communities of learners and how the knowledge they are generating benefits others; and, second, efficient dissemination so that these case studies have to be acknowledged as a legitimate form of collective learning. These ideas are explored further in Chapter 11, but a key condition is the idea of critical influence, with considerable implications.

The nature and purposes of educational influence

In his *Hopes and Prospects* (2010), Chomsky suggests that social change happens less through the implementation of policy and more through the commitments of practitioners to speak for themselves and create the kind of societies they wish to live in. I agree, yet acknowledge that those same persons can be controlled by powerful others who say they are not capable of speaking for themselves. My lifelong action research has therefore focused on enabling practitioners to study their work and generate their personal theories of practice to show how they hold themselves accountable for what they are doing, and not listen to propaganda that tells them otherwise. Their published work shows how they have done this: they understand how to help themselves.

This does not happen automatically, and it usually involves practitioners learning how to engage critically in their own thinking. Practitioners across countries, sectors, professions and social formations have done this, often for higher degree accreditation, often in problematic settings. A key focus therefore becomes why it is important to encourage people to think for themselves, and how to encourage people without imposing one's own ideas on them, because people can and should think for themselves. It is the responsibility of professional educators to help them do so.

Here are some reasons why this is necessary and how it can be done.

Theorising critical influence

The adage says, 'If you don't stand up for something you will fall for anything.' Like Arendt (1958), I believe that all people have something to say, and should use their place in the world to say it. Foucault (2001) speaks about the need for *parrhesia*, 'fearless speech', the capacity and the responsibility of people to speak for themselves. *Parrhesia*, however, implies also responsibility for truth-saying, and in speaking their truth as they see it people run risks, for truth and power are often incommensurable, as Socrates and Jesus experienced. People in power will silence others who step out of line; Alford (2001) tells stories of how whistleblowers in organisations are silenced or made invisible by being deprived of information and privileges, and are put into offices down the corridor so that contact with them takes effort and people lose interest.

I believe everyone has something to say for themselves, and that all people should be seen as intellectuals, i.e. people who think and speak for themselves. There is no difference between 'intellectuals' in the Academy and people on street corners selling newspapers. In my opinion, there are as many intellectuals on the street as in the Academy. Bayat's (2009) view of 'life as politics' is right – the everyday business of engaging with others. I also agree with Said (1994) who distinguishes between academics, who reproduce the epistemological status quo, and intellectuals, who produce new, sometimes transgressive knowledge, which positions them as separate from elites. Some academics choose to remain silent, because acquiescence ensures the security of a pension.

For me, intellectuals, in all contexts, should engage in social activism, in whatever way is right for them. I agree with Susan Sontag (2004) that we should not stand by and observe the pain of others, but should work to prevent the pain; and I espouse Russell's (1992) ideas that society needs independent thinkers more than obedient citizens. I agree with Habermas's (1975: 15) ideas that in all processes of social evolution, people cannot not learn, and I ask what they should learn for ongoing improvement of the social order.

I love the ideas of Chomsky (1996a), who explains that the work of intellectuals is to tell the truth and expose lies. For me, a great lie is that people cannot think for themselves, and I am concerned at how this message is communicated through the scholarly literatures, saying that only 'official' researchers do research and write authoritative accounts, while practitioners should do the work but not generate theory (see for example Lawson 2009). This form of brainwashing constitutes, for me, an egregious strategy to prevent people from thinking and acting as fully as they might, and with responsibility.

I am also aware of people's (including my own) tendency to apathy and fear, as communicated by Pastor Niemöller (variously dated): 'Then they came for the Jews and I didn't speak because I wasn't a Jew … and then they came for me, and there was no one left to speak for me'; and I wonder why 'ordinary people' remain silent when they can, and should, speak for themselves, and, where necessary, on behalf of others who cannot speak.

This is the task I set myself through writing, and through working with as many people as possible, in their own contexts, to persuade them that should have confidence that they know what they are doing, and should be unafraid to use their knowledge for personal and social improvement, and explain why they are doing so in the interests of accountability. My responsibility is to create spaces in which people can think and speak for themselves, and resist messages to be content with group-think, for we know that 'ordinary people' can be persuaded not to think about what they are doing, as was the case of the death squads of 'ordinary men' (Browning 2001) who nevertheless killed people systematically and in cold blood.

The nature of educational influence

So what kind of practices do we develop, and from what kinds of commitments?

We need to exercise what may be seen as educational influence to help people think critically for themselves. This involves thinking about our own capacities as creative and critical thinkers.

It means appreciating that we are born with a vast capacity for original thinking, not as a 'tabula rasa'. Babies and young children are powerful thinkers and have unlimited capacity for asking 'Why?' to make sense of their world (they try to theorise what is happening). This unlimited capacity for knowledge creation can lead to an infinite number of creative acts in the world. In addition, because we are born with originality of mind, including the capacity to choose, we can use our knowledge to decide what to do. This idea of each person's originality of mind is key in educational practices, for when person A says something to person B, what A says is filtered through the capacity for originality of mind by B. Person B listens and says to themselves, 'Should I believe this? Perhaps I will accept some elements, but not all …'. They are working out for themselves what they should think and why: they engage in critical thinking.

As universal educators, we need to develop a pedagogical stance whereby we recognise the other's capacity for originality of mind and encourage critical thinking. The idea of 'pedagogy' or 'teaching' also goes beyond the teaching profession and formal settings. It extends to everyone, because speaking with any other means we are automatically in a learning and teaching relationship. The issue is what makes the learning–teaching relationship educational.

So we return to philosophers such as Buber, Chomsky, Dewey, Macmurray and Said, who say that a relationship becomes educational when both parties grow from the encounter. For me, this means growing in criticality, where person A is aware of their influence on person B's thinking, and how B responds to A, so that A also begins to critique their own thinking. This may be the nature of mutually reciprocal educational relationships, in which each person critiques their own thinking to help the other do the same, and keep the conversation open. If all people did this, the world would be a better place overnight. It is also a matter of exercising criticality of judgement about what we do and think ourselves, and resist any powerful influences that persuade us to close down our thinking or move into group-think.

The responsibility of educators, then, becomes a commitment, first, to developing dialogical spaces where people can experiment with ideas and exercise their capacity for critique and originality of mind, and second, to encouraging them to build up their intellectual resources to resist the potential exercise of unauthorised intellectual and emotional power. Challenging what Apple (1993) calls 'official knowledge', and the power of corporate and intellectual elites, can mean trouble for practitioners and academics alike.

Chomsky (2000a) explains how, in totalitarian societies, it is easy to control people through overt systems of terror. In democratic societies, however, it is necessary to resort to the more subtle terrorism of thought control, achievable through elegant propaganda systems that communicate messages through the culture. The formal education system is, according to Chomsky, a system of mis-education, and, according to Bourdieu (1990), is the most powerful aspect of the culture as a means of social reproduction. Teaching produces students as consumers who expect to be taught in a certain way (look at how student satisfaction survey feedback influences institutional practices). How people learn through conventional didactic teaching methodologies is lasting; they learn not to question. Education is used to control the thinking of the customers.

History is full of the stories of people who are silenced and made invisible because they disagreed with dominant voices. Anderson and Herr (1999) explain how higher education institutions are aware of the rising star of action research and accept it in principle so as not to appear behind the times, but in a domesticated form that does not upset the dominant elites. This has been my experience too. I know of many universities that allow and even actively encourage an ethnographic approach to action research, possibly because this approach still maintains control of practitioners' thinking and so reinforces the position of the Academy as the locus of 'real' knowledge and therefore 'real' power. I also know of universities who do not accept action research. In 2012 I examined a PhD thesis for which the accrediting university insisted the author write in the third person ('the researcher did ... '). In 2011 I was involved in negotiation with an accrediting university to allow the use of 'I' in the title of a doctoral thesis.

Case study: Julie Pearson, UK

Here is the abstract for a paper by Julie, published in *Educational Action Research*, entitled 'Adapting the boundaries in primary physical education: an account of my learning, my educational influence and improved practice' (Pearson 2011).

In this paper I explore how I have come to theorise my work as a critical emancipatory practice as a lecturer in primary physical education (PE). I give an account of what I understand to be the epistemological foundations and practices of practitioner research and my potential educational influence in my own and other practitioner-researchers' learning. I explain how I have generated my living educational theory of practice and discuss the changes in my learning from a propositional approach towards a dynamic epistemology of practice that is grounded in inclusional and dialogical ways of knowing. Within my paper I position myself as a professional educator and researcher, and share the exciting and transformational experiences of teaching and learning in evolving action research cycles of practice. I view my learning to date as an active act, working with the novice teachers I support to offer improvement and change in our future practice. I celebrate my reconceptualised view of education as a learner from within my practice and explain my move from knowledge transfer to knowledge co-creation. I make an original contribution to educational knowledge by explaining how I try to inspire others to research their practice and contribute to a new scholarship of educational enquiry.

I imagine that all universities everywhere will have to acknowledge action research in some form or other to attract customer-students who wish to do it. It is anomalous and outrageous that some universities position themselves as those-who-know yet refuse to meet the needs of people who want to have their own knowing valued – this even in contexts where universities are under increasing pressure to 'produce' people for employability (now a criterion for many universities), with appropriate skills-based knowledge. The issue remains one of epistemology and theory generation – what kind of knowledge is most appropriate for human wellbeing, and what kind of theory may best communicate ideas about the origin, nature and use of this knowledge?

The responsibility of practitioner-researchers in exercising their influence

So what do we need to know? How can we develop our work?

We need to have confidence that we are right to encourage personal enquiry on personal and professional development programmes; that we can learn with and from others; that we need to interrogate what we already know, as if we didn't know it, in order to improve it. These processes are undertaken through examining practice and checking that we are living in the direction of our values. Furthermore, we can articulate how our values can become virtues, i.e. both what we do and also what we should do. We need to know that we are right in claiming that we understand our practices, out of responsibility to the authenticity of our relationships with one another. These claims are rooted in our personal learning from experience, and should be tested against the best critique of others similarly engaged to establish their validity and legitimacy.

Polanyi (1958: 65) says that it is the act of commitment in its full structure that saves personal knowledge from being merely subjective. He says that an intellectual commitment is a responsible decision, an act of hope, which is expressed with the universal intent of personal knowledge. Any conclusion, whether given as a surmise or claimed as a certainty, represents a commitment of the person who arrives at it. No one can utter more than a responsible commitment of their own, and this completely fulfils their responsibility for finding the truth and telling it. Whether or not it is the truth can be tested against another equally responsible commitment by another.

This may be seen in the extract from the draft PhD thesis of Maria James, about how she can improve her practices as a professional educator in the discipline of religious education (see p. 83).

We need also to know that, as social beings, we are always in company with others, through time and space. Our knowledge needs to be shared with others and refined through dialogue. Although knowledge may be the product of an individual mind, that mind is always in relation with other minds, including the living mind of the planet. The knowledge is refined and shaped according to the purposes of the individual and their companions. This can never be a coercive process; negotiating what counts as knowledge has to be a shared practice through critical dialogue. This is a contested area, for while it may be possible to agree how to share, it is not always possible to agree what should be shared (see Hampshire's views earlier in the chapter). Nor should it be.

Case study: Maria James, UK

Two core concepts form the central pillars of the thesis and are explored throughout. They are:

- Values identified as grounded in religious belief emerge also as educational values, the strongest being love, faith and hope.
- When this view is communicated through practice, Religious Education (RE) becomes a living experience, not only the communication of abstract concepts.

This has profound implications for the practice and theorisation of RE, and for my practice, for an important claim made through the research is that I have learned to teach RE in ways that help people develop as better people. The term 'better', related to the idea of 'good', is of course problematic and frequently contested, and this is discussed throughout. However, in terms of this research, and in the realm of RE, it may be understood as an improved capacity for independent learning, critical enquiry and engagement with the discipline of RE. Given that learning and teaching are intimately linked, a corollary would be that better learners become better teachers. Therefore my improved pedagogical practice could be seen as enabling growth and transformation for others. And, from this transformational perspective, the process of the research itself needs to be appreciated as not aiming to achieve a final destination so much as an ongoing struggle to understand. The content and form of the thesis show the action of this ongoing journey of self-knowledge and improvement, and suggest some implications for the subsequent exercise of educational influence in encouraging others to do the same.

James 2012: 3

We need therefore to raise our own awareness of what we are doing as a form of social change; and social change begins in the mind. We also need to be aware of the politically constructed nature of our contexts, and how powerful voices, especially institutional ones, can shut down self-expression and further development. This has major implications for those positioned as supporters, for they need to ensure that people are aware of the potential risks involved in undertaking their enquiries, in terms of the possible mental destabilisation when they begin to engage in critical thinking and also of the likely backlash when they try to challenge established institutional systems of knowledge. It is the responsibility of supporters and course providers to give emotional and practical support to people who are beginning to explore their thinking and its potentials. They need to build up emotional self-defences and see the possible retaliation for what it is. They need to have courage not to submit, and to learn how to deal with the exercise of institutional power. Providers also need to encourage practitioners to build communities, so they have support and comfort in times of difficulty, and find the inspiration to carry on.

None of this is easy. I say this from experience. It is, however, perfectly realisable, provided people have the energy, courage and vision to commit to their own power as knowers, and to create their knowledge as it transforms into the creation of their lives.

Case study: Alex Sinclair, UK

The extract below is from the papers Alex produced as part of his doctoral studies.

My studies focus on whether it is possible to develop a curriculum for ecoliteracy within the science elective course. I also focus on the appropriateness of using this module for these ends and the tension I face about whether I am abusing my role in attempting to influence my students to adopt issues that are important to me.

Part of this tension is derived from the students' perception that I possess the knowledge to make decisions about what is an appropriate education (Foucault, 1980), and in this sense, unless left unchallenged, have the power to make choices over such things as what is in the curriculum, what is discussed in sessions and in what manner. I concur with Chomsky (2000a), who stresses that many teachers have been trained to accept and act upon the normative theories of the educational system within which they teach without critical reflection. Because of this, they unconsciously fulfil the requirements of what he calls 'the doctrinal system' (2000a: 17).

I believe that there is a need to empower teachers to help break this cycle of socialisation. This empowerment may come through helping my students to develop a critical stance to what I am teaching them. If they feel that they are in a position to challenge what I am presenting them, this may reduce the tension I feel about exercising my influence in this manner. I consider the creation of a learning environment built from relationships based on mutual respect is a key element in helping this form of critical thinking to thrive. I have developed ideas around what this relationship, a mutualistic relationship, may look like. In developing a pedagogy for my mutualistic practice, I wish to draw on examples from nature to demonstrate the forms of relationship that, I believe, exist within the classroom. In particular, I use metaphors from the natural world to highlight the type of relationship I hope to develop with my students.

In nature, a symbiotic relationship is defined as the association between two organisms of different species that live closely together, and where one or both of the members benefits from this link. There are two main forms of symbiosis, those of mutualism and parasitism.

Parasitism is the form of symbiosis where one of the organisms benefits at the expense of the other. In parasitic relationships, there is an asymmetrical power balance where the host is relatively powerless and accepting of the parasite. I have used this living metaphor as a starting point and framework to help me better understand my relationship and role with my students.

I am suggesting that our current education system can mimic this parasitical form of symbiosis. Members of the government, exam boards, schools and teachers can be understood as parasitical, and the other, the hosts, are the students being taught.

Fromm (1976) makes similar claims when he outlines two kinds of students and their epistemological viewpoints: those that exist in a 'having mode' and perceive knowledge as an object that can be owned, and those that exist in a 'being mode', who understand it as something that has to be constructed from within. He defines 'having' students as those that have little or no desire to interact with the subject matter and generate their own understanding. They are content to adopt the teachers' ideas without the creation of their own knowledge. Fromm believes that these students will faithfully reproduce whatever has been spoken or written during a session and subsequently replicate this at a later date in order to pass the necessary examinations or coursework. Students in a 'being' mode are those who are ready to engage with their own knowledge.

Sinclair 2012: 6–7

So, what do we need to know? Alex Sinclair and colleagues combat the technologisation of education, as did Michael Crichton, who critiqued modern-day schooling and its emphasis on certain knowledge, as follows:

One can argue that the new generation of school children will emerge even more certain. If nothing else, school teaches that there is an answer to every question; only in the real world do children discover that many aspects of life are uncertain, mysterious, and even unknowable. If you have a chance to play in nature, if you are sprayed by a beetle, if the color of a butterfly wing comes off on your fingers, if you watch a caterpillar spin its cocoon – you come away with a sense of mystery and uncertainty. The more you watch, the more mysterious the natural world becomes, and the more you realize how little you know. Along with its beauty, you may also come to experience its fecundity, its wastefulness, aggressiveness, ruthlessness, parasitism, and its violence. These qualities are not well-conveyed in textbooks.

Crichton and Preston 2012: x

In this chapter, and indeed in all of Part I, we have considered some of the philosophical and epistemological issues that inform action research. In Part II, beginning with Chapter 5, we consider more practical aspects, beginning with how to do action research, and what this may imply.

Part II

What do we do with our knowledge?

The practices of action research

We have looked at how the 'action' of action research is action undertaken to contribute to the development of personal and social learning, which in turn may inform the development of personal and social action for personal, social and environmental flourishing. Action research therefore becomes a process of generating knowledge in action for action. The 'research' of action research is to find ways of doing this, and make the new knowledge public, so that the validity of the knowledge claim itself may be tested and critiqued. Testing is essential for pronouncing the knowledge appropriate and legitimate for public use.

This Part considers how to put ideas into practice, how practice becomes the site for the creation of new knowledge, some of the problematics involved and how claims to new knowledge can be tested. It contains these chapters:

Chapter 5: 'How do we do action research? Planning and doing a project'. This chapter gives guidance about how to do an action research project.

Chapter 6: 'Monitoring practice, gathering data, generating evidence, and ethics'. This chapter deals with questions about what to monitor and how to do so; how to gather data and what methods are appropriate for different circumstances; how to generate evidence from the data; and how to ensure that the action research is ethical.

Chapter 7: 'Practical issues'. This chapter looks at some problematics involved in doing action research.

In the next Part of the book, we go on to ask questions about what the new knowledge may be for, how it is to be used, and what might be its significance for human, non-human and environmental wellbeing.

Chapter 5

How do we do action research?
Planning and doing a project

This chapter is about planning and doing an action research project. You need to plan carefully to ensure your action will be as successful as possible.

Planning involves asking questions about:

- what you are doing;
- how and why you are doing it;
- what you want to achieve;
- how you can evaluate outcomes in terms of the values you hold.

It also involves imagining strategies for how you can realise these things in practice.

Doing means implementing those imagined strategies, and checking continually to make sure your action plan is working. This means gathering data from which you will generate evidence to provide the grounds for an eventual claim to knowledge.

Keep in mind this idea of making a claim to knowledge. Research is always about creating new knowledge. When you complete your project or reach an interim consolidation phase, you should be able to say that you know something that was not known before. In action research, the knowledge is knowledge of practice. It is created through the practice, and is about the practice. Doing action research helps you to say that you understand your practice better: this is new knowledge. However, saying that you know something, especially something new, is a big claim that needs to be tested, to show that you are not simply stating an opinion or making it up. If you can show that you have done this, you can claim that your work demonstrates methodological rigour.

This chapter is organised as two parts:

- Planning your action research.
- Doing your action research.

Monitoring practice, gathering data and generating evidence are dealt with in Chapter 6. Chapter 7 looks at practical issues, and Chapter 8 focuses on testing the validity of knowledge claims.

Planning your action research

Bear in mind that the idea of action research contains two words – 'action' and 'research'. The 'action' part of action research refers to what you are doing; the 'research' part refers to how you are finding out about what you are doing. Both parts are equally important: you improve practice with a view to contributing to good order (however you construe this), and you research the practice, as you improve it, to offer explanations for what you are doing so that you can show how you hold yourself accountable for your contributions.

Detailed practical guides to planning and doing action research exist in other books, including McNiff (2010) and McNiff and Whitehead (2009, 2010, 2011). This book therefore gives a succinct overview.

General principles in planning

A basic action research process can be described as follows:

- We review our current practice;
- identify an aspect we wish to investigate;
- ask focused questions about how we can investigate it;
- imagine a way forwards;
- try it out, and take stock of what happens;
- modify our plan in light of what we have found, and continue with the action;
- evaluate the modified action;
- and reconsider what we are doing in light of the evaluation. This can then lead to
- a new action–reflection cycle …

When you plan your action enquiry, you think about something you want to investigate, a real live issue that needs your attention. It does not need to be a problem, although it tends to be something problematic, i.e. something interesting you are curious about, such as whether you are delivering a good service to clients or managing your organisation in an inclusive way. Some writers in the literature, however, do say that an enquiry begins with a problem. Whitehead (1989), for example, proposes that you begin your enquiry by identifying a situation where your values are denied in your practice: you may believe in social democracy but you do not always give people an opportunity to state their point of view. This is a valuable idea that has been used widely.[1]

The ideas above may then transform into a coherent action plan as follows:

- What do I wish to investigate?[1]
- Why do I wish to investigate it?
- How do I show and describe the current situation as it is?
- What do I think I can do about it? What will I do about it?
- How do I show and explain the situation as it develops?
- How will I ensure that any conclusions I draw are reasonably fair and accurate, by inviting the critical responses of others and myself?
- How do I communicate the significance of what I am doing?
- How will I modify my practices and thinking in light of the evaluation?

Several examples below show these kinds of question in action.

It is important to see this cycle as an integrated whole, focusing on creating knowledge of practice. You begin by asking a research question, and end by saying that you have engaged with the question and now understand things better (although you still need to find out more). The process is integrated. Think of the Greek legend of Theseus, who had to find his way through the labyrinth to the Minotaur. Ariadne gave him a golden thread to fix his starting point and unravel as he went, so he could retrace his steps from beginning to end and back again. It is like this in your research. You can trace the steps by which your question 'How do I do this?' transforms into your claim 'I am doing this' or 'I am claiming that I have done this.' When you write your report, you need to give your reader a golden thread so they can see where they have come from, how each step relates to and is grounded in previous steps, and how the end links with the beginning.

It is also important to see how the process moves from description to explanation, thus becoming increasingly rigorous. When you offer descriptions through gathering data, you describe what is happening. However, this would be insufficient to ground a knowledge claim. You need to move into explanations and draw out of the data those pieces that help to make sense of what is happening. You move from descriptive to explanatory adequacy.

Drawing up an action plan

Now let's look at how you plan to move from description to explanation in your action plan, so that when you carry it out in live action you come to a point where you can say, 'I am claiming that I know what I am doing', and produce authenticated evidence to show that this is the case so people can believe and trust you. Here is a detailed outline of the schema above.

What do I wish to investigate? What issue do I want to look at? What research question will I ask?

To begin, identify an issue you wish to investigate; this identification of an issue is methodologically central. It involves imagining a research question of the form 'How do I … ?' or 'How do we … ?' or 'I wonder what would happen if … ?' Sometimes the question takes the form 'How do I/we understand … ?' or 'How do I/we improve … ?' It can also take the form, 'How do I show how and why I feel my practice is satisfactory?' If you feel that everything is going as you wish, you need to produce evidence to show why this is so. If you feel it is less than satisfactory, you need to do something about it and explain what you are doing. The research focus and question are about something in your situation that you feel you can investigate and do something about, in relation with others.

Remember that different areas may or may not lend themselves to action research. Generally speaking, action research is appropriate when it is overtly to do with identifying personal, social and political values, and asking what these values may look like when realised in practice. Action research is not appropriate when the aim is to show, say, a cause-and-effect relationship between variables, on the basis that if you do this, that will happen. So you would not use an action research approach for issues such as the following:

- What is the link between children's socio-economic status and their enjoyment of literature?
- What do people think about the president?
- How does management style relate to organisational productivity?
- How many customers visit the store on Saturday morning?

Investigating questions like these requires a traditional social science methodology. They are important questions, and the methodology is important, but it is not appropriate for asking how you can influence new thinking or action.

Action research approaches *are* appropriate for issues such as these:

- I would like to improve the quality of relationships in my workplace. What can I do?
- We would like to use social networking more effectively in our medical centre in order to improve communication with patients in rural areas. How do we do this?
- How do we check whether or not we are delivering a good service to customers?

It is important to focus on one aspect only; this should be something you can do something about. Stay small and focused. Be aware, however, that the focus may change and become more refined, and the research question with it. You might begin by asking, 'How can I improve the quality of staff relationships?' and find that your question changes to, 'How can I improve my management style in order to improve the quality of staff relationships?' Also sometimes you begin with only a general sense of an area and the focus emerges over time. Stay with it.

Beginning action research also involves thinking about what you can and cannot achieve. In *The Action Research Planner* (1988), Kemmis and McTaggart emphasise that an action enquiry involves strategic planning, recognising that you are in a particular social situation. This involves both an initial question – 'What is to be done?' – and a strategic question, 'What can be done?' They also point out:

> What can be done in your situation will be limited. You cannot sweep away the world which currently exists in your school, [organisation] or community; you may challenge its character and boundaries, but to change it you must recognise what it is now, and where you can work to change it. Deciding where to begin is a *strategic decision* – it is a practical decision about where to act to produce the most powerful effect compatible with sustaining the struggle of reform.
>
> Kemmis and McTaggart 1988: 65, emphasis in original

Why do I wish to investigate it? What values do I hold?

A useful place to begin your action enquiry, although not compulsory, is a reflection on your values. This may give you the reasons for your research. What do you believe in? What gives meaning to your life? Values inspire and underpin all intentional practices. It can be difficult to identify and articulate your values, but it is important to do so at some point.

Remember that you can have nasty values such as cruelty and self-interest as well as socially acceptable ones such as kindness and generosity. The question then arises, how do you justify your values? It is as valid to say, 'I wish to improve my practice as a thief' as it is to say, 'I wish to improve my practice as a nurse'; how then do you explain which profession you choose and why? How do you judge the practices of Al Capone, and why do you make these kinds of judgements? These are philosophical questions to work with over time, and you may find yourself developing new values.

Also remember that the people you are working with may not hold the same values as you. In her paper 'Viruses without vaccines, or valuing indigenous research?', Pip Bruce Ferguson (2012) explains how she worked with Māori colleagues at a Māori tertiary institution who wished to enter the New Zealand funding mechanism, a main criterion of which was to cite the number of researchers' publications. This, according to Māori tradition, says Pip:

required people to 'boast' of their research achievements in a context where such boasting is anathema; to claim ownership of knowledge where tradition often indicates that knowledge is not the property of individuals; and worst, at one point I found myself accused by my Māori manager of introducing 'viruses without vaccines'. By this he meant Westernised ideas and practices which appeared to be benevolent but in fact were toxic (the idea derives from white settlers who apparently gave native Americans blankets permeated with a virus, causing thousands to die).

Bruce Ferguson 2012: 1

It could be that your research focuses on these kinds of conflicts of values, requiring you to do something about your thinking.

How do I show the current situation as it is?

This question involves monitoring your actions and gathering, analysing and interpreting data. It is important to monitor your actions and gather data through all stages of the enquiry, from identifying a research issue to producing an outline research proposal. Your golden thread takes you through all kinds of situations. If you record these along the way, they can become your data. Further advice about data and data-gathering, analysis and interpretation appears in Chapter 6.

What do I think I can do about the situation? What will I do about it?

At this point in your action enquiry, you need to decide whether you wish to do something about the situation you are in, and what you can and intend to do, i.e. what kind of action to take. There are different kinds of action. There is involuntary action, when you cough or trip over; a stimulus–response kind of action, when you laugh at a joke; and also intentional action, inspired by your values. This tends to be taken in response to what you encounter in a person, or social or organisational situation. The action you take depends on your values and your ontological positioning.

You need to consider your options carefully. Take advice from critical friends and colleagues. People sometimes take action for the wrong reasons, perhaps for their own agendas, and it turns into interference. Or they may feel that other people need help, which may not be the case: young birds do not always need help when they fall from nests – here you can help best by staying out of the way. Many people writing in the literatures speak of 'an intervention', which implies that they are intervening (interfering). But most people don't need others to intervene in their lives. In addition, the idea of taking action in a situation is tricky. I used to use this language, but I am now aware that taking action in a situation implies that you see others as separate from yourself; you position yourself as external to 'the situation' – others – and you step into their lives. If you adopt a relational attitude to others, however, you see yourself as part of the same situation, part of the same story.

So rather than think of taking action in someone else's life, think instead of taking action in your own in relation with them, specifically in your own thinking, which is where any action starts. How do you respond to what you are experiencing? How do you see yourself being violated when others are? How do you ally yourself with them, and find ways of taking action together to improve your own lives?

Below I tell some stories of how I have taken action, and some of what I have learned about myself through doing so.

How do I show and explain the situation as it develops?

As you progress, you will continue to gather data to show what is happening and how things are changing. Aim now systematically to generate evidence. By identifying your values as criteria, you can say that your values emerge in practice as your living criteria. It is important to explain this to people who are reading your report, so they will see that you are attending to matters of methodological rigour. These matters are explored further in Chapter 8.

How will I ensure that any conclusions I draw are reasonably fair and accurate, by inviting the critical responses of others?

We speak throughout about the fact that you would identify critical friends who would stay with you for the duration of your study. You would also convene validation groups at critical episodes of your study to read and comment on your progress and final reports. These are valued friends who keep you company throughout your research. You can find further detailed advice about this in *You and Your Action Research Project* (McNiff and Whitehead 2010, pp. 45–6, 195).

How do I communicate the importance of what I am doing?

You can communicate the importance, or significance, of what you are doing by reflecting critically on whether you have influenced your own and other people's thinking so that you begin doing things differently in your mental, social and physical worlds. Some of the things you could consider are whether you have:

- interrogated earlier preconceptions that got in the way of relationships;
- developed deeper understandings about how you can influence others and the kind of influence to be exercised;
- encouraged them to do the same;

- ensured the methodological rigour of your research and scholarship;
- contributed to new thinking and practices;
- influenced others in your local, organisational, social and perhaps global communities;
- written it all up in some way, even perhaps in emails, or put a clip on YouTube, or telephoned someone who can take the ideas further;
- shared your work with the others in your context – knowledge is no use if you keep it to yourself, so how do you share it?
- contributed to saving a life.

These ideas are dealt with further in Chapters 10 and 11.

How will I modify my practices and thinking in light of the evaluation?

How do you do things differently now, having developed these deep understandings? How do you celebrate your action enquiry with others? You may be at the end of this piece of your life, but more is ahead. Each new 'answer' generates more questions: this is the nature of action research, and of life itself. Things are not over until they are, and even then there may be new beginnings.

So, how to put all these ideas into action? You now need to move into doing action research.

Doing your action research

Doing action research means you consciously hope that something is going to change. You take action to try to let the change happen, and possibly to influence it. At this point, you need carefully to consider your motives in wishing to take action.

Dr Faust, the legendary character of Goethe's play (1962), rejected the idea of 'In the beginning was the Word' (the Word here carrying the dual meaning of 'Thought' and 'Word Incarnate'), in favour of 'In the beginning was the Deed'. Faust was obsessed by the grand potentials of his own power to control nature and other people, and he saw his actions leading to his own kudos. You need to check that you are acting honestly and from a context where you can help others to help themselves, rather than do things for them (or worse, do things to them). Even if you initially 'do things for them', your longer-term commitment would be to help them to help themselves. Your broken finger does not heal because your doctor sorts it out for you; your body heals itself, with help from your doctor. So you need to appreciate that the action begins in your mind, and your ideas transform into actions in the world, to enable others also to come to the same understanding.

At this point, I would like to tell you two stories about the action enquiries I have undertaken, in South Africa and the Arab Gulf States, and outline some of the big lessons I have learned from doing so. I also refer to texts that have appeared related to the projects, and show how the structure of the texts reflects the action–reflection cycles outlined in this chapter. I have told these stories elsewhere, so here I give a synopsis and comment on how my learning from my actions has influenced new actions, such as writing this book.

The experience of Khayelitsha

Khayelitsha is a township near Cape Town in South Africa. It is a largely unlovely, often violent place, comprising sections of brick-built utility houses and broad tracts of shantytown. It has a vibrancy and purposefulness about it that is belied by its dusty exterior. Thousands of people live in close proximity, many in extreme poverty.

I went to Khayelitsha in 2005, with a colleague who worked for a non-governmental organisation who wanted me to see his work in action. While I was visiting, I got talking with some of the teachers working in the schools. I asked them about opportunities for continuing professional education, but they explained that entry to a Master's programme in South Africa required a fourth-year Honours degree. While the teachers I worked with would have a primary degree following three years' study, and were qualified teachers, they had no fourth-year Honours. This (to me) unnecessary barrier was frustrating, because I had at that time just succeeded in delivering a Master's course in Ireland, using an action research approach, from which 75 teachers had received their Master's degrees in spite of what I perceived then as institutional obstacles – I immediately saw the opportunity to do the same here in Khayelitsha.

At that time, I was also working with St Mary's University College, Twickenham, UK, as Professor of Educational Research, so I went back to St Mary's and liaised with my colleague, Patricia Wade, then Head of Department, to negotiate for me to deliver a Master's programme in Khayelitsha. Pat was the institutional front-line person who took the project through the committees, and I was the front-line field person who delivered the programme and had overall responsibility for ensuring its quality. Pat became ill during the programme, but lived to see the teachers graduate at St Mary's Cathedral in Cape Town.

The story is full of ups and downs. It was never an easy ride for a range of reasons: the teachers and I had to learn how to live and work together, from our different cultural and historical legacies; we had to overcome our own internalised racialised self-perceptions, as well as overcome the influences of dominant contemporary stories of the lack of legitimacy of workplace knowledge. Over the course of the three years of the project, we also had to overcome efforts by various people to close our programme down or to belittle its significance. I recall a conversation with a South African academic before I began the project, when I explained to him what I hoped to do. There was a change in temperature, and his comment was, 'Why would you want to do this? They will only use their degree to get themselves out of Khayelitsha.' He was mistaken. At the end of our programme, 10 teachers received their Master's degrees. Most of the teachers have used their degrees to get promotion into positions of institutional seniority where they are trying to improve the quality of learning and teaching in their schools, still using an action research approach.

The project had significant influences in everyone's learning, including mine. Some of the teachers stay in touch, and some tell me that they are trying to influence the quality of learning and life experience in their schools. One colleague told me during our studies, referring to citizens in Khayelitsha: 'I want to get them to stop killing each other' – I wonder how many lives he has been involved in saving.

I have large bodies of data to show that the project did influence people's thinking. The two case studies below show this – and these are just two among many: others may be accessed at http://www.jeanmcniff.com/kayelitsha.asp/. The first is from Zola Malgas, and is taken from her dissertation, edited with her permission. Zola is now Principal of Manyano School in Khayelitsha.

Case study: Zola Malgas, South Africa

When I started my research, I asked some of my colleagues to become research participants. They came to my classes prior to and after I had conducted my enquiry. One, who also teaches the same grade ten mathematics class and who discouraged me from including the class in my enquiry because, she maintained, there would be no significance or change, asked me what I had done to influence them to such an extent that there was such a dramatic change. I explained how, through trying out a range of strategies, learners had become hungry for learning, and levels of concentration, participation and attention had increased. Their behaviour was appreciated by everyone. This was not only for my benefit or the school's benefit but for their own benefit throughout their life. I also explained that I had learnt through learners' responses that learners were not happy in class and I was too strict. I tried smiling in class and encouraged free debates to help build their confidence. I became more flexible and understanding of their needs and expectations. Responses from interviews and questionnaires given to parents and learners towards the end of my enquiry showed that learners were now happier in class and enjoyed coming to school. So I believe I have made a contribution to improving my practice by helping my learners improve the quality of their learning of mathematics.

Having thought about my values revived my reasons for wanting to be a teacher. What seems to enable some teachers to maintain positive attitudes about their jobs is their freedom to be creative and innovative, the capacity to influence students, getting feedback, recognition and support. This is a vision where teachers are heard, appreciated and respected, where teachers work with students, not teach at them and where teachers and administrators work as a team, sharing ideas, supporting one another and enjoying the privilege of being co-responsible for education in South Africa. The value you add to the lives of your learners will also enrich your own life and each student is deserving of both your time and respect. The most important achievement that I think is good for me is the improved relationship between me and my learners.

Zola recently wrote to me as follows:

> Being a participant on the Masters course taught me to have confidence in myself. I had never thought of myself as a deputy principal, let alone principal. I feel I can face any challenge today because, as you always said, 'change begins with me'. I have used this knowledge to contribute to improvement in my school and in Khayelitsha. I am delighted to say that I am founder of Betterschools. This was an idea to assist learners to come to my school who had poor LITNUM results, that is, in levels of Literacy (English) and Numeracy (Mathematics). I invited our feeder primary schools to work together with me to find ways of addressing this problem. The programme has proved highly successful, in that many schools, including high schools, have joined in. We are also developing staff development initiatives, something that is dear to my heart. This is a free service to all schools that have joined Betterschools.
>
> I draw on my Masters work as a resource when I make presentations at various places about the benefits of doing action research. I am hoping one day to be a facilitator for action research at one of our universities.
>
> Jean, you believed in us when we doubted ourselves whether we would make it. Your work is already benefiting people who have never even met you.

Case study: Arthur Mgweto, South Africa

Here is an excerpt from an assignment by Alfred Mgweto, written in 2007; this reflects some of his learning. He speaks of how he has opened his eyes to the power of his own potential agency.

Macintyre (2000: 15) says that action researchers who read are enriching their experience. To be honest, reading is not one of the normal practices for us Africans, because we have a long history of passing information orally from generation to generation, and this has made some of us hesitant in engaging with formal literatures. This Masters programme has worked wonders for me personally in this regard, and I am hoping that this piece of work will match the standard of quality set by key thinkers in the field of research.

Speaking of what his learning has done for him, he says:

All these years I have been searching for a rationale for the situation where learners feel alienated and disengaged from their own learning. When I try to enquire from colleagues about why this should be the case, some put the blame on the medium of instruction, some on the government's banning of corporal punishment, some on the parents' illiteracy, some blame the government for not providing enough resources, some educators are demotivated because of low wages, and so on. I continually ask myself whether it is possible for these issues to be addressed and improved. If it is, where do I start? If I decide to tackle at least one of them, will I get the support I need? Despite all the obstacles I have made up my mind that I will never sit back and watch the work of my own hands fall apart. I will try my utmost to help my learners gain some interest in the subject. It is one of the reasons why I am writing this assignment about improving my teaching of mathematics.

An e-book of the project, entitled 'It Takes a Township' will be available at www.jeanmcniff.com/township.

The experience of Qatar

The second example is from work in Qatar. Again I have written about this elsewhere – and about some of the lessons learned (McNiff 2011). The story is this.

In 2010 I was contacted by Tribal Education UK, a large service provider who had won a contract for the delivery of a comprehensive teacher professional education programme. I was a member of a team of four tutors, and the project involved working with over 100 teachers in Qatar, to help them develop new pedagogies and perspectives in their teaching. The programme was highly successful in the sense that teachers learned how to manage their teaching better, and evaluate it in relation to how they were encouraging learners and colleagues to develop new attitudes to learning.

Following the first phase of the project, we put together a *Teacher Education Bulletin* to show examples from the initial work of the Qatari teachers. The work may also be accessed from http://www.jeanmcniff.com/userfiles/file/qatar/Qatar_Action_Research_booklet_email.pdf. New work has begun in the form of an evaluation of the influence of the first phase, and this is being written up. Further evaluation work is in hand and will be published in due course.

Here is an example of how one of the teachers developed her understanding and practices. It is also an example of the action plan above in action, and how the methodological structure can inform the writing structure. The report, written in 2010 by Lina Mahmoud Abu-Mallouh, was entitled 'How do I encourage students to speak English in their English lessons?'

Background to the research

Lina worked as an English teacher at Al-Bayaan Primary Two School, and wished to help her students to become proficient at speaking English.

- *What was my concern?* Lina was concerned that her students spoke Arabic instead of English in their English lessons. She asked, 'How can I encourage students to use English instead of Arabic in their English lessons?'
- *Why was I concerned?* It was important for a range of reasons that young people should become proficient in English, and Lina listed reasons in her report.
- *How could I gather data to show the situation as it was?* Lina produced qualitative and quantitative data to show the reasons for her concerns.
- *What did I do?* She tried out a range of strategies to encourage her students.
- *How can I show whether the situation improved?* Lina produced data to show the gradual improvement in students' levels of proficiency.
- *How do I check that any conclusions I come to are reasonably fair and accurate?* She explained how she presented her research to her peer group and invited their critical feedback about the validity of what she was doing and saying.
- *How do I explain the significance of my action research?* Lina showed how the work she was doing enabled her to meet the National Professional Standards for Teachers in Qatar. She explained especially how these standards became live through her research.
- *How do I modify my thinking and practices in light of my evaluation?* Although this was the end of her first action–reflection cycle, Lina continued her learning in extended and different teaching areas, and encouraged her colleagues to do the same.

Other writing from the project also demonstrates how the action plan can become the structure for a written document. Two examples, both from the same project, are given below.

CONFERENCE PAPER: 'PROFESSIONAL EDUCATION FOR TEACHERS IN QATAR FOR EPISTEMOLOGICAL TRANSFORMATION IN EDUCATIONAL KNOWLEDGE', JEAN MCNIFF AND MARK MCCOURT (2010)

Following the field work in Qatar, Mark McCourt from Tribal Education UK and I gave a presentation at the British Educational Research Association's annual conference (McNiff and McCourt 2010), entitled 'Professional education for teachers in Qatar for epistemological transformation in educational knowledge'. This is a scholarly paper and uses the same headings of the action plan above.

PUBLISHED ARTICLE: 'NEW CULTURES OF CRITICAL REFLECTION IN QATAR',
JEAN MCNIFF (2011)

This is also a scholarly paper, published in *Educational Action Research*, that shows the need for critical reflection on practice, especially in light of the importing and exporting of knowledge, and the need to make public emergent understandings that engage with the problematics. It includes an account of an incident that highlights the need for critical reflection. It uses the questions above as a framework.

My own learning from Khayelitsha and Qatar

I have developed considerable insights through the experience of engaging in these projects. They include the following (and many more).

Being reasonably clear about one's motives before taking action

At the time I was working on these projects, I genuinely wanted to contribute to people's capacity in learning, and to take more control of their lives. I also wanted to circumvent barriers to their access and success. I was aware that getting involved in Khayelitsha could be perceived publicly as a form of 'doing good', a motive excoriated by Coetzee (2004), who condemns 'do-gooders' as interfering people out for their own glory. Calderisi (2007) also demonstrates how this motive inspires many aid programmes, but while people need aid in the sense of physical resources, they need aid more in learning how to combat the political forces that exclude them from engagement in their own lives. As the teachers and I got to know and trust one another, and they learned how to become critical, I forgot about others' possible perceptions of 'doing good' and focused only on 'good work', and so did the teachers, I think. Somewhere the distinction became clear in my mind, and this was reflected in the action.

The need for respect in other people's spaces

In relation to Qatar, I have learned the importance of respect and caution when introducing a particular knowledge system into a culture whose knowledge system is different. Although we were invited by the Qatari government to work in the country, we were always aware of our responsibility to propose ideas and practices that did not offend cultural or religious values and traditions. This can be a difficult lesson to learn and calls for consistent self-critique within a dialogical practice. I am constantly amazed at the arrogance of some organisations that sweep into a country, expecting to import their knowledge systems, without any regard for their hosts and their cultures – and many sweep out again.

Both learnings relate to the idea of respecting that people already know how to live their lives within their cherished traditions. Any actions we take as action researchers need to be taken with humility and caution, for no one has 'the answer' to another's life. Everyone needs to work things out for themselves, in patience and commitment, and not expect everything to turn out right. It is engaging with the problematics of trying that helps; perhaps it is this engagement that constitutes 'the good', without any expectation that there will be concrete or desired outcomes.

This is, I think, where many of the current action research literatures can be misleading for their readers. They emphasise that action research is about achieving outcomes. Not for me it isn't. For me, it is about taking action in your own thinking, so that your actions in the world work for other people's benefit, and therefore for your own; for it is through working together that we can get rid of shantytowns and imperialist behaviours that smother opportunities for critical thinking, and encourage people to engage in their own lives, for universal wellbeing.

Now, having considered some ideas about what is involved in doing action research, Chapter 6 offers ideas about monitoring practice, gathering data, generating evidence, and ethics.

Chapter 6

Monitoring practice, gathering data, generating evidence, and ethics

This chapter is about monitoring practice, gathering, analysing and inter-preting data, and generating evidence to ground and support a claim to knowledge. Chapter 8 deals with testing the validity of claims to knowledge.

In order to gather data, you have to monitor your own and other people's practices, which means observing what is going on and keeping records; capturing records of the action as data; analysing this; and interpreting it in order to generate evidence. This all needs to be done within an ethic of care and respect for others and self. The chapter is organised as four sections to address these issues:

- Monitoring the action
- Gathering and analysing the data
- Interpreting the data and generating evidence
- Ethical issues.

Monitoring the action

Monitoring the action means monitoring what you and others are doing. It first involves you being clear about your positionality: you may be researching yourself with people, or helping them to do action research, or conducting a collective enquiry. In action research, all situations are possible; you need to decide where you stand. It is not possible to do action research on people or use them as data: this would be empirical or even positivist research.

Monitoring means keeping track of things, which involves gathering data and keeping records of your thinking and actions. Are you achieving what you aimed to do? Do you need to act differently? Monitoring the action is a first step in evaluating it. Keep the following in mind:

- Action research is always collaborative.
- The aim of your enquiry is to try to exercise your educational influence in other people's thinking and your own.

- Your thinking influences your actions, and your actions influence your thinking.
- You hope that your thinking and actions will inspire and influence other people to reflect critically on their thinking and actions.
- Their revised thinking and actions in turn influence your thinking …
- … And so it continues to develop …

The whole system becomes interrelated and mutually reciprocal. You are in a web of critical thinking and action that aims to influence new ways of thinking and practice in the wider world. These ideas are set out fully in McNiff and Whitehead (2010).

This has implications for what you monitor and how you gather data about it. You need to monitor and gather data about:

- your own thinking and practice;
- other people's thinking and practice;
- how you are influencing one another;
- how you are developing new insights and practices through the interactions.

Your records can therefore take a range of forms to capture these individual and collective actions. Here are some ideas:

Monitoring what you are doing

You need to monitor your thinking and your actions, as well as try to capture how your thinking has informed your actions. A lovely example of this appears in the case study of Peter Hyde (see p. 186). To monitor your thinking, you could use a research diary, in written, audio- or video-recorded form, and keep copies of emails, texts, interactions on social networking, letters and blogs.

To monitor your actions, you can use any or all of the data-gathering techniques identified on pp. 106–7. Note any shifts in emphasis in your data. You can also invite others to observe and monitor your actions. This might take the form of written, oral or visual feedback. Also invite your critical friends or validation group to look at your data and make suggestions about interpreting them or modifying your actions. Critical friends stay with you throughout your project and give formal or informal feedback about progress. You can convene validation groups to look at your progress reports at strategic intervals and offer formal critical feedback.

Monitoring what other people are doing

Other people become participants in your research. Only they can monitor their thinking, probably through keeping a written or multimedia diary, which they may share with you. You should never insist that they share their diaries – diaries are people's private property.

To monitor their actions, you and they can use those same research diaries, or you could interview them regularly, or invite them to make videos of themselves for sharing with others. When you monitor others, or invite them to monitor themselves, check that all accounts are reasonably in agreement. Triangulation can be helpful; this occurs when the data from at least three different sources are scrutinised and the analyses compared.

When you monitor actions, you gather data. In the first instance, you gather and analyse the data to make sense of them. Later you begin to interpret the data to generate evidence (see below). Here are some ideas about how you can gather and analyse data.

Gathering and analysing data

When gathering data, you ask these kinds of questions:

- What do I want to find out?
- Where am I going to find it?
- Who can tell me?
- What should I look for? How will I recognise it when I see it?
- What will it tell me when I find it?

There are no hard and fast rules about how to gather data, but here are some general guidelines.

Gathering data

You gather data to show the situation as it is now and as it emerges; that is, you offer descriptions according to what the data show you now ('Here is a photograph of our group talking') with a view to turning those descriptions into explanations ('We are talking because we are planning our next steps'). Moving to the level of explanations involves turning data into evidence and explaining how you have done so (see p. 112).

When you gather data, you often find, especially in the early stages, that you have probably gathered too much. You can discard unwanted data, but do not reject anything too soon because it may be useful later.

Many good books offer advice about forms of data and how to gather them. Some distinguish between quantitative and qualitative forms, but these distinctions should be seen as flexible, and sometimes the categories become blurred. *Quantitative* data can be useful especially if you are trying to get a sense of trends. You would gather data using some kind of tally or record sheet, on paper or on a computer. An everyday tally sheet would look something like this:

Record sheet to show clients interviewed

Times	9.00am–9.45am	10.00am–10.45am	11.00am–11.45am
Clients interviewed	Mr Green Mrs Black	Ms White Mr Grey	Dr Blue Ms Silver

Record sheet to show number of times employees speak at a staff meeting, 10 am–11 am

Employees	Number of contributions
Mr Green	⊬⊬ ⊬⊬ II
Mrs Black	I
Ms White	⊬⊬ ⊬⊬ I
Mr Grey	III
Ms Silver	⊬⊬ ⊬⊬ ⊬⊬ ⊬⊬

You could also use a Likert-scale type tally sheet, for example:

	Strongly agree	Agree	Don't know	Disagree	Strongly disagree
Camel racing is an exciting sport					

Many other kinds of devices for gathering quantitative data exist. You can usually find them in psychology and sociology study guides and some research methods books. They are useful at many points of your enquiry. Some people use them to show a 'before' and 'after' situation, for example how many people took part in staff meetings before and after you introduced more participative forms of leadership. However, this kind of 'before-and-after' strategy does need care because it tends to be associated with cause-and-effect or stimulus–response strategies, and could easily stray into behaviour management.

You can also use *qualitative* data-gathering methods, such as (1) documentary methods and artefacts;, (2) live methods, (3) ostensive methods, and (4) visual and multimedia methods. Here are some ideas.

Documentary methods and artefacts

These kinds of data take the form of field notes, observations, questionnaires, reports, and diaries and logs. New forms of electronic data-gathering devices are available, as well as traditional paper-and-pen exercises. It is your choice how to create and store documents, taking into consideration issues of storage space and ease of access. During her early PhD studies, for example, Margaret Meredith from York St John University kept a record of her preliminary reading electronically (see http://participationict.wordpress.com).

The data themselves may take the following forms.

FIELD NOTES

Keep notes of the situation you are investigating in the field. The 'field' can be a workplace, a bus queue, a classroom or a home. Aim to document significant aspects, for example whether a colleague raised an important question during a meeting. Try to record your observations as quickly as possible after the event; if you leave it too long, you may forget what happened and distort your own and other people's interpretations of the action.

DIARIES AND LOGS

Aim to keep your own diary, and encourage research participants to do so too. You could keep your diary as a written document, an audio-taped recording, a video diary or a blog. It can be useful to organise your diary into columns, screen boxes or other devices, labelled 'What I did', 'What I learned' and 'The significance of my learning'. It is easy to say what you did, more difficult to say what you learned, and sometimes really hard to identify the significance of your learning and its potential implications.

If you invite participants to keep diaries, reassure them that their diaries are confidential, unless they wish to make the diaries public. People often like to be identified and have their work celebrated. Negotiate these things with them.

Diaries are valuable sources of data because they show developments in the action and in thinking and theorising. You can document how your own perceptions changed over time and how you used new learning to help make sense of a situation.

REPORTS

Reports take a range of forms – accounts, letters, memos and emails – and can be communicated using forms such as paper, the spoken word, ostensive methods and video-taping. To find out what people feel about a situation, you might ask them to write you a text or an email or text message. You can also solicit feedback about your own practice, but this can be risky and takes courage. What will you do if feedback suggests you should change? Building an archive of reports can help you keep track of the action, and see how issues and opinions have changed over time.

QUESTIONNAIRES

Use these only if you must. Questionnaires can be helpful but are notoriously difficult to construct. They are also liable to misuse. In action research, use a questionnaire or survey only to get an idea of trends. Further analysis of the data is often necessary using more qualitative forms that aim to see the extent to which values are being lived out in practice. Open-ended questions can provide richer data than closed questions, but analysing the responses is usually more labour- and time-intensive.

LIVE METHODS

You can gather data using live methods such as those described below.

SURVEYS

These are often the spoken equivalent of questionnaires, in which a researcher documents the responses of people to specific questions. The same comments of caution apply as to questionnaires.

INTERVIEWS, DISCUSSIONS AND FOCUS GROUPS

These are valuable sources of data that capture the live responses of people. They can be recorded using field notes or audio- or video-recording. They are time- and labour-intensive and involve you doing some analysis as well as drawing up a report to show your conclusions. In interviews, aim to adopt an open-ended approach, otherwise it would be as sensible to use a questionnaire or survey. Interviews need special consideration for the interviewee and require refined interviewing and counselling skills.

LIVE AND ONLINE DISCUSSION FORUMS, AND VIRTUAL WORLDS

These are becoming increasingly used to share information and engage in discussion. If you record them, they can provide rich sources of data. Similarly, blogs and websites are live and interactive, and can provide data about the developing learning of individuals and groups. Social networking sites such as Facebook and Twitter can be a valuable source of data, and mobile phones, tablets and computers can be useful data-gathering devices.

Ostensive methods

These include all kinds of presentations, including PowerPoint presentations and talks, especially when made available through multimedia, for example on YouTube. You can see many presentations of research on YouTube, as well as validation meetings (you can see several YouTube presentations by me, for example: http://www.youtube.com/watch?v=uGyuQ1uTrzM). These ostensive methods are everywhere because of the interest in multimedia methods.

Visual and multimedia methods

Multimedia methods have become especially popular with the availability of technologies such as websites and online journals. Many action research websites show a range of ways in which people network and learn with and from one another. Presentations made at conferences and live presentations may be communicated through streaming video and webcam conferencing. Virtual learning environments and virtual worlds are increasingly used, especially for distance communication and blended learning programmes. These ways of communicating are useful for supporting learning, as well as acting as sources of data, and there is much debate about whether they will actually change the face of the learning experience, including professional education, because online learning opportunities provide easier, wider and less expensive access for learners.

Interestingly, a call for papers was distributed on 12 June 2012 from the journal *Teaching and Teacher Education*, for a special edition on 'Scholarly Work Beyond Written Texts'. This made the point that although visual and multimedia representations may communicate the live nature of the action, there must still be a verbal text to interpret and explain the meanings of the action. Explaining things verbally is still central.

Summary

So, to return to the questions asked above, we can respond:

- *What do I want to find out?* I want to find out what is going on in the research setting. I can do this by gathering data at any point in the research to help me show the real–life situation as it is, so I can describe what is going on and how I am making sense of it.
- *Where am I going to find it?* I can find what I am looking for in the interactions between people, recorded in documents and artefacts such as diaries and logs, and in responses to questionnaires and surveys. I can watch recorded presentations and videos, and look at messages on texts, videos and blogs via mobile phones and computers.
- *Who can tell me?* All participants in the research can tell me what is going on. I need to find different ways of asking them, also using the same methods identified above.
- *What should I look for? How will I recognise it when I see it?* I will look for data that tell me whether I am influencing people's learning to enable them to become more critical, to exercise their curiosity and originality of mind, and to develop the kind of relationships with others that will help them find ways to do so.
- *What will it tell me when I find it?* The data will tell me whether or not I am succeeding in what I hope to do. Not all data will tell me this – some

will show me things happening that I was not expecting to see and that may lead me to rethink the situation (disconfirming data), so I have to be selective and analyse my data in relation to identified criteria. Here is how I can do this.

Analysing data

To analyse anything, you need to identify some kinds of categories of analysis, using identified criteria and standards to guide your choices. Recall we said above that you may use quantitative and qualitative analysis of data as appropriate. First, we will consider quantitative analysis, and then move to qualitative.

Quantitative analysis

You would use quantitative data-gathering and analysis if you wanted to show that certain things were happening at a specific time. This would mean considering the data you had recorded on your tally sheet and drawing up some kind of chart to show the results, such as a bar chart or a pie chart.

Qualitative analysis

Analysing data qualitatively involves:

- identifying criteria for what you expect to happen, and standards to show the extent to which it is happening;
- analysing and interpreting your data in terms of these criteria and standards;
- coming to a conclusion about how well this has been done – this moves the idea of analysis into evaluation.

In action enquiries, you expect to see improved learning, so improved learning becomes a criterion: you analyse the data in relation to whether improved learning is evident in the data. Showing this would mean showing the situation 'before' as well as 'now', as you take action to encourage improvement (but see a cautionary word above on 'before and after'). You would also need to explain how you understand 'improved' – for example, whether the nurses on your ward show an increased awareness of the need for good service delivery, perhaps when caring for fragile elderly patients. Search your data archive for instances of what you consider improved learning, and show in what way it is improved.

You could then go on to analysing in what way the learning had improved and how you make judgements about its quality. This would involve identifying standards, that is, saying how well you thought the criteria had been achieved. If you really wanted to refine your work, you could explore the extent to which the learning had influenced the practice.

Also remember that you are not focusing only on analysing data about other people – you are doing the same about yourself in relation with others. This means you should be able to show the interrelationships between your thinking and actions, and their thinking and actions, and how they interact and mutually influence one another.

When you gather data, you store them in your data archive – your desk drawer, or computer, or a box. Keep your archive live and visit it regularly. Aim to sort your data into appropriate categories, which may change from time to time; you may organise your 'letters' file into 'emails' and 'text messages'. Try to manage your data systematically otherwise they will quickly get out of hand.

Now let's look at interpreting the data and generating evidence.

Interpreting the data and generating evidence

Interpreting the data means making sense of what you find, using your chosen categories of analysis. You would make a judgement about the success (or not) of what you and others are doing. Coming to a judgement, a first step of which is analysing, means identifying criteria, and in action research, these criteria are related to our values. For example, if we feel that a successful meeting is one in which everyone participates, the value of 'participation' becomes a criterion. You would search the data archive for instances that show participation in action. You would then select those pieces of data that show your values in action, drag them out of the data archive and drop them into a new evidence archive. You will draw on this evidence to ground your knowledge claims. So when you say, 'Motivation is higher', as Linda Clifford does in the case study below, you draw out pieces of evidence to show the real-life enactment of what you are saying. These matters are dealt with further in Chapter 8.

Ethical issues

Ethics is not only about taking action; it is also about doing research. In action research, both are related.

Ethics in action

Gathering data involves other people, and you must ensure that your practice is ethical. This means taking care about confidentiality, ensuring access and withdrawal from the research if participants wish, and securing permission from all parties. You must get permission to monitor other people, particularly if they are vulnerable, such as children. If you are engaged in an accredited learning programme, your institution's ethics committee will want to approve your research. When you produce your report, especially for academic accreditation, you should explain to your readers how you sought and were granted permission to do the research, and include any letters of permission as appendices.

Anonymity is an issue for action research. Accrediting institutions often insist that participants' identities are kept secret. In action research, this could actually be perceived as unethical, for people rightly wish to be recognised for their contributions. However, to be on the safe side, get their written permission that they are happy for their identities to be made public, and put this permission somewhere in your report. In addition, make these permissions available to institutional ethics committees.

Being ethical involves, however, more than just observing protocols. It involves an attitude towards other people and the world. This is a dialogical attitude, in which you show yourself to be open to others' opinions and insights, and to be prepared to learn with and from them. This means that your practice becomes praxis, i.e. morally informed action. Detailed guidelines about ethics are given in McNiff and Whitehead (2010).

Ethics in research

Ethics in research is about how you conduct your research in a morally committed manner. This includes avoiding sins, both sins of commission and sins of omission. There are many of these, and here are some obvious ones.

Sins of commission

PLAGIARISM

The most usual sin is copying pieces of text, or reading ideas from the literatures and cobbling them together so that they appear as your original ideas. This is dishonest and you may be found out: people who are familiar with the literatures, such as your supervisor or examiner, will know immediately. In addition, technology is available to identify plagiarism. Plagiarism is mean – intellectual debts need to be paid the same as financial ones. You should always reference your sources and attribute ideas to the people who created them.

The same thing can happen, all too frequently, when you talk through ideas with colleagues but then hear them talking about the same ideas the next day as if their ideas were original. You have choices, depending on your attitudes: you can keep the ideas to yourself until you make them public by writing or putting them on your website, in which case you lose the earlier interaction with colleagues that may help you develop the ideas; or you can share your ideas, knowing that there are plenty more original ones in your head to come after those that have gone to other people. Your ideas will in any case change over time.

NAME-DROPPING

Do be careful of how you use the literature when writing your reports. Bassey (1992) speaks about this as 'sandbagging' – when we drop names into a sentence to make it look stronger, without necessarily reading the original text or even a secondary source. If you do this in a doctoral examination for which you have a viva, be sure that your sins will find you out because your examiner will have read the same literatures as you and may ask you about them.

PEDANTRY

People often take a particular stance in relation to a research methodology or method, are dogmatic about issues such as data analysis or interpretation, or rage about the merits of qualitative rather than quantitative data … I have probably been dogmatic in this book and raged a bit. I try to take a balanced view but this can be difficult in the face of outright pedantry that verges on intellectual bullying.

Sins of omission

Some of the most common are as follows:

*   *Not stating your positionality as researcher*: you need to explain to all in the research, including the readers of your reports, how you position yourself in the research field, whether as a participant, an external researcher or other.
*   *Not observing conventions*: people sometimes write reports that show a blissful disregard for literary or academic conventions – incorrect forms of reference, gaps in the references lists, no page references, spelling and syntactical errors … and so on.
*   *Not coming out and speaking your truth*: it is perhaps as great a sin not to commit to what you believe in as to become pedantic. Sitting on the fence never moved the fence forward, although it may have helped it to collapse so the field could move ahead without you.

The wages of sin can be severe, and sinners might even get away with their sins; but sins run deep and have long-lasting effects in people's lives. You need to explain how and why your action and research should be seen as good, to show how you are contributing to improving practices, and explain how and why you are prepared to say so.

Case studies

Three case studies here will show these principles in action. The first is from Anne Marie Villumsen, who speaks about the problematics of gathering data. The second is from Rita Jentoft, who uses multimedia technologies for gathering and presenting data. The third is from Linda Clifford, who tells a lovely story that shows the realities of what we have considered in this chapter.

Case study: Anne Marie Villumsen, Denmark

My action research aimed to encourage collaborative practices among childcare, social services personnel and health-care professionals. I convened meetings of 20–50 people, hoping to encourage learning in groups of two or three. The dilemma was how to capture as many interactions as possible, while ensuring transparency. Transparency in documenting how the data is generated is important if action research is to be valid and ethical. However, data-gathering is also a living activity, which means that it is impossible to control. The focus of my research was on process and outcome, so how could I capture both? How does a multidisciplinary dialogue influence the thinking and behaviours of every participant? Probably in as many ways as there are people and changes occur in their moment-by-moment interactions.

Case study: Rita Jentoft, Norway

Rita Jentoft, at the University of Tromsø in Norway, has been working with occupational therapy professional educators at Bethlehem University in Palestine, with a view to supporting students from Gaza. You can see her work at http://seminar.net/index.php/volume–5-issue–1–2009-previousissuesmeny–126/116-facilitating-practical-knowledge-by-using-ect and read her Project Report at http://www.ub.uit.no/munin/bitstream/handle/10037/2294/article.pdf?sequence=1

Case study: Linda Clifford, Dubai, United Arab Emirates

While undertaking my daily walk around classrooms to engage with students and check on our learning and teaching programme, I overheard two students outside their tutor class:

'I'm going to get into trouble with this homework because I don't understand any of these stupid words …'

This conversation was a genuine caught 'on the spot' reflection between two students who were having trouble understanding key words in a homework task. I was surprised by this as I knew this student was capable, although he was an English language learner. I decided to observe and chat with other students about using key words in their work, and found many struggling and frustrated students. Considering that 68 per cent of our students are English language learners, I shouldn't have been surprised.

I value the importance of providing learning opportunities for all, so I wondered how I could provide additional vocabulary support, scaffold the reading strategies already in place, and add a more multifaceted approach to making our students more confident when writing and reading English.

I gathered further data. On analysis, it became apparent that I needed urgently to work alongside a group of Arabic and Islamic teachers, reflecting together how we could best support student learning.

Many scholarly articles explain how a lively learning environment can influence student learning, and since many Arabic/Islamic classrooms had no displays (Figure 6.1), I decided that the classroom environment was a practical place to start. I set about taking photos of the Arabic and Islamic classrooms to show them in their initial state, and also transcribed and collated the interview data from the students.

Figure 6.1 An Arabic and Islamic classroom before the action research

On sharing this information with the teachers, I initially found the Arabic teachers very defensive, as if I was criticising their practice rather than being constructive. I explained the need to make the school learning environment print-rich, but they still actively resisted.

Language, ironically, was part of the barrier, so after much thought, and a few sleepless nights, I got a bilingual English/Arabic speaker to assist me. I also arranged to take the teachers on a learning walk to the Primary section of the school, where the lively, print-rich Arabic department had wonderful displays. The conversation that evolved was quite remarkable; I became the English language learner! Ideas began flowing – content words written in English and Arabic of the Hadith, five pillars of Islam, numbers and simple commands in Arabic. For further support, I enlisted the practical support of a teacher's aide to laminate key words and displays.

Upon re-interviewing the students a term later, I found they enjoyed going into the now positive and helpful environment (Figure 6.2), their motivation to learn was higher and there has been a measurable improvement in key word usage in writing.

Figure 6.2 The Arabic and Islamic classroom after the action research

We now consider some practical issues of doing action research in Chapter 7, and then turn to how to generate evidence in Chapter 8. This involves identifying criteria and standards to judge the quality of your work and thereby engage in testing the validity of your knowledge claim.

Chapter 7

Practical issues

Action research is practical. Here is some advice about what to do and what not to do when undertaking your action enquiry.

Stay small, stay focused

There is a big difference between the scope of your work and the scope of your project. Even though the area you are researching may not be small, the study itself should focus on one aspect of the overall picture so that it is always clear what you are investigating. Although, in a wider sense, work and practice are research, and research is practice, in a practical sense you need to see your research project as an extrapolation from your wider work and keep it in perspective.

You are researching how you are trying to influence people's learning so they can reflect on and change their mental and physical behaviours as they see fit. Therefore one piece of your practice is going to be symptomatic of the whole, in the same way that, according to complexity theory, one segment of a fractal is part of the whole and holds the whole always already within itself.

You could find that researching one aspect will reveal other interconnected aspects: you and your work are integrated as a constellation of interests, commitments and intents in which everything is interconnected and mutually influential. Don't try to research everything at once. Stay focused on one issue, get on the inside of it and understand it, and put the others on hold. Concentrating on only one part of your work also helps you understand the nature and processes of your own learning. Once you have come to where you feel you have made progress in one aspect, you can then progress to other areas that will themselves become new research projects.

Identify a clear research question

Try to be reasonably clear about what you are researching. Action research questions usually take the form 'How do I ... ?' or 'How do we ... ?', for example, 'How do I improve the quality of my relationship with Ms X?' or 'How do I ensure good service delivery to the clients?' The questions emphasise several things:

- Although the research is about the individual or individuals working collaboratively, it is also about their understanding and about improving their practice as a means to wider wellbeing and social good. All the case studies in this book are about people reflecting on what they are doing and taking action on behalf of others. Research questions communicate the idea that research is about showing the responsibility of the 'I' to others, not about claiming the individual's rights. It is seldom about 'me', more about 'I in relation with you'.
- The idea of 'centre' disappears (see also p. 42). In action research, everyone becomes a centre, and therefore there is no discernible 'centre': notionally, 'I' as centre encounter 'you' as centre, so we become a new kind of centre, as drops merge with others to form a pool. But this 'centre' then transforms into wider 'centres' as we encounter other people through space and time. The idea of 'centre' melds into an image of people living lives of enquiry in relation with one another where boundaries dissolve or become permeable. The focus is on the relationships that keep people and their environments together.
- Any action research question is therefore about people contributing to social and environmental good. All questions are part of an emergent order that keeps things in balance.

At a practical level, you need to be aware of asking the right kind of question. You would not ask questions of the kind 'How many people have achieved a specified level of expertise?' or 'Is there a relationship between room temperature and degree of concentration?' These are social science questions, where the aim is to establish facts and figures and show a cause-and-effect relationship between variables in the quest for certain knowledge and predictable outcomes. Although action researchers appreciate the value of these approaches and are interested in the same kinds of question, they put their energies more into developing ways of contributing to enhanced experience of life for all.

Also be aware that your research question may change as you develop the research. The question 'How do I help my students concentrate?' may transform into the question 'How do make my presentations more interesting so that my students want to learn?' As you dig down into your thinking, you will come to new understandings about yourself and the problematics of your situation, and begin asking new kinds of questions.

Be realistic about what you can do; also be aware that wider change begins with you

Can you do anything about the unsatisfactory infrastructures of your organisation? Possibly not immediately, especially if you are trying to influence processes of change from the outside – it is much more feasible to think of change as happening from within. You can, however, certainly contribute to

---

Case study: Vicci Carroll, UK

Vicci Carroll is a beauty therapist who is studying for her Certificate of Education. She wrote asking advice.

The young ladies in my beauty therapy class work well, but it is a struggle to get them motivated. I tried a range of strategies, including peer assessment, but to no avail. A difficulty is that some of them attend class because they want to be with their peers, and this makes peer assessment difficult because they don't want to give one another any negative feedback, even if it is constructive. If I pair them with strangers, they don't achieve their best because they want to work with their chosen peer. Do you think this may be a case of do the best I can? I would much prefer them to excel, and I know some of them are hiding a lot more talent than they show.

---

changing wider systems by focusing on a smaller piece within the system, as a participant. You can understand and modify that piece of the infrastructure that constitutes you working with others, and you can influence others on an increasingly wider scale by producing accounts of your work and showing how others may learn with and from you. You cannot expect the world to change immediately, but you can contribute to your piece of it, and you can influence others to contribute to changing theirs.

This is a powerful methodology for social change. It is a process of individuals deciding that they want to change their own lives and then coming together as communities of like-minded practitioners who mobilise themselves for action. I remember listening to John Hume, then leader of the SDLP in Northern Ireland, when the fragile peace process was in danger of collapse because of the issue of decommissioning. He said that decommissioning begins in the mind, not in the laying down of arms. I also think of the wonderful TomTom GPS advertisement that says, 'You are not stuck in traffic. You are traffic' (I was stuck in a traffic jam when I first saw this). Personal and social change are long term and labour-intensive, but people are resilient and determined, especially when they come together as a group. You are never alone.

Plan carefully

This means having a broad outline of where you hope the research will lead you, but it does not mean setting specific objectives. The research will often develop in ways different from what you expected, and you may need to shift the focus and change the research question. From the beginning, set yourself working criteria for how you are going to judge your effectiveness and the quality of your research and practice. You may need to refine and modify your criteria and your thinking as you go. An example of this is in the correspondence from the case study at the end of this chapter.

Criteria are grounded in and informed by our values: our values transform into criteria and standards of judgement. If we identify criteria such as 'speaking for oneself', we hold values around the need for people to speak for themselves, to exercise their freedom of mind and action. Our values inform our work, and our work can be judged in relation to whether we are living our values in our practices.

Case study: Sólveig Zophoníasdóttir, Iceland

Sólveig Zophoníasdóttir is a specialist in school development at the University of Akureyri in Iceland. She writes:

The aim of my action research into my practice as a professional educator is to gain a deeper understanding and stronger awareness of myself and my professional theory of practice through examining my ideas, thoughts, values, attitudes and practices. Action research is a form of enquiry that enables me to investigate and evaluate my work. I need to be aware of what influences my practice, and how it changes and evolves. This means being aware of what lies behind my words and actions in order to improve what I am doing. The justification for my research and my work lies in my genuine will to ask critically how I theorise what I am doing and renew my professionalism in order to live more fully in the direction of my educational values and build a professional knowledge base about what I know and how it may influence my daily work and thinking.

Set a realistic time scale

The wider project that is your life is long term and goes on; you adopt an enquiring attitude to everything. The specific project you are working on is short term and bounded. Aim to set time limits, but make these realistic enough to cope with unpredictability and changes of direction. Also, instead of thinking in terms of deadlines, think about when you will start a piece: when will you start gathering data or writing up? You do have to finish, but developing a 'starting' attitude can help to get jobs done. You need to show others that you are managing your project appropriately. If you have set deadlines, perhaps for you to return an edited transcript, ensure also that you honour commitments. It is important to maintain credibility, not only for yourself, but also for the knowledge you stand for.

Involve others

As a social being, you are always in company with others. They may not be present, but you and they are still influencing one another: you are in relationships of influence. You are not doing research on them, you are researching with them (Reason and Rowan 1981). You are inevitably involved with others in doing your research. Here are some of the relationships you will probably experience.

As research participants

You will invite others whose situation you are involved in and whose learning you are nurturing to become research participants. If you are exploring how you can increase the degree of workplace participation in decision-making, you will monitor how you are achieving this. You will aim to get feedback from them on how well you are helping them to help themselves. While the research focus is you and your learning, you also appreciate how your learning is potentially influencing the quality of learning of others.

As observers

Be public about your research so that it does not appear mysterious. Invite others to observe you, and ask for their feedback. At a public relations level, others will warm to you; at a research level, you are showing that your research is rooted in an ethic of respect for others' opinions.

As critical friends and validators

Submit your research and its findings to critical friends and validation groups for scrutiny to ensure that any conclusions you may come to are not just your own opinion but are also agreed by others. It may be that your ideas come in for critique. Colleagues may make suggestions about how you should revise your research and your ideas. When you produce your report, aim to build in these factors and show how you took action on the advice of others to help you think and act more purposefully.

As potential researchers

As an on-the-job researcher, you are inevitably involved in wider systemic change. You are part of a living system with others; if you change, others will also change. In the 1930s Schrödinger demonstrated what came to be called 'the observer effect', i.e. that the very presence of an observer influences the attitudes and therefore the behaviours of the observed (see Barrow 1990). The same applies to you: if you encourage others to regard their practice as research, you are contributing to the development of communities of action researchers who are studying how they can improve their learning for mutual benefit, moral accountability and social evolution.

Ensure good ethical practice

Be aware of your own positioning in the action research and the setting in which you are doing it, and the potential abuse of your own position power. Be careful not to encourage people to become dependent on you or wait for you to give them direction. This is possibly one of the problems with charismatic leaders who attract other people and then use those people as means to further their own ends of self-promotion. Perhaps the only way out is to take the advice of Habermas (1979), who says that it is only possible to judge over time whether people are engaging or simply pretending to engage in communicative action.

There are other widely accepted aspects of doing ethically informed research, and many good books are available, such as Mason (2002) and Robson (2011). Key principles include the following (see also McNiff and Whitehead 2010, 2011):

- Negotiate access – with authorities, participants and parents, guardians, caregivers and supervisors.
- Promise confidentiality – of information, identity and data (but identify people if they wish to be named, to recognise their contributions).
- Ensure participants' rights to withdraw from the research.
- Keep others informed.
- Maintain your own intellectual property rights.
- Keep good faith throughout.

Concentrate on learning, not on behavioural performance, as the outcome of action

It can be tempting to focus only on activity and produce a report that offers descriptions of the activity, what you did and how you did it. This descriptive level is important but insufficient. It stays at the level of descriptive adequacy, but does not move into explanations. Because action research is about doing research, and doing research is about knowledge creation, it means that your research can contribute to wider fields, both about specific subject areas and about how knowledge is created and used in a range of settings. To show this, you need to explain the processes of learning that informed the activities, why you did what you did, and what you hoped to achieve.

If you take this view, you will think in terms of two complementary processes. One is to do with your activities with others, the other to do with your learning with others. The way we develop our learning with others influences the way we develop our actions.

Case study: Hjördís Thorgeirsdóttir, Iceland

Colleagues and I have created ourselves as an action research group in our college. We aim to create knowledge about classroom practices from our practices, in order to increase students' responsibility for their learning. From 2009 to 2011 we linked action research and activity theory in a 'Change Room', where we engaged in expansive learning. This was based on the Change Laboratory, one of the methods of developmental work research established by Yrjö Engeström.

Our learning was a mix of individual and collective learning, with an agreed motive, and with individual goals and ways of implementing projects. The group meetings provided a space for teachers to discuss their work, values and conflicts, and collaboratively create their own living educational theories. The Change Room provided the tools, the conceptual framework and the historical analysis to understand the conflicts that teachers experience in the classroom and analyse what changes are needed to try to solve these tensions. Action research provided the approach to guide participants when carrying out and evaluating these changes.

Be prepared to problematise your thinking

Many philosophers emphasise that research is not about finding solutions as much as about asking new questions. Collingwood (1939) says that the aim in human interaction is always to keep the conversation open, and Said (1997) emphasises that there is no such thing as an 'end' because whatever appears to be an end is in fact the beginning of something new.

Ideas like these have implications for judging quality in research and trying to understand what counts as 'good' in 'good practice' and 'good research'. For if we say that action research is about studying and reflecting on one's learning, and how that learning influences practice in order to improve it, there is nothing to stop the likes of Al Capone from claiming that they are contributing to a good social order, as much as Gandhi or Jesus might say. Al maintained order in a commendable way by stopping the gang warfare in Chicago (Stockdale 1996); he ran a legitimate business to meet the demand for prohibited products (alcohol); he spent time and energy on improving his practice as a gangster and influenced people like J. Edgar Hoover to engage critically in ideas about how to stop him … and so on. Whatever we may think about whether what Al Capone did was 'good' or 'not good', it is important to problematise our thinking about these things.

These ideas are relevant to the field of action research. If we are prepared to say that what we are doing is 'good', we also need to be prepared to justify what we are doing within a particular world philosophy of what counts as 'good' and who says so. It is no use simply saying, 'This is the way things are because this in the way things are'. You have to justify why you think things should be this way, and this requires critical thinking, including critical thinking about your own thinking.

This leads to the idea of being cautious about aiming for solutions and happy endings, as follows.

Beware of happy endings

A widespread mythology is that life is full of episodes with happy endings. This is seldom the case, because happy endings imply working towards closure. For some, it means working towards a utopia where everything will be perfect (which could also be rather boring). Life is always problematic – but this does not mean it is not happy; it means that life is always interesting because it is never quiescent. Given that we are choice-making beings, and choices involve conflict, it does not make sense to think in terms of coming to closure. The idea of closure itself is part of a traditional epistemology that sees everything as working towards an end point where questions will be resolved (see Berlin's critique cited on p. 73 of this book). Iris Murdoch may have a point when she comments (1985: 62) that Jesus should not have said, 'Be ye therefore perfect' but 'Be ye therefore slightly improved' (although perhaps the state of slight improvement is perfect for its own time and place).

Action researchers do, however, work towards the creation of a good society, and any improvement, no matter how small, is still improvement. We struggle to take incremental steps to where we wish to be. Horton and Freire (1991) spoke about creating the road through walking. We also need to be aware how, in the creative process, we are changing our own present realities so that our vision of where we want to be is also changing. Insofar as the future is in the present, we create the future as we change the present. We are aiming not for happy endings as much as new beginnings. Each moment is a new beginning.

Be aware of politics

All research is political, especially action research. Its entire mandate is about emancipation and change (Carr and Kemmis 1986), but change can be threatening to some. Many people feel comfortable with the status quo even though they complain about it. Familiarity often gives security. Byron (2006) explained in *The Prisoner of Chillon* how we come to love our chains; and Red, in the film *The Shawshank Redemption*, spoke about the comfort of institutionalisation. We might rant about being colonised, but we learn to collude in it (Memmi 2003). We say, 'Blame the system', forgetting, as Habermas (1979) says, that we made 'the system' in the first place. What we make, we can make again, differently. You are not stuck in traffic; you are traffic. Some people are comfortable with the status quo because it suits them, particularly if they have position power and are unwilling to encourage public participation in decision-making.

Action researchers are beset by these kinds of external pressures, as well as by the logistical issues of resources and support, government policies, and cultures of control and creeping managerialism. They are also beset by their own internal constraints of lack of confidence, or their capacity to take action, or the possible challenge from colleagues. It is not easy. It is not straightforward to recreate yourself and find ways to help others do the same, as well as articulate reasons why this is necessary; many people, understandably, give up the struggle as the pressures begin to bite.

We all make our own decisions about who we are and who we want to be, and what we wish to do with this wonderful life that we did not ask for but that was freely given. It is hard, and anyone doing action research in this way is to be admired.

Case study: Ruth Seabright, New Zealand

Extracts from email correspondence, May 2012

19 May 2012: 5.14 am
Hi Jean,

My name is Ruth and I am a mature 40-something Masters student embarking on an action research project for my thesis.

I just found your website and am busy reading, reading, reading. I have found myself in a bit of a dilemma and although I feel totally embarrassed by my confusion, I thought I would write to you to see if you can help in clarifying my thinking. I totally understand if you choose not to respond – it is a bit of a long shot on my part and I expect you have many other pressing priorities.

My issue is that I feel lost in how to structure my thesis/proposal – perhaps because it is different from the traditional theses my peers are embarking on, or perhaps it's just my complicated over-analysis. I think sometimes I think too much!

I am studying towards a Masters in Applied Psychology (Community). As part of a directed study this semester, I have been working with a local community house here in my hometown, investigating the level of interest in Time Banking. There are twenty-two Time Banks across New Zealand, but none in my hometown. I am really drawn to Time Banking as a concept and believe it has an immense amount to offer on many levels. Unfortunately, there are several barriers which I identified in my study, including funding, staffing and physical space.

By the end of my practical time, I had made many connections within the community and had identified several community groups who were interested in Time Banking. My project is to work within the community, bringing individuals and group representatives together, to set up a citywide Time Bank. Where I come unstuck is with the research/thesis side. I can't seem to get my head around the action on one side, and the research on the other. Am I best to think of this as a self-study action research project where I write about my reflections on the experience of being part of the team setting up the Time Bank? This would involve reflection on my practice, the challenges, decisions and consequences encountered along the way?

Any words of wisdom or clarity you can offer would be much appreciated. I gather it is not uncommon for students to feel totally incompetent at some points along this journey. Sometimes it just feels like there is some small 'aha' moment that I am missing here.

Many thanks in advance for taking the time to read my email.

Yours with gratitude
Ruth Seabright
New Zealand

19 May 2012: 6.30 am
Hi Ruth,

Lovely to hear you and many thanks for writing. I was in New Zealand last November, and isn't it a lovely place?

I think you have a lovely thesis in the making. Perhaps the overall thing is to see your action and your research as interwoven. It may help to think about the 'action' part of your action research as what you do, and the 'research' part as how you find out about what you do. So you are interested in supporting others in Time Banking as your action, i.e. this is what you do, and you are finding ways of doing so as your research part, i.e. you are finding out about what you do as you get involved.

Maybe a first step would be to ask yourself, 'What do I do, as my work?' This would involve writing about your work. And then ask, 'How do I find out about my work in a systematic way?' This would involve writing about how you find out, i.e. identify an issue that needs investigating, say why it is an issue, monitor your practice and gather data to show the situation as it is, look at the data carefully to help you decide on a course of action, take action, review what you had done, think about whether it is what you want, and if not, take a new course of action.

Could you clarify for me how you understand the concept of Time Banking?

I also have to say that, while I can talk with you about general issues, as we are doing here, I would not respond to anything about your formal studies. That would be unprofessional and unethical. I am sure you understand.

Let me know if you feel this is a useful way to go.

I am actually working on a new edition of 'Action Research: Principles and Practice' right now, so it's nice that you are focusing my thinking on the idea of the inter-relationship between action and research.

All good wishes,
Jean

19 May 2012: 7.21 am
Hi Jean,

Wow, that was a fast reply. I had imagined you asleep in bed at this time of the morning. Yes, I think New Zealand is lovely, but then I am biased.

To clarify about Time Banking: Time Banking is a reciprocal volunteering system which uses time as the unit of measurement. I like to think of it as a pay it forward system that encourages neighbours to help neighbours. The basic principle is 1=1: that is, my time is worth the same as anyone else's time, so it doesn't matter what you offer, it's all the same in Time Banking. The beauty of Time Banking for me is that it contributes to community capacity-building, encourages social capital and trust, and helps to break down stereotypes and prejudice by reconnecting people with each other. Time Banking is based on reciprocity, social justice and most importantly the valuing of everyone. If you are interested you can read more about Time Banking in the UK here http://timebank.org.uk/.

I will need to sit down and think over your questions. My initial response is that part of my attraction to action research is that it reflects my natural approach to life. I have always been a flexible and responsive person in my working life. Problem-solving is one of my fortes. However, I haven't given much thought to theory as such in the past; it's been all about intuition. As I train towards becoming a community psychologist, I want to be more mindful and conscious about what I am doing and how I do it so I can be more helpful to groups I work with in the future. This project offers me that opportunity to be involved in something I am passionate about, while at the same time being critically reflective about what I am doing and why.

I agree about professional sensitivities and I am respectful of roles. I am so grateful for your thoughtful reply. I have been feeling more than a little dense of late – luckily I have a good sense of humour, a healthy perspective on life and a husband with great listening ears!

Yours with appreciation & thanks
Ruth

19 May 2012: 8.27 am
Hi Ruth,

The reason I wrote earlier is because I tend to wake up very early, do some writing, and then go back to sleep, so here I am again, awake for the second time. ...

I really like your insights that action research is not only about doing projects but involves an attitude to life – I wish more people saw it like this, but one of the unfortunate aspects (as I am writing about now in this book) is that too many people want to box it up and see it only as something to be applied rather than a way of living.

How would you feel about meeting with a colleague I know who happens to live near you? Perhaps I could contact them and see how they would feel about having a chat?

Look forward to hearing back when appropriate,

Best wishes,
Jean

Many more emails later ...

29 May 2012: 6.34 am

Kia ora Jean,

Just wanted to let you know that Jo and I met late last week, which was extremely helpful. We talked through the general principles of action research and I got a lot of clarity in my thinking. Action research needs a different mindset from traditional social psychology research. It is so nice not to feel like I am 'lost in space' any more. I feel more in control of my research and have actually started writing my proposal, and am able to visualise how my thesis will come together.

Conversing with you has been immensely helpful. Yesterday morning I awoke with my mind alive with connections. I had to grab a piece of paper and write to get the thoughts out. It was really inspiring to see how my mind was connecting past experience and knowledge with my current situation in ways I hadn't seen before. It is so nice to feel I am moving forward, rather than chasing my tail.

Thank you for your kind and supportive emails, and for connecting me with Jo. Somewhere in there I found confidence in myself again.

Arohanui (big hug/love)
Ruth

Chapter 5 set out ideas about designing and planning an action enquiry, and this chapter has offered practical advice about what is involved. Bearing in mind that doing action research is about generating claims to knowledge, you now have to test the validity (truthfulness) of the claim so others will take it seriously. This becomes the focus of Chapter 8.

Part III

How do we share our knowledge?

Writing up and making public

When we do action research, we conduct an enquiry and then make it public in some way, for different reasons but mainly to test its validity so that we can be confident in its usefulness and truthfulness when putting it to use in the interests of the flourishing of all living things.

The Part contains the following chapters:

Chapter 8: 'Testing the validity of knowledge claims'. Here we consider necessary strategies for testing and demonstrating the validity of emergent knowledge claims.

Chapter 9: 'Writing and presenting action research reports'. This chapter offers advice about what goes into written documents, and how the validity of the text can be demonstrated.

Chapter 10: 'Judging quality and demonstrating impact: The significance of your action research'. Here we consider the potential influence of action research for the development of personal, social and environmental formations.

Part IV goes on to consider how these practices may inform personal, social and institutional transformation, and how this may contribute to good order within personal, social and environmental orders.

Chapter 8

Testing the validity of knowledge claims

In Chapter 5 we discussed designing and planning your research. This involves asking research questions, gathering and making sense of the data, and generating evidence with a view to making a knowledge claim. We looked at how a research question can lead to a claim to knowledge: you begin with a question, and go through a range of transformational steps whereby you transform the question into a statement. However, if you make serious statements such as, 'I know what I am doing', you have to be prepared to stand over the claim, ground it in concrete evidence, and subject the whole process to the critical evaluation of sceptically minded others.

This chapter therefore deals with the questions:

- What is validated?
- Who validates?
- How is it validated?

It also deals with matters of legitimacy.

What is validated?

Chapter 2 made the point that practice is rooted in personal knowing. Throughout the book, I have suggested, drawing on the work of Polanyi (1958, 1967), Bateson (1972) and Chomsky (1986), that humans possess a vast reservoir of tacit knowledge that guides their practices in the world. Polanyi says (1958) that we know more than we can say. This has implications. On the one hand, you do not have to be able to use clever words to show that you are clever. Quality work does not depend on knowing the literatures: we need not have heard of Piaget, Habermas or Schön to be good practitioners. Sometimes rational thinking can even get in the way, as Kevin Costner in the film *Tin Cup* showed when he thought too much about his golf swing and lost his capacity to hit the ball straight.

Many practices can, however, be enhanced when we reflect consciously and critically on what we are doing and decide to investigate and improve it.

In action research, this means becoming aware that we have this vast fund of personal knowledge, valuing it and understanding how to use it to contribute to people's, animals' and the planet's wellbeing. We raise our deep tacit knowledge containing our knowledge of our values up to an explicit surface level where we try to live those values in our practices. We come to understand how our I–knowledge embeds and informs our practices in the world (Figure 8.1).

For me, the most important part of this visual representation is the process of transformational emergence. What happens in the process of making tacit knowledge explicit? How do we do this? The struggle to make sense of one's practice, says Mellor (1998), *is* the research.

Case study: Gabriella van Breda, USA

When I think about action research, this quotation comes to mind:

> Imagine a map ... drawn from your memory instead of from the atlas. It is made of strong places stitched together by the vivid threads of transforming journeys. It contains all the things you learned from the land and shows where you learned them ...

> (Patton, 2002: 27 quoting Tallmadge 1997)

The quotation captures the essence of action research for me. The cartographic abilities of our predecessors provided the framework wherein we can engage in a critical assessment of our own learning and experiences. Furthermore, we are now able to create our own maps through the explicit expression of what we have known tacitly and continue to know and learn through our enquiries.

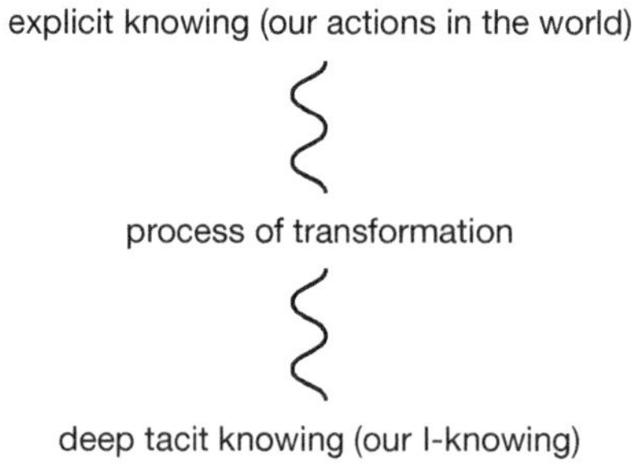

---

explicit knowing (our actions in the world)

process of transformation

deep tacit knowing (our I-knowing)

Figure 8.1 Transforming tacit into explicit knowledge

The struggle to make sense is an ongoing process. We never get to closure. Everything in life is full of potentialities for growth: unstable, unstoppable, transforming itself into a new, more fully realised form towards ongoing life. Reality exists in a balanced state of tension, an inherent harmony of contradiction. Whatever is, is changing. What appears as a new balanced state is already realising its own potential for change. This includes processes of knowing and knowledge creation, involving a dialectical and transformational process of making tacit knowledge explicit, becoming aware of embodied knowledge and drawing theories out of practice, so that theory becomes embodied practice, which potentially emerges again as new theory. Here is the balanced tension where, as soon as we say, 'I know', we also know that we do not know and need to learn further.

People working in traditional forms of scholarship often find it difficult to accept this volatile process of knowing and coming to know as legitimate (see for example Newby 1994). They cling to the idea that rational knowing is the only legitimate form; justifiable belief is a belief in an objective reality. Subjectivity is suspect; the complexity and unpredictability of life are factored out or ignored, as is the values base of human living. Reality can be understood as a unified and predictable whole, and people and their practices should be adjusted to fit accordingly. Anyone who does not conform is regarded as anarchic. An example of this occurs in the film and book *Jurassic Park* (Crichton 2006), where dinosaurs were created on a model of mechanics: it was assumed that their behaviours could be predicted and controlled. Humans were in for a nasty shock when they found that the creations, once brought to life, developed a mind of their own. 'Life finds a way,' says the scientist Malcolm.

When you create knowledge that you want to use, say, to influence people's thinking, the knowledge has to be tested for validity, so what you say you have done (your knowledge claim) has to be justifiable. It also has to stand up to scrutiny, in the same way as when you design a new car, you put it through its paces to make sure it will do the job it was designed to do. This means identifying and agreeing specific tests, such as brake tests and impact resistance. Knowledge also has to go through tests. In traditional social science forms of research, rational knowledge is tested using traditional forms of data analysis, usually statistical (Schön 1995), and the research needs to be shown to be objective and replicable. Much social science research aims to show a cause-and-effect relationship between phenomena through the manipulation of variables to predict future outcomes. This is regarded as good scientific research. Research rooted in personal knowing is regarded as unscientific and lacking in rigour.

These rationalists have a point. While personal claims to knowledge may be claimed as valid without evidence (for example, if I say I have toothache, I am making a valid claim to knowledge but it cannot be demonstrated as true), those claims are best served when they are grounded in some form of corroborating evidence. If a practitioner claims to have improved their practice, they need to provide supporting evidence to show in what way the practice has improved and by what criteria they are making the claim. Within these parameters, action research may be seen as a disciplined enquiry, in which a practitioner systematically investigates how to improve practice and produce evidence for the critical scrutiny of others to show how the practice can be judged to have improved.

What is tested are the knowledge claims of people who have undertaken their I-enquiries to generate knowledge about their work in company with others, and to show the transformational processes of coming to know. They explain what they hoped to achieve and how they feel they have achieved it by pointing to critical instances from the data that can be regarded as evidence. They explain how they are generating their own theories of practice from within the practice, how the process of theorising is an ongoing engagement with inherently volatile living systems. Testing the validity of practical theories involves moving beyond standardised categories of analysis – not an easy thing for some people who may refuse to recognise the claim, or the need to develop new ways of thinking themselves.

Who validates?

Who do we choose to help us test the validity of our knowledge claims and the quality of the work from which the knowledge has been generated? A range of validity tests is available (see p. 140), and it then becomes a matter of who we invite to use the tests, and how we know we can trust their judgement.

In any process of judgement, it is less problematic to invite friendly critics than sceptical ones to look at the work, but if we want our work to be judged in the wider community as worthwhile research, we need to ensure from the start that appropriate rigour is built in. Action research accounts need to stand on their own feet. Even though some people may disagree with the idea of action research, they should not have grounds to find fault with the methodological or epistemological rigour of the account. It is perhaps wise to begin with the most supportive but perceptive critics, but at some point you should also invite critique from those unfamiliar with the principles and values of action research.

You would invite at least the following people to look at your work closely and judge whether it does what it says it does.

Yourself – processes of self-validation

Aim to become your own best critic. This involves interrogating the assumptions that underpin your thinking, and checking that you are speaking out of respect for others and their potentially divergent viewpoints. Although you might disagree with some people's points of view and try to persuade them to think and act your way, you need to respect their right to hold their opinion, while recognising the right also to hold your own. Gray (1995b) speaks of this as agonistic pluralism, which becomes the basis of debates about freedom of speech and information.

This is essential though problematic, especially in these days of instant electronic communication, when racist and homophobic propaganda can be whizzed around the world in seconds and hate mail on mobile phones becomes a feature of daily life for many school children. Do we allow freedom of speech, and freedom of the press, or suppress it in the interests of a good social order, while recognising that freedom to speak is itself at the heart of a good social order? The exercise of responsible freedom of the press has been jeopardised by recent revelations of unethical behaviour in the UK press. Action research emphasises the need for personal critique about one's own normative assumptions – but getting to this level does not always happen.

Colleagues – processes of peer validation

Recognising that we are all liable to self-delusion and to making factual errors, we need to invite others to look at our work and the assumptions that underpin it, and to give honest feedback about the possible validity of the knowledge claim. People we may invite include the following.

Critical friends

Invite one or more colleagues or friends to become critical friends throughout the process of your enquiry. Their job is to be familiar with your research and offer advice and criticism. They should be supportive, but not so supportive that they do not point out real or potential flaws. Listen to their advice and act on it. Sometimes you can become too close to your own action, or fail to see potential flaws in an argument, so always welcome fresh perspectives, even though you may not accept them in light of your own responses to the critique.

Validation groups

Aim to convene a validation group of several people for the duration of the research. Their commitment is to meet with you, perhaps every few months or so, depending on how long your project will last, to look at your work and to offer feedback. You may convene the group at critical points, such as when you feel you are making progress in fulfilling identified criteria or exploring the value of a new conceptual framework.

A procedure for convening a validation group is usually as follows:

- Well before the validation meeting, circulate a report of the research so far, and say clearly what you are claiming to know and how this represents a development from earlier stages of the research.
- Ask the members of the group to consider questions such as:
  - Does the report accurately describe what is happening?
  - Does the evidence ground and support the claims being made?
  - Can they see instances that show the living-out of values?
  - Are emergent knowledge claims tested within the report itself?
  - Is there evidence of awareness for methodological rigour?
  - Is there evidence of the need for linking knowledge and practice?
- Look carefully at the claim and its evidence base at the meeting, discuss it and invite agreement with it (although you may not get this). Also invite suggestions about how the research might be modified and strengthened: McNiff and Whitehead (2010) give a comprehensive account of convening a validation group.

Supervisors and assessors – academic validation

If you are presenting a formal report, you hope that the claim contained in the report will be recognised as adding to the existing body of knowledge of your field. At the moment, the Academy is still the highest authority for what counts as legitimate knowledge, although the situation is changing with the emergence of more democratic forms of debate and their communication through web-based systems using multimedia technology. In an academic context, therefore, the work has to stand in terms of its academic rigour. This means you have to show engagement with traditional academic criteria and standards, such as respect for correct referencing and engagement with debates in the literatures.

As a practitioner, however, you also need to communicate ideas with the authority of your personal professional knowledge, while recognising that many university-based people still use the criteria of the social sciences, such as generalisability and replicability. In recent times, there have been calls for new criteria and new standards of judgement for judging quality in practice-based research (see Furlong and Oancea 2005). A main strategy is to appreciate how your values come to act as criteria and standards as they come to life through your practice. The implementation of such new criteria is now widespread, although some more traditionalist institutions still insist on traditional scientific and social scientific measures. Perhaps you just need to wait until they become aware of the contemporary realities of massive world changes, including epistemological changes, and in the meantime ensure that you go to an institution that recognises the validity of practice-based research.

And a new form of validation group is emerging too, as follows.

Readers and users – professional validation

We live in a world where information is instantly accessible through print- and web-based media, and ways of accessing it are increasingly easy and affordable. This means that, if you put your work on the web or write a text, millions of people can access it at short notice, so it can become public property to be judged by people whom you hope know what they are speaking about and can appreciate its quality in its own terms (have a look at the feedback on Amazon or on other websites, and think about how this may influence possible readers, even though it may be factually inaccurate). It therefore becomes your responsibility to explain to your readers what you are claiming, how you are testing its validity in relation to the criteria you have selected, and the standards you wish them to use, and produce a report they can understand without struggle.

This has implications, for it means you have to develop a dual perspective to your work: first, you need to do research that will stand up to methodological scrutiny, and second, you need to produce a report that will stand up to literary scrutiny. You need to become a good writer as well as a good researcher. 'Writing' may mean any form of communication 'written' on a page or screen (Derrida 1997). This issue is political too, for example, in relation to questions such as which language should be used for writing texts, how texts should be disseminated, what counts as a 'scholarly' text and who makes decisions about these things. It also raises questions about how the publishing world works with traditional scholarships. Some publishing houses remain traditionalist, while others accept innovative and experimental texts. These are vital debates that have implications for the future careers of practitioner-researchers. You are already implicated in them by producing your own professional or scholarly text to go into the public domain and be judged for validity. And this also raises the issue of legitimacy (see below).

Case study: Alison Joy Barton, UK

As a manager in Further Education, I could be perceived as the person who is constricting teacher educators by giving them a forced curriculum framework, a 'box' they have to step into and comply with. I (and the university) are gatekeepers for Initial Teacher Training national standards, endorsement and inspection. We are accountable to external agencies. I overcome the tension by encouraging diversity and challenge. Colleagues and I have created a learning culture that is not about compliance, but is committed to quality. All teacher educators are free to deliver the programme in their own way, so their individual professionalism is not undermined and they are trusted. When we evaluate their work together, we agree that we are looking for equal standards of provision but not replication of practices.

How is it validated?

When you present your knowledge claim, you do so through a report of some kind; the claim is contextualised within a research story. This has big implications for you, because it means you need to produce a narrative that shows awareness of methodological, social and textual issues. Your text therefore needs to demonstrate explanatory adequacy at the methodological, social and textual levels.

- *At the methodological level*: you demonstrate methodological rigour by explaining that you have identified a research issue and question, gathered data and generated evidence in relation to identified criteria and other methodological issues; i.e. you show that you have conducted a systematic enquiry with personal and social intent.
- *At the social level*: you show how your claim to knowledge may be judged in relation to criteria you consider important. Rorty (1999), drawing on the work of Dewey, says that a major criterion for research is to demonstrate social hope. I like this idea very much. I would also say that social hope is about the realisation of human nature and capacity – critical awareness, curiosity, choice and unlimited creativity – and the need for attachment supported through dialogical forms of communication. Unless people can exercise their curiosity, there can be little hope for them to understand themselves as in the world; unless they recognise that they are social beings and that an individual's wellbeing is linked with the wellbeing of others, there can be little hope of appreciating that they are a creative part of the world. This becomes an exercise of how we can realise our creativity through the way we live with others.
- *At the textual level*: you communicate your claim through your report; you have moved into 'making public'. You need to communicate what you are doing so people will appreciate what you saying. It is not just that you have performed certain steps; you can also show how those steps work together. It is as if you are performing in a dance competition: you need to execute a sequence of dance steps with technical accuracy and also transform them imaginatively into a dance. You are judged on technique at the level of competence, creativity in association, and imagination in performance.

This is where the field still sometimes comes undone, because many assessors still prefer to stay at the level of technique only, when judging both knowledge claims and the reports that communicate them. Many ignore the social dimension altogether. Other scholars complain about this: Thomas (1998), for example, speaks of 'the tyranny of the method', complaining that a focus on the technical issues of terminology and the emphasis on conventions such as a literature review can lead to stereotypical reporting and foster stereotypical thinking about practice.

Technical competence is of course necessary, but this is not the only way in which knowledge claims should be judged. Action research is real-world research; for claims to knowledge of practice to be judged as valid, the effects of the knowledge need to be seen at work in the real world. We need to show how we have influenced the quality of people's thinking and lives through the way we ourselves think and live our lives. These issues also influence the content and form of action research reports (see Chapter 9).

Richard Winter's work (1989) has been influential in suggesting new kinds of criteria for assessing quality in action research reports. He says they should demonstrate six principles (Winter 1989: 43–65):

- Offer a reflective critique in which the author shows that they have reflected on their work and generated new research questions.
- Offer a dialectical critique which subjects all 'given' phenomena to critique, recognizing their inherent tendency to change.
- Be a collaborative resource in which people act and learn as participants.
- Accept risk as an inevitable feature of creative practice.
- Demonstrate a plural structure which accommodates a multiplicity of viewpoints.
- Show the transformational and harmonious relationship between theory and practice.

These linguistic criteria, essential starting points, now need to come to life. Action research reports need to show these criteria in action, in terms of people's real living. This means that values need to be seen to emerge as living practices and come to act as criteria and standards to judge the validity of knowledge claims (McNiff 1989).

This becomes a key criterion for judging quality in action research. Furthermore, if our values include equity and social justice, we can show how we are contributing to improving the quality of life for others and, by doing so, for ourselves.

Like Winter, Habermas (1987) also identifies criteria for judging quality in practice, and there is an overlap between the practice of work in the social world such as in health care, management and teaching, and the practice of communicative action such as writing and speaking. Habermas identifies these criteria to be fulfilled:

- The claim is comprehensible: it makes sense to a listener or reader.
- The claim is truthful: the speaker-writer explains how they are telling the truth.
- The claim is authentic: the speaker-writer produces evidence to show how they have done what they say they have done, over time and through interaction with others.

- The claim is appropriate: the speaker-writer shows they have taken normative assumptions and traditions into consideration when telling their story.

Yet another matter arises – the structures of power that do or do not grant legitimacy to validated knowledge claims.

Matters concerning legitimacy

Validity is to do with establishing truth. Legitimacy is about demonstrating power. It often becomes a question of demonstrating either the power of truth or the truth of power (Foucault 1980). Each of us decides for ourselves which one wins.

To appreciate what legitimacy means, think of the Harry Potter stories. Harry Potter is a boy wizard, with magical powers to show this is the case; yet he is denied his identity as a wizard by his opponents. Or think of some romances, where the hero or heroine genuinely love each other, but someone casts doubt on their honesty (or reputation, or something like that), so the love affair is in danger. Many stories and legends have this as a main plot (*The Lion King, A Tale of Two Cities*), that the person who we, the listeners, know is actually a hero is unjustly treated. You can see a similar situation with historical figures like Socrates and Galileo. The person could show that what they were saying was valid and they were justified in claiming legitimacy, yet their claims were denied legitimacy because of the exercise of power.

Sadly, this can still be the case in judging action research accounts, and supervisors often play safe to ensure that candidates get through. I have examined several PhD theses recently (during 2011 and 2012) in which the candidate has written in terms of 'the researcher did this and that … '. When I have asked why they chose to write in the third person, they responded that they had been advised to do so, 'to be on the safe side'. This is understandable although sad, and does not speak well of the current situation where people are afraid to exercise creativity, or what Dadds and Hart (2001) call 'methodological inventiveness':

> Perhaps the most important new insight for both of us has been awareness that, for some practitioner researchers, creating their own unique way through their research may be as important as their self-chosen research focus. We had understood for many years that substantive choice was fundamental to the motivation and effectiveness of practitioner research (Dadds 1995); that what practitioners chose to research was important to their sense of engagement and purpose. But we had understood far less well that how practitioners chose to research, and their sense of control over this, could be equally important to their motivation, their sense of identity within the research and their research outcomes.
>
> Dadds and Hart 2001: 166

Much pressure has, however, been brought to bear on traditionalists, and new forms of criteria are being established in the Academy that show how candidates may request that their own criteria be used for judging their work, alongside identified institutional criteria. The following case studies are examples of how this may be achieved.

In her draft writing for her PhD studies, Jill Wickham, a physiotherapist and lecturer at York St John University, outlined her values and asked for them to be used in judging the quality of her work (see the case study). Similarly, in his thesis 'Helping eagles fly: A living theory approach to student and young adult leadership development' (2008), Chris Glavey identifies his living standards of judgement as love, justice, humility and authenticity, as communicated in the biblical verse Micah 6:8, as well as drawing on his experiences and understanding of the concept of liminality.

Case study: Jill Wickham, UK

- The service user is central to my work as a lecturer in physiotherapy. I hold values in respect to the service user as an individual, whether patient or student. In offering an account of my practice, I explain how this practice is informed by the questions, 'So what?' and 'Who cares?' and then adjust my practice accordingly. I hold myself accountable in terms of whether I show that I care and that it influences the quality of the service user's life.

- All students deserve encouragement to succeed as emerging physiotherapists with the capacity to offer excellent quality of care to the service user and to enhance service delivery. Dewey (1938) understood that success is not measured only by the acquisition of abstract theory but can also be achieved through inquiry. In my inquiry I value the students as inquiring beings.

- Students are critical thinkers. Clydesdale (2009) states that if we are to respect students as thinkers, as lecturers we need to reveal our intellectual journeys and be overt about the intellectual transitions we have made.

- I value my life experiences and the opportunity to learn from them and use this learning to contribute to improvement in my own practice and the practice of others.

- I value the passion that others and I have for the profession of physiotherapy. In my work, I try to help physiotherapy students integrate practical knowledge and theory and academic knowledge and theory. Both are important, and when both are combined physiotherapists can deliver optimum care to the service user. Polanyi says that we know more than we can tell (1967). I hope that the process of explaining how my values come to act as my living criteria and standards of judgement will enable me to show that what I know I will be able to tell.

Case study: Chris Glavey, Ireland

My living standards of judgement

Were my research to remain purely at the level of narrative, however, my claims to knowledge would have little validity or significance. Conscious of the fallibility of ideological bias and illusion, my research addresses the issues of truthfulness and meaning as the basis for the credibility, coherence and significance of my account. I emphasise the 'dialectical reflexivity' (Winter, 2002: 148) of the narrative, acknowledge the contingent nature of my understanding and the possibility of alternative interpretations. The collaborative nature of my research is fuelled by a dialogical engagement with the views, insights and perceptions of others – teachers, students and young adults ...

Glavey 2008: 32

The issue therefore now becomes: 'How do you communicate the amazing genius of what you have done? What kind of story will you tell that will make people want to listen to and learn from you?' Chapter 9 gives some ideas about this.

Chapter 9

Writing and presenting action research reports

This chapter and Chapter 10 deal with the criteria and standards used for judging quality in action research reports. Although the two concepts of criteria and standards are interlinked, it is important to appreciate the distinction between them. A criterion refers to something you expect to see, so is set in advance; a standard is how that something is judged in relation to the identified criteria. For example, you would expect a hotel to be clean, warm and welcoming; these are the criteria you would expect of any hotel. However, you would choose to go to Hotel B because it is cleaner, warmer and more welcoming than Hotel A. Hotel A does not come up to the same standards as Hotel B. You make judgements according to your own standards about what you expect from a hotel. The same principles extend to writing an action research report. You expect to see certain criteria achieved in a report, and these criteria are identified in this chapter. However, you would make judgements about the level to which those criteria are achieved according to specific standards; these matters are dealt with in Chapter 10.

Recall that Stenhouse often said that 'research is a systematic enquiry made public' (see Stenhouse 1983). In 1975 he said that practitioners should be doing research as a form of professional education:

> A capacity for autonomous professional self development through systematic self-study, through the study of the work of other teachers [practitioners], and through the testing of ideas by classroom research procedures.
>
> p. 144

In the 2002 edition of this book, I added the words 'with social intent', and this has been expanded now to read 'with social and environmental intent'. In this chapter, we move first into the part about 'making public', to do with writing and presenting your action research report in order to communicate the knowledge you have created of your practice. Later, we consider what might be some of the implications of 'with social and environmental intent'.

In an earlier chapter, I referred also to Foucault's (2001) idea of *parrhesia*, the right and responsibility of citizens to speak for themselves. As noted throughout, the emphasis shifts from rights to responsibilities: you need to share your knowledge, so that others can make judgements about what you are doing and can learn from and with you. The theme therefore develops into writing as a practice. As a writer-practitioner, you need to know what to say, how to organise your ideas, how to say it, and how what you say will be judged.

This does not mean that writing becomes just a technical exercise. We continue to create knowledge as we write, because the process of communication is itself a process of knowledge creation. It is a realisation of Schön's (1995) idea of reflection in action on action: you reflect on writing through the process of writing. It also represents your best thinking at the time, so shows the journey in your thinking. Writing becomes both content and form, the message and the medium. Furthermore, writing itself becomes an artefact such as a book or blog. It is durable. While your spoken words are durable only inasmuch as they settle in the mind of the other, your written word is durable in the physical world and lasts as long as the material it is written on.

So if the process of action research is to find ways of improving practice, this needs to be communicated through the report. The report explains what you did, how you did it, why you did it, what you believe the significance and some of the implications may be, and how you make judgements about what you have done. The report itself is judged in terms of how well you communicate what you have to say, and whether your capacity for communication may be judged as being of sufficient merit that people will listen to you and take your words seriously. If writing is a practice, you should bring the same level of critical scrutiny to this aspect of your action research, conducted at your desk, as to the action research conducted in your workplace.

The chapter talks through these points, which are organised as follows:

- What you say: the content of your report (this may be your work-based report, or your dissertation or thesis, or your e-portfolio)
- How you organise your ideas: the form of your report
- How you say it: writing for communication
- How you reflect on it: judging your writing capacity.

As always, these sections act as organising categories; in reality they are integrated, so aspects from one inevitably appear in another.

What you say: the content of your report

> *Criterion*: An action research report speaks about action and research, and explains the relationships between them.

In your report, you tell the story of your action research. This means you speak about the action you took, as well as how you researched the action. The action was about how you could understand and improve what you were doing, and how you could influence other people's thinking so they could do the same. At this point, you are speaking with your practitioner's voice. However, you are not just writing a description of what you did; you are also giving an explanation for how and why you did it and what you hoped to achieve. Giving explanations requires you to reflect on your action, so you step in and out of your text, now speaking with your researcher's voice. You speak with your reader and draw their attention to specific things you are saying. You make sure your reader appreciates that they are reading an explanatory document and not only a descriptive one.

It may be helpful to consider the philosophical frame outlined in the Introduction that guided your action research, while considering the real-time practicalities. From a real-time perspective, the action you took was to show how you found ways (researched) to work with others so you could all contribute to one another's growth and wellbeing. You did this through trying to influence their thinking and work towards fulfilling their human capacities (an unlimited capacity for creativity, curiosity and making choices) and growing mentally, physically and spiritually through recognising yourself as always in relation with others. This required negotiating the conditions that would foster that growth (freedom, mutuality, dialogue, openness) and engaging with the processes involved (emergence, generative transformation, self-organisation). You may choose not to write explicitly about these more philosophical frameworks, but they inform your writing throughout.

From a practical real-time perspective, the action you took was to work with others to understand what was going on in your contexts and to find ways of taking action so that the situation was more in line with your values. It is vital to be aware of what the core issue is, because this provides the golden thread that runs through your research story. Your reader needs this golden thread so they can see where they have come from, how each step relates to and is grounded in previous steps, and how the end links with the beginning.

You would therefore include the following issues in your report.

Be clear about your claim to knowledge, its starting point and the processes involved in testing its validity

Tell your reader what you know now that you did not know before: state your claim to knowledge. Say this right at the beginning of your report to orient your reader and keep it in mind throughout. Your research issue becomes the golden thread that runs through your report; it starts life as a question and transforms into a claim. If the key idea is to provide better quality care for patients by improving collaborative working among care-givers, the golden thread is the issue of how you have provided quality care. In academic language, you could speak about 'the unit of enquiry', that is, the thing you are investigating (your claim) and how you are testing its validity; to do so, you would have to tell the research story.

Give descriptions and explanations for what you have done

Describe the actions you took, including how you worked with others, and the different strategies you tried in order to improve what you were doing individually and collectively. Give explanations for what you have done, i.e. say why you did it and what you hoped to achieve, your reasons and purposes. It is absolutely not enough just to describe things: this would give you a professional development report but not a research report, and, as noted throughout, it is not enough just to show that you have engaged in professional development only at a skills level; you also have to show that your professional learning and development is grounded in and informed by a research base.

Show that you can analyse and appreciate the significance of what you have done and its possible implications

Explain to your reader what you think the significance is of what you have done. This is important. Make every effort to analyse and explain what the significance is (although it is often the case that other people can appreciate the significance of our work more quickly than we can). For good communication, however, it is your responsibility, as a researcher and research writer, to explain to your reader what you think they should know; it is not their responsibility to have to work it out for themselves. You need to offer ideas about the significance of your research to show that it was not just ad hoc or a one-off project, but that it made a lasting contribution that could influence new thinking and practices in the field and perhaps beyond.

In the case study, Martyn Rawson reflects on his work, and what he has helped other people to do, and he includes a sub-text that draws his reader's attention to what they should note about the story and why it is important that they do so.

How you organise your ideas: the form of your report

> *Criterion*: An action research report tells a story, which shows the transformation of a research question into a knowledge claim, and gives explanations for how and why this happened.

Action research reports tend to take a narrative form: you tell the story of what you and others have done. This is an explanatory story, where you weave descriptions of action and explanations for action together, so your reader can see how you had clear ideas about what you wished to do, how you did it and what happened. Show wherever possible the transformational connections between these descriptions and explanations. It can be helpful also to draw on other people's theories-in-the-literatures to help you make sense of what you are doing. In academic studies, this is essential, and usually a criterion for success.

Structure your report so your reader can see the unfolding of the action over time. They would see the original plan, including how you thought through the different phases of the research and what you needed to do to keep your golden thread running through. For the actual structure, you could consider using the same headings as those of your action plan, as follows:

- Say who you are and outline your context. Say whether this was an individual or a group project, and, if a group one, what part you played in it.
- What did I/we wish to investigate? Say how you identified an issue that needed investigating.
- Why did I/we wish to investigate it? Say what was going on in the contexts – personal, professional, social and historical. This involves articulating your values and making your implicit knowledge explicit.
- How could you show the situation as it was? Say how you gathered data to act as a baseline from which you could think about taking action, and what this involved at a practical level, such as involving others as participants and ensuring ethical conduct.
- What did you do? Say what your options were and what you decided to do, and what prompted this decision.
- How did the situation change? Say how you generated evidence from the data to show the situation as it developed.
- How did you check that any conclusions you came to were reasonably fair and accurate? Say how you tested the validity of your emergent knowledge claims against the critical feedback of others, using your values as your nominated criteria and standards.
- What do you think is the significance of your action research? Say how you believe what you have done may have influenced other people's thinking. Say what you think may be some of the implications.
- How have you modified your actions and thinking in light of the evaluation? Say how you are doing things differently, and whether your new thinking and practices are working.

You do not need to use these headings to write your report, although you can if you wish, but you do need to organise your ideas to show the process of how you carried out a systematic enquiry in which you engaged with these kinds of issues. A more detailed outline of how you can develop these headings appears in McNiff and Whitehead (2009, 2010).

Different forms of representation

Also be aware that you can now use all forms of representation in report-writing, even in academic writing. Most universities accept multimedia representations, showing videos of practice as part or the whole of evidence bases, or that refer their reader to web-based work – see Eisner (1997) for the philosophical underpinning of these new forms of representation; see also the case study of digital portfolios at Pepperdine University.

Case study: digital portfolios at the Center for Collaborative Action Research, directed by Margaret Riel, USA

Margaret Riel at Pepperdine University has been recognised for her superb innovative work in promoting and supporting action research using digital forms of technology. Margaret describes the work of the Center for Collaborative Action Research (http://www.cadres.pepperdine.edu/ccar/) as support for the process of conducting and teaching action research:

> The Center for Collaborative Action Research at Pepperdine University links educators, researchers, and community members with the goal of creating deep understanding of educational problems in a range of different contexts including but not limited to schools, and to encourage evidence-based reasoning to solve these problems ... The Center provides support for both action researchers and those who teach action research. It was created as both a way to help action researchers share their work with a larger community and to help those new to action research.

> Riel 2010: 1

The Center publishes a small number of peer-reviewed action research digital portfolios that share findings and can be used to help other action researchers as they formulate their action plans. The portfolios are arranged in two groups; action research in instructional settings with students; and action research within community and corporate settings with colleagues. The Center provides for community interaction and knowledge-building through the use of a wiki (http://ccar.wikispaces.com/). It is organized around each phase of the action research process and provides suggestions for the writing process, as well as suggesting a rubric for self and other assessments of the quality of the action research portfolios.

As part of these open environments, Margaret also organises a yearly interactive web-based conference on 'Action Research with Technology', in late June. This web-casted event provides amazing opportunities for people to come together in dialogical encounters and share their ideas and writings without having to travel thousands of miles. Invitations to participate can be found at the Center for Collaborative Action Research.

A range of online journals also exist to show action research reports in action, for example the *Canadian Journal of Action Research* (http://cjar.nipiss-ingu.ca/index.php/cjar/), the *West Virginia Online Action Research Journal* (http://www.wvcpd.org/PLAJournal/index.html), the *Turkish Online Journal of Qualitative Inquiry* (http://www.tojqi.net/) and *Action Researcher in Education* (www.actionresearch.gr/). Some academic reports, especially those linked with professional development initiatives, accept performance, such as dance or music, as part of the dissertation or thesis. How these are judged, however, is a different matter, and calls for new forms of standards of judgement that may be negotiated according to the values of the presenters and their audiences.

How you say it: writing for communication – developing capacities in knowledge and skills

> *Criterion*: An action research report positions the writer as 'I' and the reader as a 'You'. It takes a dialogical form where answers turn into questions, through a commitment to new beginnings.

Writing an action research report means writing for a particular audience, whether this is work-based or university-based. This idea has consequences because you need to know what your audience expects from your writing, and then learn how to give it to them. Therefore, as well as learning how to do research and ensuring that your research matches the standard your audience expects, you also have to develop capacity as a writer. This can be difficult for some people, but it is essential. If you do not communicate what you have been doing and its significance, your readers will not appreciate what you have achieved and may not give you the credit you deserve.

Here are the key skills you need to develop in order to produce a good quality report for any audience.

Research the market

Do your homework around what your readers need. If you are writing an academic report, make sure you know what the criteria are for academic report-writing and write according to the criteria. If you are writing a work-based report, find out what your readers (e.g. in your organisation) expect.

Be prepared to practise and produce multiple drafts

It is said that good writing requires a small amount of talent and a lot of hard work:

'Talent alone cannot make a writer,' said Ralph Waldo Emerson, more than a hundred years ago. And how right he was. While talent does help ... success in writing, particularly writing for which you will be [recognised], depends mostly on market analysis and commitment to satisfying market requirements.

O'Reilly 1994: 1

Any experienced writer will agree. Do not expect to produce a report in a weekend. Good writing takes time, energy, determination and stamina. Most experienced writers spend more time on editing than on producing a first draft. Regard writing multiple drafts as practice – it is. Each time you write a new draft, you are practising your skill. It took you time to learn to play the piano or drive a car; it takes time to learn to write for a particular audience.

Write for a reader; write like a reader

Develop the capacity of writing for a reader. Your reader does not know who you are, what you do, what your research is about and why you are doing it. The only thing they know about you is what they read on the page. You need to tell them. Practitioners sometimes write on the mistaken assumption that their reader knows these things already, which is not the case. They write things like, 'We discussed the issue and decided ... ', but often forget to say who did the discussing and what the issue was. To write like a reader, practise putting yourself in your reader's shoes and reading your own work with a critical eye, or perhaps ask someone who is unfamiliar with your work to read it for you, or even to you. This also means organising your ideas and providing signposts such as section headings and summaries that will guide your reader in appreciating the significance of what you are saying.

Organise your ideas

You need to organise your ideas into some kind of structure. This need not be a linear structure, of the kind a → b → c → the end. It can be transformational, where ideas and narratives are embedded within other ideas and narratives. It can be as creative as you like, using poetry, artwork or a mix of different forms of representation; but there must be a golden thread running through all the other themes so your reader can see where they are going and make sense of their journey. This should be integrated in form and content.

Use section headings

Using section headings can be useful to help your reader stay on track, especially if those headings are of different fonts and weights (as in this book) to show where they are in the organisation of the ideas (avoid using '1.1, 1.2' forms of organisation). You need to lead your reader through your text and provide signposts for them to know where they are. It is not your reader's job to work out where they are.

Use good grammar

Watch your language when you write. It is assumed that you will have good skills in grammar and punctuation, but if in doubt, get some good books on writing techniques and study them. And practise. If necessary, send your work out to a copy-editor, or hire a consultant who will tidy up the work for you. Do not, however, ask or expect a copy-editor to write the work for you. It is their job to make sure your writing is intelligible, not to produce your copy. Also, do not, under any circumstance, copy material from the Internet or any other source without giving credit. This is plagiarism, and if discovered, which is highly likely, you could have your degree or certificate withheld; or, in the case of writing a work-based report, you could find yourself without credibility or, in extreme instances, without a job.

Proofread

It is an expectation of all reports that you will produce an error-free document, but this is easier said than done. You do need to proofread your work multiple times before submitting it. It will not guarantee that your text will be perfect because you will probably find on each reading that yet another error appears; but keep at it until you have a text that you are proud of and that you feel does you justice.

How you reflect on it: judging your writing capacity

> *Criterion*: An action research report demonstrates critical reflection and, where possible, meta-critique.

Writing a report for a degree does not mean that the report has to be perfect, but it needs to be good enough to meet at least minimum standards. To achieve at least a minimum standard, you would have to fulfil all the criteria identified above. If, however, you wanted to produce a really good report, and not just a 'good enough' one, you would need to demonstrate critical reflexivity in your research and in your writing.

Critical reflexivity is referred to by a range of writers, including Lankshear and Knobel (2011), Said (1991) and Winter (1989). It refers to your capacity to step aside from yourself and reflect on your own behaviours and, more importantly, on your own thinking. In the case of writing for publication, it means being able to reflect on your text and make critical judgements about its quality. This is one of the most difficult things to do, because you have to use the way you are thinking to critique the way you are thinking. Consider the following.

Bourdieu (1990) says we are all born into a habitus. By this he means that we are born into a culture that has certain norms, values, practices and customs. These elements become normative, that is, they are taken as normal and they are also expected to be normal; the idea of 'normative behaviour' or 'normative assumptions' therefore takes on the meaning both of 'what is' and 'what ought to be'. Not only do these normative assumptions tend not to be challenged, they also tend not to be noticed. For example, it is normative in Western societies to consider that democracy is the desirable form of social order (see for example Fukuyama's 1999 ideas about state-building in *The Great Disruption*), or that justice should be tempered with mercy. If you are doing your action research in any context, you need to show your understanding of normative customs and cultures.

As well as demonstrating awareness of these socio-political aspects, you also need to show awareness of the fact that a culture has its own epistemology (ways of knowing) underpinned by its own logics (ways of thinking). For example, Everett explains how the Pirahãs, among whom he lived and worked for years, have a different way of thinking that informs the structures of their language. He writes of the difficulties of legislating about 'correct forms of thinking':

> As a scientist, objectivity is one of my most deeply held values. If we could just try harder, I once thought, surely we could see the world as others see it and learn to respect one another's views more readily. But as I learned from the Pirahãs, our expectations, our culture, and our experiences can render even perceptions of the environment nearly incommensurable cross-culturally [let alone conceptions of the nature, origin and use of language, as Chomsky (1986) says].
>
> Everett 2009: xvii

Everett develops these themes in his *Language: The Cultural Tool* (2012), where he promotes the idea that 'all human languages are tools. Tools to solve the twin problems of communication and social cohesion. Tools shaped by the distinctive processes of cultural niches' (p. 6). Our epistemologies (how we know) inform how we act.

At a deeper level of complexity, it is not enough only to demonstrate awareness of normative assumptions; you also have to show that you can demonstrate critical awareness of your own ways of thinking and normative assumptions. Take for example the idea in the UK that women take their husband's name on marriage. This is not the law; it is a normative assumption: women the world over keep their own names on marriage. Or think of how you regard a person of a different skin colour, or with tattoos, or with Down syndrome, or who can't hear properly … How do you communicate your critical perspectives about these things?

Reflecting on one's thinking can be the most difficult thing because it means challenging your own normative assumptions; and if 'normative' means 'the way things should be', this means you are actually deciding to change your mind about something. In the film *Kinky Boots*, Simon, a man who dressed as a woman, says to Don, the stalwart self-identified 'Northern lad', 'Change your mind about something. Change your mind about someone.' This is what is required in action research, to change your mind as the first step in changing your practice.

When you write your text, you need to show that you have interrogated your normative assumptions and actually changed your mind about something, or given good reasons why you choose to maintain your current position. Furthermore, you need to communicate this to your reader by commenting on what you are writing, rather like a Greek chorus in a play, who comment on the action on the stage while intermittently stepping in and out of the action. It is no use saying you have developed critical capacity unless you can show and explain how you have done so, and how it has made you act differently. Changing your mind is for ever; there is no going back once you step over the threshold. Recall Polanyi's words in Chapter 4: 'My eyes have become different; I have made myself into a person seeing and thinking differently. I have crossed a gap, a heuristic gap, that lies between problem and discovery' (Polanyi 1958: 143). And once your mind is changed, it is difficult even to remember how you thought before your current insights, which is why documenting every step of the process will help you when you are ready to write about the changes you have experienced.

This is what we do in action research; we create and cross gaps in the mind, which can make learning so problematic and uncomfortable; in writing, we show how the meaning emerges through the text by highlighting those pieces of text that show this crossing of gaps between the normativity of assumptions and the dismantling of them. This book, for example, is a case of how I have changed my mind. It is different in content, form and tone from the first and second editions; and I have radically changed some of the underlying principles, and am able to articulate the differences. It is also an example of the power of journalling, when we 'see' earlier perspectives in writing: in this case, books and other texts come to stand as a form of maintaining a research journal.

This process of interrogating your text, if you can show it successfully, will speak to your reader's interests. Chapter 10 explains why this is important, in terms of what standards are used to judge the quality of what you write about and how you write it. This is where Habermas's work is also central, for he explains the significance of writing a text that is comprehensible, authentic, sincere and appropriate, as the case study from Martyn Rawson now demonstrates.

Martyn Rawson is a teacher in a Steiner Waldorf school in Germany. He is also a teacher educator and researcher, and frequently acts as an interpreter in the course of his work. The text in the case study is a modified extract from an article that was in preparation for the *Journal of Education for Teaching*.

Case study: Martyn Rawson, Germany

Non-verbal reflection in action research: a report from Kosovo

The Pre-School Peace Education Programme in Kosovo (here abbreviated to PPE) is an in-service teacher education programme that was started by Beatrice Rutishauser Ramm, a Swiss Steiner teacher, shortly after the war in Kosovo in 2001. It currently has 42 teachers teaching over 800 five-year-olds mostly in rural municipal primary schools and within a Roma colony. The educational concept is a blend of Steiner education (Rawson and Richter, 2000), peace education (Rutishauser Ramm, 2011) and what the PPE has developed. Mentoring and teacher education is now carried out by the first cohort of teachers supported by some external tutors from Germany and Switzerland. Sustainability, resilience (Cyrulnik, 2009) and salutogenic health-promoting growth (Antonovsky, 1979) are core aims for teachers and children. Reflection and action research are important in this aim.

I was involved in the programme between 2006 and 2010 as tutor and researcher (Rawson, 2008). Data was continuously collected using observation, interviews, focus groups, non-verbal and narrative inquiry methods, and artefact analysis for self-study and evaluation.

Biographical drawings

Not speaking Albanian can be a problem while doing research with Kosovan people, most of whom do not speak English. We external tutors and researchers were dependent on the few English-speaking participants for interpretation. Whenever data was collected in interviews or focus groups, I checked via the interpreter that we had understood what the participants meant. Participants listen attentively to the translations and summaries, and clarify points with the interpreter.

Towards the end of their apprenticeship, I asked a group of novice teachers to make drawings within the context of narrative biographical discussions aimed at supporting what Biesta *et al.* (2011) call 'learning as becoming' and Goodson *et al.* (2010) call 'narrative learning'. The use of drawings in the style of children's drawings suggested itself partly because the novice teachers were familiar with studying children's drawings as a diagnostic method (Rawson and Rose, 2003) and partly because drawing is non-verbal. Being non-verbal, it had the double advantage of not needing translation and the fact that drawing enables participants' social and/or emotional understanding of themselves.

I asked the teachers to draw such pictures depicting how they felt about their roles as pre-school teachers at the beginning of the programme and how they felt then, near the end. When they finished, each person told the story of her picture to the group.

Analysis

I have not attempted to interpret the drawings psychologically. The images were not simply illustrations and bore little resemblance to the physical environment in Kosovo, but appeared to use a more universal set of symbols to represent and identify experience. Typical images included a central narrative figure, a path leading to a house with doors and windows, often with a fence around it; sometimes a river with a bridge, a sun in the sky and usually mountains in the background. The mountains clearly represented geographical realities as well as the sense of many Kosovans that their lifeworld is an enclave, isolated from the world by a ring of real mountains and political and economic restrictions. One Kosovan colleague described Kosovo as a cultural prison, which, like many prisons, is rife with drugs, power struggles and corruption, fenced in by mountains of peace-keeping bureaucracy.

The analysis of the pictures representing 'after being on the PPE programme' showed they were more colourful and harmonious; the person was clearly on the path moving towards the house or in the garden of the house, in many cases full of children and flowers. The pictures representing 'before' were often less colourful, less detailed, the person was far from the house, which had no windows or doors, or the path was missing. The narrative figure was often separated from the path by a river or jagged obstacles, or in one case was absent. The path clearly led from a past full of fear, pain, uncertainty and darkness, or was obscured. The future appeared to be represented by the sun, order, vitality and play. When questioned, the teachers indicated that the order and harmony was not what is, but what they were creating.

Taken together, the pictures give a sense of transition, a journey towards a coherent, optimistic and more self-directed present and future, a reading confirmed verbally by the participants. The meanings given to the pictures were often more complex than the apparent naivety of the images. One woman told me via the translator: 'the drawing shows the child in me – not when I was really a child, but now – because the child is still there underneath [pointing to her heart] – and that's why I want to understand about children.' Another referred to the hurt child within her who hid her scars but knew they were healing when she was with the children in her class. Many other equivalent observations showed subtle levels of self-insight. Another teacher told me that she often repeated this drawing at home when she felt stressed because 'the drawing shows me as I like to feel – it gives me hope', thus showing that the pictures could also have a therapeutic aspect. Together with the verbal narratives, they tell a story of transformation and inner perspectives, of new values and positive relationships.

Conclusion

It is important that the participants interpret the pictures themselves. Their primary value is in support of biographical learning. In such cases, a teacher-researcher can only note that people are experiencing transformation. Deeper and more personal, specific meanings remain obscured, which may sometimes be a good thing. Non-verbal representations need to triangulated by other data and rich descriptions of the context. They do however offer a means of articulating visceral levels of experience that are hard to verbalize, let alone translate.

So now you have done your research and produced your report, the question becomes, 'How do you judge its quality?' You must be able to do this and articulate how you make these judgements if you are prepared to put your report into the public domain, especially if you are hoping to gain accreditation. As part of a professional development review, for example, your assessor would ask you to comment on what you see as the significance of what you have done; in a viva voce for a PhD, you may also be asked to comment on the quality of the writing itself. This process of making judgements about quality becomes the focus of Chapter 10.

Judging quality and demonstrating impact

The significance of your action research

This chapter is about judging quality: in action, research and writing. When you write your action research, you hope to say that you have conducted some good quality action research and have produced a good quality report, as part of your good life as a practitioner. The issue therefore becomes, 'How do you judge "good" in action, in research and in writing? How does this reflect a good life?' This involves:

- identifying criteria and standards for judging quality (a technical level);
- coming to some understanding of what 'quality' means in relation to the work you do (a practical level);
- appreciating how you judge it, and what this may mean for yourself and others (a theoretical level);
- explaining how your research reflects what you understand as a good life (an ethical level).

The chapter is organised as five sections that reflect these issues:

- What do we mean by quality?
- What does this involve?
- How do we test the validity of knowledge claims?
- How do we justify what we are doing?
- How do we articulate the significance of what we are doing?

Chapters 11 and 12 consider some of the implications of these ideas.

What do we mean by quality?

These days, the idea of quality is everywhere, and quality assurance agencies flourish. While it is important to have quality control, it is first necessary to establish what we mean by 'quality', how to judge whether it is good or bad so that it can be assured, and how to explain the thinking behind the judgements.

Linguistically, we know what we mean by good quality; it refers to something we believe is worthwhile. You say, 'This work is high quality', or 'I will not purchase this paper because it is of lower quality than I normally use.' By this you mean, 'This paper is not good enough for my purposes', or 'This paper does not meet my standards.' You are therefore identifying what you believe is 'the good'. When you assess something, you assess it in terms of what you believe is good, your standards.

Your idea of 'the good' is to do with your values. Values give meaning to our lives because they represent what we believe in; and because we believe what we deem worthwhile, our values represent what we think constitutes 'the good'. 'Good food' is food we enjoy and choose to eat. 'Good practice' is practice that meets our standards, what we believe practice should be like, as a realisation of our values. When we make judgements about what counts as good, we do so in light of our values commitments.

The ideas of 'quality', 'good', 'values', 'judgements' and 'standards' therefore become linked. From the perspectives of practitioners, they refer to what we hope to achieve in the world, and how we hope others will agree with our judgements. Making judgements involves identifying criteria and standards, related to our values. Criteria refer to what we expect to see, and standards refer to how we judge the quality of what happens when the criteria are achieved (these ideas are developed shortly). These are transformational processes: criteria transform into standards, and abstract values such as freedom transform into living practices of freedom. As an action researcher, you try to live in the direction of your values as much as possible.

So far so good. Now comes a tricky bit.

Different people have different values (Berlin 1997), so they have different conceptualisations of what counts as 'good' or 'good quality'. Al Capone had different values from J. Edgar Hoover. In Hoover's idea of a good social order, everyone abided by the law, even if the law was inappropriate at the time, as some deemed prohibition to be (Coffey 2008). Al Capone's idea was that people obeyed what he said – Al's law: and he did bring order to the streets of Chicago by negotiating, frequently forcefully, that other gangs would agree. J. Edgar's and Al's interests may have been different: Hoover's to do with creating safe streets for citizens, an other-centred philosophy; Al Capone's as creating streets as contexts for his business, a self-centred philosophy (or you may say that Hoover wanted to enforce his ideas, while Al supplied an otherwise unavailable service – it depends on your point of view).

So if people have different values and understandings about what counts as 'good', they may also have different standards of judgement, i.e. how they make judgements about something. When it is a matter of judging quality, in your action research and your research account, the field gets muddy, because judgements are made by a person who was born into a *habitus* (Bourdieu 1990), with its own criteria and standards, and who brings these criteria and standards of judgement, as well as their own past and current experiences, to the event. When you present your account for accreditation, you do so to a person who is prejudiced towards what they understand as 'good practice', 'good research' and 'good writing', according to their existing standards.

Be aware, too, how the language we use tends to communicate 'official' mindsets. Take, for example, the word 'impact', nowadays a major criterion for judging quality. We are all now judged by the 'impact' we have on others. However, there are differences of opinion about the term (see Francis 2010). 'Impact' would be appropriate for the likes of Al, who believed in impacting people. He had no compunction about bludgeoning to death any opposition. Nowadays, our bureaucratic corporations seem quite happy to bludgeon practitioners and service users, wheeling in technocratic values and standards of judgement as weapons.

So if 'impact' implies violence, the word 'influence' may be more appropriate. We are trying to influence other people's learning and encourage them to think for themselves and to realise their always already capacities for originality of mind, creative thinking, reflective thinking and choice-making, in dialogical relation with the other. They choose what to think and whether or not to accept our influence. They can also choose their interests, whether these are the interests of self-service or of other people's interests, for example whether to follow Dewey (1916) and Rorty (1999) in seeing work as contributing to social hope and wellbeing. A key issue is that being aware of the language used to communicate ideas enables us to see those ideas for what they are, and to become more aware of how we are possibly being persuaded to close down our capacities for agency and toe the party line.

The two case studies here show the exercise of agency in action. The first is from Eric Yuan, a doctoral candidate at the Chinese University of Hong Kong. Eric writes about the transformational changes he experienced in his thinking, using an action research methodology, as he tried to help others do the same. The second is from Timothy Golden, a teacher studying for his Master's degree in America.

Case study: Eric Yuan, China

From 2010, I was involved as a research assistant in a university–school collaboration project, working with two school teachers undertaking classroom-based action research. The two teachers went through a systematic process of inquiry and also a dramatic process of change in terms of their beliefs about teaching, students and themselves. One explained how, through her research, she had stopped thinking only about her workload and focused more on students' learning. She found, she said, that her students suddenly became 'smarter' and more autonomous; and concluded that this was because she had critically interrogated her practices. On reflection, she said, 'I am no longer a "fisherman" who feeds the students but have become an "educator" who teaches students how to fish for themselves.'

During the project, 12 more teachers from five secondary schools conducted research into their teaching, assisted by university personnel. Sharing experiences and exchanging ideas became a form of mutual learning for the school teachers and the university staff. In addition, teachers who were not part of the project asked to come to our research. A community of practice (Wenger 1999) thus came into being to promote the collaborative improvement of education in specific contexts.

Case study: Timothy Golden, USA

As a graduate student working towards my Master's degree in school counseling, I spent a year working on a project titled 'Creating a Community of Kindness at the Middle School Level'. This was an action research project at a middle school in San Diego, California, to bring together school counselors and students in creating a school-wide program for increased acts of kindness, to reduce acts of bullying and unfriendly behavior. The program was led by school counselors and comprised teachers and students.

Major themes included coming together as a community and the role bystanders play in how students treat one another. Students' survey data helped us develop strategies that included school-wide assemblies and classroom lessons. We used a combination of video clips, songs, and magazine articles to facilitate classroom discussions about bullying-related issues.

Some months later, results show that most students report greater awareness of how their behavior affects other students and say they have tried to be kinder to others. Most students surveyed believe the school is a kinder place. Gathering data regularly reminds us of the importance of evidence-based knowledge. We have used the data to strengthen practice and meet students' needs, and have made recommendations for future actions based on our analysis and reflection.

Throughout I began to see how action research fits naturally in an educational setting, where educators attempt to engage with issues on an iterative basis. I have learned that action research can and should be part of a school counselor's practice, and can provide a structure for improving practices. I feel fortunate to understand this as I move into the profession of school counseling.

What does this involve?

What to do, then, in situations where there are varying values, standards and forms of language, and all claim theirs as the right version? Or when your account, showing that you have learned to think independently, is judged by someone from a managerialist background, who does not appreciate the basics of action research and uses their own standards of judgement from a different philosophical and values perspective?

At this point, you need to do two things at least. The first is to recognise that you are in a political game, with established rules and practices (see Habermas's 1987 view of 'systems' below). These rules are not for negotiation; they are part of the game, in the same way as chess and football have their own internal rules. If you work in an organizational culture of managism (Watson 2006), you will not get far if you talk the language of dialogue and respect without acknowledging the prevailing cultural discourses. Similarly, when you write a dissertation or thesis in an academic setting, you do so having bought in, often literally, to the game. In doctoral-level work, for example, the rules are generally that the work:

- makes an original contribution to knowledge of the field;
- demonstrates critical engagement;
- contains material worthy of publication;
- engages with appropriate literatures;
- is of appropriate technical merit and the document is error-free.

You have to fulfil these criteria and produce a work that meets academic standards. Similarly, when submitting your work to, say, a refereed journal, you must obey the journal's rules and meet the editors' standards. However, by getting your work recognised, you manoeuvre yourself into a position from which to begin to influence new thinking. This may appear as manipulation, but it may also be seen as exercising political commonsense in contributing to a professional order that honours all participants' capacities for agency.

The second piece of advice is to theorise the situation so that you can live by your own standards of dialogue and respect for others, show that you can engage with issues at the same level as your assessors, and use forms of discourses as appropriate. You then need to go public by sharing ideas with others in the same settings, writing for publication, going on a degree course or using any strategy available to you to celebrate your work. The process of theorisation begins with thinking things through, supported by ideas from other colleagues, theorists and writers, to understand how they also theorise the situation. Theorists would include authors such as Machiavelli (1998) and Sun Tzu (2006), who offer practical political strategies, and authors such as MacIntyre (1985) and Bernstein (1991), relating to how you can justify your position when you claim your work demonstrates good quality.

First, consider how MacIntyre (1985: 187) defines 'a practice' as an intentional human activity to achieve certain goods internal to that activity. He also says, 'A practice involves standards of excellence and obedience to rules as well as the achievement of goods' (1985: 190), recognising that different people have different standards for different contexts and traditions that need to be negotiated. Similarly, Bernstein (1991) calls for dialogue, because 'there is no single paradigm, research program, or orientation that dominates philosophy' (p. 338). Habermas (1987) also believes in negotiation: he speaks of the need for intersubjective agreement in discourses concerning human interactions – we need to talk through ideas to reach agreement.

However, recognising that, while laudable, intersubjective agreement is unlikely to be achieved because it is an idealised concept, he theorises how real-world change comes about. He explains the importance of interrogating normative practices to make judgements about them and change them. He speaks about systems and the lifeworld: systems are those structures and institutions to do with the political state and administration, and the lifeworld refers to people and their practices within the systems. Habermas consistently makes the point that people create their own systems; they talk about what they should do, and how and why, and then they do it. Thus discussions can become policies, which can become normative.

If, however, people become complacent about things and do not critique, but go to sleep, the system often takes on a life of its own and becomes reified (turned into a thing). This suits many people, however, because they can say, 'Blame the system', as something outside themselves, so they are exonerated from personal responsibility. The system becomes a great place to hide. Drivers see traffic as separate from the car they are in, so traffic becomes a problem to be solved, not one they are contributing to. The issue is, how do you locate yourself? Do you become part of the normative system, or exercise your agency in the lifeworld and try to influence people's thinking to create their own intellectual and practical systems?

So, to summarise, criteria and standards feature in judging quality: technically, criteria are objective and descriptive (they identify what we expect to see), and standards are subjective and explanatory (they give opinions about how we would like things to be). In reality, criteria are also subjective because they are the criteria of someone who is a human being with values.

So, still thinking about judging the quality of your action research, criteria may be understood as related to the values you hold, such as 'participation' and 'freedom'; you expect to see participation and freedom in action. The values therefore transform into criteria. You also transform these criteria into standards when you make judgements about how the criteria are achieved. You say, 'I expect to see participation in organisational decision-making, but this must be participation by everyone, not only a few.' Or you say, 'I expect to encourage freedom, and this must be people's freedom to challenge my thinking, not freedom to do as they are told.'

Criteria are relevant to the 'action' piece of action research, to check whether we are living in the direction of participatory and emancipatory values, and to the 'research' piece, when we claim that the research is rigorous and relevant to its purposes (see McNiff 2010, and McNiff and Whitehead 2010, 2011, for ideas about how values transform into criteria and standards of judgement).

These ideas are especially relevant in debates about judging quality in action research reports, especially those for academic accreditation. Most award-granting institutions accept that candidates may negotiate the criteria by which they wish their accounts to be judged, while expecting also the fulfilment of institutional criteria – see Maria James's draft writing for her PhD thesis in the case study here. Furthermore, work like this has been tested stringently within the Academy and pronounced valid: people have been awarded their doctoral degrees. This is a case of establishing legitimacy as well as validity: doctorates are earned, never awarded simply because you are a nice person.

Case study: Maria James, UK

The following extract is from Maria James's draft PhD thesis (James 2012: 3).

Introduction

This thesis is an explanatory account of how I have generated my living theory of practice as a professional educator in a University College of Education and as a Religious Education specialist. My intent in undertaking my research has been to make explicit my understanding that my practice is purposeful intentional action, and to clarify embedded assumptions about the reasons for and purposes of this action. Throughout, I have asked how I can legitimately be a Christian teacher-educator. My main claim to knowledge arising from my study is that I have developed an epistemology of practice that I term 'theopraxis' (James, 2007), that is, a morally committed and thoughtful practice in the light of my belief in my God. The focus of the work therefore becomes the development and generation of my theory of theopraxis; in other words, to offer explanations for how I claim to have developed a morally committed and thoughtful practice in the light of my belief in God. ...

This has profound implications for the practice and theorisation of RE, and for my practice ... In terms of this research, and in the realm of RE, it may be understood as an improved capacity for independent learning, critical enquiry and engagement with the discipline of RE. Given that learning and teaching are intimately linked, a corollary could be that better learners become better teachers. Therefore my improved pedagogical practice could be seen as enabling growth and transformation for others. From this transformational perspective, the process of the research itself needs to be appreciated as not aiming to achieve a final destination so much as an ongoing struggle to understand. The content and form of the thesis show the action of this ongoing journey of self-knowledge and improvement, and suggests some implications for the subsequent exercise of educational influence in encouraging others to do the same.

Maria asks her examiners to judge the quality of her practice in relation to the aims outlined in the passage above. She asks whether her evidence shows that she has encouraged independent learning, critical enquiry and engagement with the discipline of RE, and that she has enabled growth and transformation for others and thereby for herself.

However, claiming that you are achieving your criteria and standards is a big claim whose validity needs to be tested through rigorous checks and balances, including a range of validity tests, as described below.

How do we test the validity of knowledge claims?

We considered earlier the idea that you need to invite others such as critical friends to look at your work. We now look at the nature of the validity tests we ask them to carry out. Such tests ensure higher quality research. You are claiming that your practice and your research are good, and that you are communicating your story effectively. To be legitimated, these claims need to be subjected to the critique of a range of peers (see pp. 137–9), who, when considering your evidence, will ground their judgements in the following validity tests.

Internal validity tests – personal validity

First you judge the validity of your claims in relation to whether you show that you are living in the direction of the values that have inspired your research; these constitute your internal validity tests and help to demonstrate the validity of your claim to have influenced your own learning. You provide evidence, for example, of whether you have helped health-care practitioners to encourage greater autonomy among patients, or managers to help trainees learn to develop interpersonal skills appropriate to working with customers. Your evidence shows that you have realised the values of autonomy and dialogue. You could say you have realised your capacity for critical thinking and creativity in finding ways to help others do the same.

You can link this with the literatures and draw on the work of, for example:

- Fromm (2001): you have resisted the fear of freedom and can engage with the freedom to think for yourself.
- Foucault (2001): you are practising *parrhesia*, the right and the responsibility of speaking for yourself, while also welcoming critique.
- Arendt (1958): you have realised your natality and are using your rightful place on earth with social intent.

External validity tests – social validity

You have also used external validity tests to see whether you have contributed to the improvement of others' life experience. You can show that clients found your support helpful in developing their capacity for self-determination and critical reflection about how to help themselves. Helping them realise their sense of wellbeing contributes to your own. These tests help to demonstrate the validity of your claims that you are influencing the learning of others in your professional or social formation.

For this you could draw on the work of, for example:

- Buber (2002) and Bohm (1996): you show how you have engaged in a life dialogue where you kept the spaces open for other people's learning.
- Kristeva (2002): you show how you are developing your singular talents in relation with others who are doing the same.
- Macmurray (1957, 1961): you show your developing sense of self in relation with others, a sense of community.

Shared validity tests – peer validity

You have used peer validity tests, inviting peers to comment on your claims, and using triangulation techniques, to ensure intellectual and methodological rigour and avoid bias. You have established the relationship between self and others in methodological terms, and brought the concept of I-in-relation to research processes, and to actions in the world. These tests help to demonstrate the validity of your claim to capacity for peer influence.

For this, you could draw on the work of, for example:

- Wenger (1999): you show how you have helped develop communities of practice.
- Sacks (2007): you show how you have worked with others to build a sense of purposeful community.
- Winter (1989): you show how you have observed the need for methodological rigour and critical reflection.

Testing the validity of your practice of communication – communicative validity

You have demonstrated capacity in communication and have made yourself intelligible, so people may engage fully with your ideas. They will learn from your ideas and your writing. Your writing shows that you communicate critically and with self-reflexivity. These tests help to demonstrate the validity of your claims to capacity for communicative action.

For this, you could draw on the work of, for example:

- Habermas (1987): you show how you have attended to communication criteria, including the need for comprehensibility, authenticity, truthfulness and normative understanding (Chapter 8).
- Lankshear and Knobel (2011): you show how you have engaged critically with your thinking to check that you have shown awareness of normative contexts.
- Said (1994): you show how you have exercised intellectual engagement and critical thinking about that engagement: you have demonstrated meta-cognitive awareness, and you respect the rights of others to disagree with you.

All these validity tests act as objective tests for whether you communicate how you judge the quality of your practice, research and writing. However, the question remains about how you justify your research as a reflection of what you understand as a good life.

How do we justify what we are doing?

Identifying criteria and standards for testing the validity of knowledge claims is fine so far. However, in considerations about how action research may contribute to leading a good life, or how it might reflect a good life, we are still short of the mark. Although we analyse how we justify our action, research and writing, we still do not demonstrate how we justify the values underpinning those practices. This must be a key ethical criterion in making judgements about the quality of action research, or indeed any research. Staying at the level of technical analysis allows Al Capone to justify his practices of killing people to achieve his idea of good order. We cannot therefore justify what we may consider to be a universal value, for example that no one should ever condone wanton cruelty.

Therefore, offering justification for the values that inspire action research means moving beyond testing the validity of claims. Focusing only on the details of analysis and what this may contribute to the field can mean losing sight of the field itself; and in drawing up formulae for justifying practices, we may forget the real-world purposes of the practices. Perhaps this is where the world of action research needs to rethink itself, as noted in the Introduction, for the aim of the dominant epistemology, representing the interests of dominant corporate and intellectual elites, is to try to analyse everything into independent elements that can be dealt with separately (Bohm and Peat 2000), and we run the risk of losing sight of wider purposes in the world. It is, as Bohm and Peat say (p. 16), rather like smashing a watch: 'for what results is not an appropriate set of divisions but arbitrary fragments which have little or no significance to the working of the watch'.

So, as in the Introduction, I return to the idea of human nature and its unfolding through the life of a person: how individuals realise their capacities for unlimited creative acts, their curiosity, creativity, original thinking, the use of language to reflect on these capacities, as well as attachment and loving relationships. In Chapter 11, I suggest that the realisation of human nature is homologous with the realisation of the natural universal order, as emergent, dynamic, transformational and coherent. If we can justify our values, we can do so in relation to how those values become realised as practices that show the reality of our human nature, in all its aspects. Some people realise some aspects, but not others; Al would have shown great creativity, yet not a great capacity for dialogue, because dialogue implies openness to speaking with everyone. It could be a case of arrested development in one area while other areas develop to their full potential.

So I will take human nature as my yardstick for justifying my choice of values: do my values count as the basis for how I am realising my human potential through enabling others to do the same? Do I enable others to grow, and make wise choices about how they grow? Do I encourage dialogical critique, to find better ways of thinking and being?

If so, the issue then arises whether we can articulate the significance of what we are doing.

How do we articulate the significance of what we are doing?

The realisation of these ideas could have far-reaching significance for new ways of judging quality in action research. Here are some possibilities.

You are contributing to a more rigorously theorised conceptualisation of the origins, nature and uses of action research, and its justification as a preferred methodology. The contemporary literatures of action research, including my own previous contributions, aim to describe and explain action research processes and justify them in relation to methodological, social and political issues. They show, for example, how action researchers are contributing to the education of themselves, their peers and their social formations, drawing on their values as their dynamic standards of judgement. They do not so far aim to justify why they choose those values. Al remains free to exercise his law at the expense of other people's wellbeing.

You can explain and show how you are realising your humanity, and providing the conditions for its realisation. Al could not do this because he could not demonstrate a dialogical stance in relation to all that is a feature of human nature. You are showing how you are doing this at the level of practice (you are realising your capacity for agency) and theory (and for critical thinking). You are also communicating what you are doing in a way that demonstrates your responsibility to the other by being honest and clear about your meanings, speaking in a language they will understand

– and using this capacity for communicative action to influence practices in the social world.

You are contributing to new understandings of how values may be articulated as virtues (the good), at epistemological, personal, social and political levels. You are contributing to theorisations about which values should count as good – virtues – and how this can be done. Virtues, for me, would be those values-transformed-into-practice that show the realisation of human nature in its full structure. Al had strong family values but few dialogical ones, except for those people he cared about (see Deirdre Capone 2011).

In my view, what makes a value a virtue is when the practitioner holds the value as normative and can justify this stance by showing its unfolding in practice and explaining this as an aspect of human capacity. You explain why you hold as normative a value of, say, kindness, rather than cruelty, while acknowledging that entire groups of people may be persuaded to believe in values that deny kindness. Your task in action research and in your reports is to explain why you are articulating some of your values as virtues, such as when you say you practise in the direction of kindness. For example, you could claim *parrhesia* as a virtue, because you show that you are accepting the responsibility of speaking for yourself out of a sense of accountability to the other. Or you could say you are developing new practices of client-centred care aimed at serving the interests of your clients; you judge the quality of your care in relation to clients' feedback, and you explain the justification for your choice of this value as a virtue in relation to how you are contributing to the realisation of their and your humanity, as part of the unfolding of the natural order.

Contributing to new thinking about what counts as good quality practice, research and communication, and how good quality may be judged. You are contributing to new ideas about what kind of epistemology is appropriate for person-centred practices and how this may transform into living practices. This kind of epistemology is informed by inter-relational logics that enable people to exercise their capacities for original critical thinking and choice-making. You are reconceptualising action research from its current focus on improving procedures and techniques to a holistic view of how you live well in the world. You are moving from knowledge to wisdom: you explain and justify why you choose to live like this. You are influencing people's thinking so they can realise their potentials for changing their own systems.

Here is a case study from Pip Bruce Ferguson of the University of Waikato, which shows how she made judgements about the quality of her work using identified criteria and standards, and related it to wider human purposes. This was a presentation at the 'Value and Virtue in Practice-Based Research' conference, held at York St John University in July 2012.

Case study: Pip Bruce Ferguson, New Zealand

Passion and pitfalls in action research practice

I first became aware of action research when undertaking my tertiary teacher training in the late 1980s. I did a two-week course in action research, and completed a small project. I was so enthused by the potential of action research that I based my PhD study on the approach.

Our institution needed to get staff 'on board' with research quickly, and I was able to introduce action research courses into their tertiary teaching programme as an option. I could then monitor how they used action research and so come to understand research processes better and write for publication.

I continue to find working with action researchers stimulating. In my PhD (Bruce Ferguson, 1999), I cited words that Jean wrote in 1994:

> For me, in my perhaps idiosyncratic understanding of action research, it is that ability to be able to share the passion, the awe, the wonder, the beauty, the delight in your own life with somebody else, to show that you really do delight in your own life, and each moment is better than the last, and help someone else to share that delight, and find it in their own life.
>
> McNiff 1994: 19

While sharing that 'passion and delight', I have also increasingly become aware that there are tensions in some of the ways I have worked with others. In my Master's thesis (Ferguson 1991), I explored injustices applied via the education system to Māori students, so many were disadvantaged throughout their lives. In subsequent research, I have come to see that challenging such injustice can be fraught with danger when 'the goldfish doesn't see the water' (Ferguson and Ferguson 2010). Sometimes, even with the best intentions, we take action that aims to improve practice but can have pernicious effects that we hadn't anticipated.

This situation has caused me to engage in rather more introspective and critical action research than when I first came across the approach. I am challenged in this development by Whitehead's living educational theories work (see, for instance, Whitehead 2010). On the front page of his website www.actionresearch.net, Whitehead writes:

> In a living educational theory approach to action research, individuals hold their lives to account by producing explanations of their educational influences in their own learning in enquiries of the kind, 'How am I improving what I am doing?' They do this in contexts where they are seeking to live the values they use to give life meaning and purpose as fully as they can.

This can often be uncomfortable, as we strive to achieve what Freire (1970) referred to as 'emancipatory' education, but which can sometimes have constraining and occasionally even negative effects for those involved in our practice. The 'goldfish' paper and two papers presented to the Value and Virtue in

Practice-Based Research conference at York St John University in 2012, describe some of these tensions, where I concluded:

> If we, as educators, are to hold ourselves accountable for our values as articulated in our speech and lives, we will not necessarily have peaceful, safe lives. In our attempts to live out our practice and to be 'virtuous educators', we may give offence, cause dissension or expose ourselves to abuse even when our best intention is to rectify injustice. But if we exercise constraint in our practice in order to protect ourselves from these possibilities, we run the risk of perpetuating structural privilege; of operating hypocritically when we know we should do better; of preaching messages of social change that we are not prepared to practise ourselves. It may be dangerous, but can we ethically do otherwise?
>
> Bruce Ferguson 2012

So, how do we judge our practices and how do we justify them? How do we develop knowledge of practice – i.e. how do we say that we know what we are doing and why we are doing it, and show the rationality and justification for what we are saying? Furthermore, how do we use our knowledge, and what do we use our knowledge for? How is the knowledge legitimised by others?

These issues are explored now in Chapter 11.

How do we use our knowledge?

Action research for good order

This Part is about how we use our knowledge for good order, within different types of personal, social and environmental order. The Part contains the following chapters.

Chapter 11: 'Action research for personal, social and institutional transformation'. The chapter contains ideas about how to use your knowledge in ways that will help others and yourself create new futures.

Chapter 12: 'Action research for good order'. This chapter is about ensuring balance in the external and internal world through enquiry, and how people's stories of how they do this can constitute a people's history of action research.

There never was such a time for practitioners' knowledge to be valued and celebrated; practical theory has possibly come of age. However, dangers continue to lurk, and the field is not without its problematics. The question becomes, where is it going and will it last? These questions form the basis of Part V, with words of caution, while always emphasising the hopes and prospects in store for action researchers.

Chapter 11

Action research for personal, social and institutional transformation

These ideas about knowledge production and its uses now need to be located within broader contexts to do with human purposes. The questions 'What do we know?', 'How do we come to know?' and 'How do we use and share our knowledge?' need to be contextualised within questions that ask, 'Knowledge for what?' Also, the 'what' does not necessarily imply benefit for everyone. If education is about encouraging people to re-create and speak for themselves, we must accept that they will say and do things with which we do not necessarily agree. The 'what' could be to do with the distribution of instruments of torture as much as with food to the hungry. The 'what' is deeply problematic.

Remember that knowledge is the basis for action: we act in response to what we think is true. If we think that people and the world are in a constant process of self-development, as part of a natural order, we will try to provide appropriate conditions to support that development. If we believe that people should do as they are told, as part of an imperialist order, we will do our best to make sure they do so. It becomes a conflict of visions (Sowell 1987) and a struggle for the legitimation of a particular view of order.

Remember also that action research is always conducted within a socio-economic, political and historical context; the current mood of the times appears right for its widespread take-up. Intensified epistemological and social change through practitioners' communicative action can be shown in the political world, disseminated through increasing levels of social interaction using Web 2.0 technologies (see below). This is forcing a rethinking of the existing epistemological and social order, away from the imposition of the established form of abstract knowledge, to the creation of dialogical forms. This also shows the strong relationship between your action research and the global order.

This spirit of change of course does not suit corporate or intellectual elites. Arms manufacturers would not wish for peace or public engagement in world affairs. So remember that, as soon as communities of practitioners decide to take communicative action for democratic practices, those same intellectual and corporate elites also take action to suppress it. Given that knowledge, action and power are tightly interpenetrated (Foucault 1980), it becomes a battle for knowledge, what counts as knowledge and who says so. (Ironically, the same struggle is now being played out within the action research community – see the Introduction and Chapter 13.)

The chapter explores these issues and is organised as three parts:

- The significance of your action research for the education of your intellectual and social formations.
- The struggle for the control of practitioners' knowledge and action.
- Examples of action research-based social and political change.

The significance of your action research for the education of your intellectual and social formations

Consider how your action enquiry can contribute to wider development. Consider what intellectual and spiritual resources you have in yourself, your companions and your action research, and how you can use these for social good, which may in turn be used for environmental good. Consider how you need to do your best to work for a social order in which people care about one another and their environment in safety and kindness, where they are free to exercise their unlimited capacities for curiosity, creativity and attachment, in equal measure, in whatever way is right for them. And consider how you can enable them to recognise that these inherited capacities, and therefore human and natural rights, are mutually reciprocal in relation with others.

Hannah Arendt (1958) considers this. Her two main guiding principles are freedom and plurality. By 'freedom' she means that we are each able to do something new, that life is about new beginnings, and our history ought not to stop us from engaging in the future. Arendt speaks about 'natality', the idea that when a person is born they bring something new to the world: 'the new beginning inherent in birth can make itself felt in the world only because the newcomer possesses the capacity of beginning something anew, that is, of acting' (1958: 9). 'Thy life's a miracle', says Edgar in *King Lear* (Berry 2000). Beginning something new, however, requires us to move into action: and the fact that we are born and have our place in the world means we need to use that place well, to speak with authority about those things we know to be true. This introduces what Arendt calls plurality, for we live in a world in which others are born too. We must be in relation with them, first, because they exist and become our public, so we need to act with them in mind; and second, because we need others to help us and to build networks and alliances for getting things done in the world.

This has implications for action research, for in the world of education and professional education, each one of us who is able to think and speak bears the responsibility of speaking comprehensively, authentically, sincerely and appropriately, as Habermas (1987) says, on behalf of ourselves and of others who are not able to do so. It also becomes our responsibility to use our knowledge to create the conditions for all to speak for themselves. As an action researcher, you achieve the power of speaking with the authority of your knowledge, to offer descriptions and explanations for your practices. And although the capacity to know is yours by birthright, you have earned your present knowledge by dint of diligent and systematic work. Ian Malcolm, the scientist in the book and film *Jurassic Park*, makes this point when admonishing the initiators of the dangerous experiment of creating dinosaurs for their attitudes towards knowledge and power:

> Most kinds of power require a substantial sacrifice by whoever wants the power. There is an apprenticeship, a discipline lasting many years. ... You must give up a lot to get it. ... And once you have got it, it is your power. It can't be given away. It resides in you. It is literally the result of your discipline ... that kind of power has a built-in control. The discipline of getting the power changes you so that you won't abuse it.
>
> But scientific power is like inherited wealth, attained without discipline. You read what others have done, and you take the next step. ... You can make progress very fast. There is no discipline lasting many decades. There is no mastery: old scientists are ignored. There is no humility before nature. There is only a get-rich-quick, make-a-name-for-yourself-fast philosophy.
>
> And because you stand on the shoulders of giants, you can accomplish something very quickly. You don't even know exactly what you have done, but already you have reported it, patented it, and sold it. And the buyer will have even less discipline than you. The buyer simply purchases the power, like any commodity. The buyer doesn't even conceive that any discipline might be necessary.
>
> Crichton 2006: 306–7

It is the same for you and your studies. You set out with the capacity to learn, but no one gave you the knowledge you now have. You earned it. If you had simply picked it up somewhere, there would be doubt about the legitimacy of your claim that it is your knowledge, your original contribution to the field, and therefore about your status as a knowledge creator. Wenger (1999) speaks about this, too, when he says that belonging to a community of practice means you must live in it and not just be a visitor. Having earned it, it becomes a property of your thinking; and now it is yours and part of your being, it becomes your responsibility to share it as you share yourself with others, and with justification.

Also, by thinking and speaking for yourself, you have identified yourself as an intellectual, alongside other intellectuals. As noted earlier, everyone can be an intellectual if they have something to contribute to new thinking. Your next-door neighbours are intellectuals as much as are university workers, thinking and speaking their truth, albeit over the garden fence or in the pub. When we think anew and challenge received wisdom, we position ourselves as intellectuals, bringing new ideas into the world. But this raises the questions, 'How does one speak the truth? What truth? For whom and where?' (Said 1994: 65). And any responses to these questions have implications, because speaking one's truth usually comes with a price, as explored shortly.

Furthermore, the sharing of neighbours' and other practitioners' knowledge is now easier than ever before, in that what were once called 'alternative' forms of print-based literatures are now legitimated and even mainstreamed, as is the use of multimedia technologies. Print-based texts such as popular magazines, fanzines and diaries, once legitimated only within cultural and literary studies, are now widely used in educational research (Jenkins 1992). Collins (2010) speaks about 'bringing on the books for everybody', and technologies such as Kindle and audiobooks make reading more portable. Publishers also acknowledge this opening up by providing access through online interactive journals, online portals, virtual learning environments and book repositories. Knowledge creation, sharing and legitimation, through YouTube, listservs and social networking, have never been so fast, accessible or legitimate.

I see this emphasis on interaction between knowledge and technology as the onset of a third cognitive revolution.

A third cognitive revolution

In the Introduction, I suggested that we are entering a third cognitive revolution, in which different perceptions of the nature, origin and uses of knowledge become central. Here I wish to develop the ideas by linking technological and epistemological issues, and show how technology may be seen as a means of supporting the creative use of knowledge, and itself be seen as such.

The first cognitive revolution in the seventeenth century, says Chomsky (1996b), was grounded in a mechanical worldview and gave rise to an era of structuralism and behaviourism. This view was gradually replaced in the twentieth century, to make way for a second cognitive revolution, through the emergence of computers that represented human enquiry as interactive and autonomous. Pioneering cognitivists such as Chomsky, said Gardner (1987), 'showed little concern with the human brain or nervous system', focusing rather on 'the properties of thought ... simulated by the computer, or embodied in the symbolic products of a culture' (p. 394). Now, he said, there was a swing towards 'a different "modal view" of cognition, where psychological, computational and neurological considerations are far more intricately linked' (p. 394).

This heralded a more integrative future, achieved in the late twentieth/ early twenty-first century through a transformational process from analogue to Web 1.0 to Web 2.0 digital communication technologies, where information was increasingly easily manipulated and users offered a greater range of options (with Web 3.0 just around the corner). The transformation also emphasised that knowledge is embodied and resides in intuitive interactions. The differences between Web 1.0 and Web 2.0 forms of communication are that, while a Web 1.0 television screen or a website may be a digital form of communication, they offer fewer opportunities for interactive engagement than Web 2.0 forms of communication, such as Moodle or iPhone.

Web 2.0 communications technologies offer opportunities for the realisation of unlimited creativity, connectivity and communicative action, and provide the means to realise the embodied knowledge of persons as dialogical beings involved in communicative action. These technologies enable instant messaging to many, on a peer-to-peer basis. This was demonstrated through recent social movements, such as the Arab Spring and the London riots of 2011, when efforts were coordinated largely through mobile technology. Equally, mobile technologies were used by forces aiming to control these social movements, including the police and armed forces. Questions may arise about their different purposes, but the point remains that new means of communication are potentially available to all, to be used as they see fit (see below).

By analogy, these ideas enter debates concerning knowledge. Analogue technology is premised on a more linear form of thinking, paralleling the use of propositional 'know that' and procedural 'know how' forms of knowledge. Digital technologies, however, represent the dynamic interface between people, appreciating the user's intuitive, personal knowledge and the responsiveness of technology to it. So technological structures become paralleled by, and linked with, epistemological structures. Web 2.0 technologies represent both the freer unbounded use of knowledge as well as a shift in the ownership of knowledge with the users themselves assuming the power for knowledge creation in interaction with others.

This, however, represents bad news for those who wish to remain in control. Especially if they wish to remain in control of forms of theory, for the physical switch from analogue to Web 2.0 communications technologies parallels the cognitive switch from E-theories to I-theories, from the dominance of abstract propositional theory to an acknowledgement of personal theory as of equal status, where the knower is authorised to create their own theories of practice, which embed propositional knowledge and objective information within them. These shifts represent a political shift from the external control of thinking to its control by persons themselves.

Furthermore, Web 2.0 forms of interaction tend to be dialogical, anticipating that new insights will emerge through interaction, so all possibilities need to be kept open. The focus therefore becomes the nature of the relationships between participants in the dialogue, as the grounds for the development of new participative futures. Thus, the interrelated and transformational nature of interrelationships between mental and physical phenomena, and knowledge and culture, are highly evident.

Knowledge and power

These ideas need, however, to be considered against the fact that people are always caught up in socio-political contexts, in which the ownership of knowledge/power is perhaps the major issue (Foucault 1980). Those already in power will never give it up without a struggle, especially in the case of education, and professional education in particular. Education represents the future; autocratic power maintains the legacies of the past as the means for controlling the future. But this is no use in fostering the wellbeing of everyone: 'Knowledge has no real value if all you can tell me is what happened yesterday', says Feynman (1999: 25). This again raises issues about how people's thinking is controlled in democratic societies.

Chomsky (2000a) comments that, in totalitarian societies, it is easy to control people's thinking through torture and death. In democratic societies, this is more difficult, so those in power need to find more subtle means of control. One of the most powerful strategies is to play the opposition at its own game; thus, democratic means are used against democratically oriented citizens to ensure their compliance. Voting can be used to vote out the just as well as the unjust, and rhetoric can be used in ways that persuade people to accept false arguments and come to see the arguments as their own. People are seduced by a false consciousness to do what they are told and to claim that these were their ideas in the first place.

Here some examples from some current situations to illustrate these points.

The struggle for the control of practitioners' knowledge and action

Several recent major initiatives in the UK show how education and the professional education of practitioners are under attack across the age ranges, sectors and disciplines. Here are two examples. The first is the Cambridge Primary Review (Alexander 2009), focusing on primary education, an example of the control of education and knowledge. The second is the Lingfield Report (Department for Further Education and Skills 2012), focusing on further education, an example of the control of professional education and knowledge. In both cases, knowledge is controlled in the interests of established power-holders.

The Cambridge Primary Review represents a unified resistance to the state regulation of education and the imposition of an external theory of learning and education on primary teachers and pupils (Alexander 2009). Contrary to some official opinion, says the Review, primary education remains in good shape and is valued by parents, teachers and children, albeit recognising that some aspects need attention, similar to the situation in the secondary sector.

The Lingfield Review (2012 and ongoing), in relation to further education, also contains a sub-text about the politicisation of professional education. Following raging debates about whether or not teachers should pay membership for the Institute for Learning (the professional body for further education), the report recommends the removal of membership fees, while also recommending, as an unexpected broadside but as what now appears to be possibly the original intention, that teachers need not be qualified in order to teach: decisions about the suitability to teach would rest with employers.

Familiar issues about the legitimation of forms of knowledge re-emerge, as well as about the degree to which professionals should be knowledgeable, and what kind of knowledge is right for the job. The new criterion of 'employable skills', used now by universities in the accreditation of work-based learning, becomes a substitute for 'professional knowledge'. 'Employability' is frequently understood as the capacity to carry out tasks, not the capacity to think or ask questions or engage in policy formation. The overall organisational aim remains for managers and corporate elites to create policy, and for practitioners to implement it. Corporations remain in control of what counts as knowledge and who should be regarded as a knower. They dictate policy and pay lobbyists to support their strategies in limiting the amount that people can think; this may be seen as short-term thinking with a long-term price to pay.

Given that they also control most of the media, it is easy to endorse a view of corporate hegemony, such as the encroachment on small communities of large supermarkets, putting smaller firms out of business, while wrapping it up in the attractive neologisms of 'widening participation', 'customer choice', 'excellence' and 'improving standards'. So the culture of Big Brother and a stable world is perpetuated, underpinned by an epistemological tradition of not rocking boats and not fixing it if it ain't broken, frequently achieved through prioritising the desirability of factual and procedural knowledge that maintains a conservative agenda of stability. It acts as an equivalent for the Roman agenda of 'bread and circuses' as an appeasement to the masses, while covering up the real agenda of the exercise of power. 'Render therefore to all their dues: tribute to whom tribute is due; custom to whom custom; fear to whom fear; honour to whom honour', says Paul the Roman (Romans 13:7, Holy Bible, King James version).

'Fear to whom fear' – we learn to do as we are told, and are led to think this is our idea in the first place, a kind of false consciousness. We learn to welcome colonisation, and see it as a natural state:

> the native has been conditioned to perceive [the coloniser] as the most worthy subject of emulation. The native has been convinced, unbeknownst to himself [sic], that his authentic self is a worthless thing,

and that his only salvation resides in imitating his master, whom, at a conscious level, he imagines himself to despise. Who, then, is in charge? What is the nature of authenticity? What is to be made of the liberated native's determination to again become 'himself', if his sense of direction is provided by the indoctrination he has received?

Waters 2010: 9

This is where action research is basic to the argument, because you have researched your practice and produced your critically reflective account that offers explanations for what you are doing and what you know. You move into Web 2.0 forms of knowledge and into new public spheres; you interact with your knowledge and claim your place as a full participant. You are not a technician who applies others' theories, or offers only descriptions of your work: you are a knowledge creator, a theorist, who offers explanations for it. You are on a par, an epistemological equal, with others in the academic and corporate world. Your explanations of practice are as valid as anyone else's for contributing to policy formation and implementation. You potentially stand with the best.

Action research takes its place as a real-life dialogical practice within real-life socio-political contexts, not as a ready-made set of techniques in a toolbox. All practitioners may and should engage in knowledge creation with potential for personal, social and institutional hope for transformation.

Examples of action research-based social and political change

Here are two examples of action research projects that show these potentials, from Norway and Ireland.

Example 1: Norway

I work with colleagues in the Department of Health and Care Sciences at the University of Tromsø who are charged with the responsibility for recommending widespread government-authorised reforms in the nursing and health-care professions and service delivery, and for overseeing the implementation of these recommendations. My colleagues are university-based professional educators, with advanced knowledge and understanding of the profession and the field, and with pedagogical and academic knowledge. We are developing an action research approach to their work, on the basis that they need to develop new democratic and relational epistemological frameworks appropriate for the democratic and relational practices they are supporting. My work with them is to advise on methodological and epistemological issues to contribute to the smooth implementation of the reforms.

Three examples of the work are shown in the case studies in the form of proposals (edited from their originals) submitted to the 'Value and Virtue in Practice-Based Research' conference at York St John University, July 2012. The first is the proposal submitted by Bente Norbye, research leader. The second is from Anne-Lise Thoresen, a professional educator for midwives; the third is from Odd Edvardsen, coordinator of the practical training in the BA programme for nursing.

Case study: Bente Norbye, Norway

Decentralised nursing education – prepared for the future?

In Norway, Tromsø University promotes the development of flexible learning methods to reach out to students in the region. The system of decentralised nursing education admits students from rural areas of North Norway, using a blended learning approach that combines ordinary teaching methods with a variety of distance learning tools, such as videoconferencing and streamed lectures.

The research focus is to study the students' experiences from participating in an online module with a subject focus on the nutrition of the fragile elderly. This has a national focus in nursing. The research investigates whether it is possible to improve the quality of nursing students' learning through the use of online module delivery.

Focus group interviews were conducted with two groups one month after the students completed the module. The interviews were transcribed and analysed by two researchers using qualitative content analysis.

The provisional findings were as follows. The students found the online module motivating. Variety in teaching methods was important even if the discussions online were initially intimidating. The compulsory module challenged the students in group discussions online: the discussions went further and deeper than the students initially thought was possible and allowed time for them to reflect on the group's contribution; this was especially valuable for the more withdrawn ones. The subject was important for the students in their preparation for clinical practice. The flexibility of the module gave the students time to study as and when it suited their schedule, and links to research articles, national guidelines, online discussions and written work were clear. Taking the students' voices into account became a key criterion in assessing the quality of the research.

Case study: Anne-Lise Thoresen, Norway

Improving mentoring for midwives in clinical practices

This is a report of research in progress, about encouraging midwives in a practice setting to improve their capacity for mentoring midwifery students. The midwifery education postgraduate programme at the University of Tromsø lasts for two years full time (120 ECTS – European-validated credits), and during this period midwifery students are in direct clinical studies for four periods of 12 weeks for each of the two years of their studies. However, currently there is no demand or provision for formal mentoring education for midwives. The situation therefore becomes complex because some midwives do not necessarily see mentoring as a regular part of their practices, so it is important to help them see the reasons for focusing on mentoring.

The aims of the research were to help midwives develop pedagogical practices in relation to midwifery students; and to promote greater cooperation between university-based midwifery lecturers, practice-based midwives and midwifery students. We therefore developed a project structured as a series of university-based meetings for midwives. They then met, now as mentors, with midwifery students, in a clinical practice setting. This has been going on for six months (at the time of writing in July 2012). During the university-based meetings, we put in place a range of strategies, including reflective teams, lectures and seminars, reading groups, and logs as a form of reflective writing. The analysis of the logs became a key aspect of the research, because from the transcripts it was possible to identify four levels of analysis:

1 Writing up as a record of activities at the end of each day (reflections on learning achieved during the activities above).
2 Transcribing the learning logs to form one common narrative, which I then emailed to all participants before the next university-based meeting for discussion.
3 Identifying and extracting common themes from the analysis of the common narrative.
4 Writing up a research report and sharing significant ideas.

This research is potentially significant in that it contributes to new practices about learning logs as a means of professional education for midwives, and also to new thinking about the role of midwives as mentors in clinical practice settings.

Case study: Odd Edvardsen, Norway

Improving the experience of clinical placements for nursing students

Clinical placements and the supervision of nursing students on the BA programme in nursing at the University of Tromsø have been a priority in the curriculum. Nursing teachers are involved in the supervision of student nurses in different sectors of the health services. A collaborative pilot project was conducted, involving a group of university-based nursing education tutors (including me), and a group of nursing teachers from different parts of the health service. These were paired with nurses in the practice field, to explore how to improve the quality of their learning for the benefit of patients' wellbeing. The areas and settings we selected were a medical ward in a university hospital, a home-care unit in the municipality and a nursing home in a rural setting. Three pairs of nurse teachers and nurses took part in activities both in the practical field and in the university setting. Twenty per cent of their overall workload was allocated to their involvement in this project, aimed at improving the quality of nursing education in the clinical programme.

From data gathered in seminars and written reports from the pairs of teachers and nurses, preliminary results show improved cooperation between the university and the different health-care services, with an increased emphasis on the role of the nursing teacher as a supervisor in the practice field. Additional day seminars in health services, with a focus on students' learning, promote an awareness of educational responsibilities in clinical settings. Changes in the internal organisation of nurse teachers' responsibilities for the supervision of nursing students have added to the overall cooperation between the nurses involved in the students' clinical studies.

We are now considering whether these kinds of collaborative practices can contribute to improvements in the practical training of nursing students. We are also considering what may be the potentials of this closer cooperation between the health services and nursing education.

In Chapter 12, another story from Odd appears, to demonstrate how he has influenced learning beyond his own sphere, showing in detail the potential of transformational practices for social good.

Example 2: Ireland: The National Centre for Guidance in Education

The next case study is from Linda Darbey, Guidance Programme Coordinator for the National Centre for Guidance in Education (NCGE), Ireland. I have worked with Linda and the NCGE since 2005, on developing guidance programmes.

Case study: Linda Darbey, Ireland

NCGE is an agency of the Department of Education and Skills, established in 1995 to support and develop guidance practice in all areas of education and to inform the policy of the Department in the field of guidance (see www.ncge.ie). NCGE's remit includes the provision of Continuing Professional Development to guidance counsellors.

In 2004–5 NCGE developed the Whole School Guidance Planning programme to support guidance counsellors and schools in developing Whole School Guidance Plans, a requirement of the 1998 Education Act. The programme consists of three stand-alone modules, each delivered over a three-month period using a blended learning (a combination of face-to-face workshops and e-learning; http://vle.ncge.ie) and an action research approach. This methodology takes account of the unique context of each school and enables guidance counsellors to develop their reflective practice. To support the development of reflective practice guidance counsellors submit a learning journal and three reports, using an action research framework, for each module.

Guidance counsellors who successfully complete all three modules receive a Higher Education and Training Awards Council (HETAC) Special Purpose Award – Certificate in Whole School Guidance Planning at level 8 of the Irish National Framework of Qualifications. On successful completion of each module (10 ECTs), guidance counsellors receive a HETAC Single Subject Certificate.

Module 1 of the programme was first delivered to guidance counsellors in September 2005. Since then NCGE has delivered Modules 2 and 3 of the programme. To date, 279 guidance counsellors have participated in Module 1.

Peter Hyde, a Deputy Principal in a Cork school, has been a participant on the programme for several years. The case study box is an edited version of his final learning journal.

Case study: Peter Hyde, Ireland

5th May 2012

I have learned much by attending this course and engaging with others in what I term critical and reflective conversations, as well as from the inputs of the course tutors. I have learned about the need for teachers to make a greater contribution to debates on education reform. This was brought home to me when I attended the Association of Secondary Teachers, Ireland (ASTI) Conference last week for the first time, and I realised the power that teachers' contributions, grounded in evidence-based research, would make to national debates on education and education policy. What we do when we undertake action research, action planning and evaluation in whole school guidance (especially in the light of the increasing importance of self-evaluation) has importance and application wider than just guidance.

10th May 2012

Typing this in Helsinki as I am on an Academia exchange. When they talk about whole school here, they really mean whole school! Everybody works together for the good of the students and their learning. The guidance counsellor I am shadowing has many meetings with the team in the school: principal, school psychologist, school nurse and special needs teacher. They see it as everyone's concern to ensure students are learning and are happy. There is a huge emphasis in this school, and in schools in general, that it is the student's responsibility to learn. They talk things out with the students and ask them for their opinions and suggestions. They try things out and see if things improve and if they do, good, and if they don't, then back to try something else out: very much like an action research cycle.

6th June 2012

Since my last entry, I have given some thought to what this module and previous modules have meant to me. It has made me think especially about the profession of teaching and how individual it can be. Whole school anything, never mind guidance, can be a great challenge to staff in schools as it takes a shift in mindset from individualism to collaboration. I am not sure if all teachers are ready or open to engage in such a mindshift.

My learning has enabled me to think about things at a much deeper level, because it admits of values and their importance. This is different from the model of research that I thought to be 'real' research – the traditional or linear approach. It has made a real difference to my thinking about power and legitimacy in relation to knowledge. I think it was only during the second or third workshop in Module 2 that I realised what action research really involved, as a living practice. For me, the actual process was and is of far greater importance that the actual end product of what we achieved or perhaps did not achieve in our schools.

I found keeping a learning journal to be useful. It has allowed me the space to put down my thoughts, and in so doing to see what might be relevant to my practice. I don't mean only what I might do in my practice, but also how I might be in my practice. While the doing is important, I think the being is of greater importance as this is part of who we are and how we are: for me, these are the really important elements of teaching.

Action research can contribute significantly to personal, social and organisational development. How, then, can this be seen as a realisation of human capacity, and how is this relevant to debates about educational research? Chapter 12 aims to provide some ideas.

Chapter 12

Action research for good order

In the Introduction, I said that the book worked at several levels: as a guide to doing action research, as a report on my knowledge, and as a reflection on my practice. Here I synthesise these perspectives through the explanatory framework of order. 'Order' has different meanings, including 'arrangement' (the way things are) and 'community' (the groupings we live in). We need good order for balanced living; when things are out of order we lose our way. We need good order in our various orders so we know where we stand, not in a hierarchical sense but in that we feel rooted. We can use action research to help us.

In this chapter, I consider how, in explaining the potential significances and implications of our action research, we may contribute to good order in different orders. I call these a personal order, a social order and an environmental order, all embedded within and generated through a natural order. I also introduce the idea of history, because you need to know where you have come from to understand and explain where you are and where you wish to go.

There are different views of 'history': some people see it as the deeds and dates of famous people, told by an objective commentator (a linear order); Zinn (2005a) and others see it as a collection of generative stories, told by the people who make up history (an emergent order). This raises questions such as 'Whose history is it?', and issues of whether people must be represented or can represent themselves. I will go with Zinn, and show how the stories of action researchers have transformational potential for good order within emergent orders. I therefore link the idea of good order in human orders with the natural order, i.e. the way things are in the universe. I also make the point that self-interested people try to turn their own imperialist orders into a kind of natural order; whether they succeed is up to us.

The chapter is organised as follows:

*   Different orders, different visions
*   Orders and history
*   Action research stories for a new history for a natural order

Different orders, different visions

Consider the idea of natural order. Some writers speak about life as a realisation of a natural order (Bohm 1983; Feynman 2001; see especially Spinoza 1996, and also Deleuze 1988). They explain how everything is interconnected, in process of emergence and transformation; according to Spinoza (Yovel 1992), everything is immanent in and emerges from itself, and transforms into more developed forms of itself. In Bohm and Peat's language (2000), the natural order is implicate and generative; in the language of complexity theory, everything is self-embedded and emergent. Whatever is, contains its own past, present and future already within itself and emerges out of itself, in an unstoppable process of growth. Growth in one part of the system means growth in all, so the whole becomes more than the sum of its parts. We are always growing.

You need not go far to see this. You can see an environmental order in action in gardens, where plants, foxes and hedgehogs thrive, provided they are left alone to do so. Animals, including humans, sleep and wake according to cycles of day and night, spontaneously self-organise (Ridley 1997) and grow together (Abrams 2011). Systems are interrelated: 'nature has a simplicity and therefore a great beauty' (Feynman 1992: 173). Spinoza (1996) says this is the way things are; the system is self-justifying. Nature is ethical. Growth of everything together is the nature of the natural order, the way it should be. The environmental order and the natural order are commensurable.

However, descriptions of how things are are not the same as explanations of how things work. Nature does not need to give explanations for itself: 'what happens in nature is true and is the judge of the validity of any theory about it' (Feynman 2001: 97). When humans begin to explain how nature works (theorise it), problematics arise, for one person's explanations are not necessarily the same as another's. Sowell (1987) says that these differences of opinion often end up as conflicts of visions. He identifies two main kinds of vision: a 'constrained vision' that is grounded in self-interest; and an 'unconstrained vision' that sees openness and potential in everything.

This is where conceptual and political problems arise, and a strange structure of power emerges, because people's choice of vision and interests influences how they perceive their relationships. Many consider their interests more than they consider what they are interested in, and these interests themselves transform into a specific form of order. When people are mainly interested in profit, their technical and practical interests become the dominant order; this is an imperialist order, because the aim is to control: imperialism becomes a legitimate form of order. By clever sleight of hand, the imperialist order then transforms itself in the public mind into the natural order, the way things should be. It even gives itself the new name of globalisation.

This is happening in action research too. Instead of being seen as a methodology that helps us care for one another and our environment, action research is put into the services of those who wish to legitimate an imperialist order. They turn action research into a kitbag of techniques, to be applied to what they see as a gullible world and an opening for opportunism.

I resist this view, for it does immense disservice to practitioners and community, reinforcing messages that people may be used and that the imperialist order is the way things are. The outcomes can be grotesque. I was in Kuala Lumpur recently, confined to my hotel room because the open burning of the neighbouring rainforests, to make space for palm oil, created such a thick smog that I could not go out. In that same room, was a notice inviting me to re-use my towels to protect the planet. We are not protecting the planet when we re-use towels. We are protecting ourselves, for the planet will not die. It will survive in its own way and, unless we blow it up, run its due course. It will not be destroyed. We, the destroyers, will be; we are destroying ourselves. 'Protecting the planet' becomes another euphemistic sound bite used by imperialist corporations whose interests it serves to burn rainforests and, through subtle doubletalk, win public collusion in their crimes against nature.

Let me make clear this link between human interests and form of order. The natural order exists, and will continue to exist with or without us. The imperialist order also exists, fanned by the greed of elites, who manipulate the public mind so that people learn to agree with the status quo. They aim to persuade people that the imperialist order is (1) right, (2) the only order, and (3) the way things should be. It is little wonder why action research has always met with opposition, given that it actively challenges imperialism; and, now that overt imperialism is frowned upon, why it is being co-opted by governments to keep the 'common people' happy by thinking they have triumphed.

What is needed is for 'common people' to reclaim action research as their own, and create the kind of order they wish to have. Your action research is significant here, for you can show the generative transformational realisation of your own nature through the following.

Your influence in your own learning: you and your personal order

You keep yourself in good order. You show how you are influencing your learning through questioning normative assumptions and communicating your work in a form acceptable to accrediting bodies and the reading public. You legitimise yourself through demonstrating the validity and legitimacy of your research. You use this knowledge to help you influence the learning of others. You become a shape-shifter, like Berlin's (2009) fox that knows a lot about many things, and the hedgehog that knows a lot about one big thing. You see potentials for educational influence within the big idea that a natural order means change.

Your influence in the learning of other people: you and the social order

In their rationale for the 2012 American Educational Research Association (AERA) annual conference, the organisers said:

> The initial steps in preparation for this year's meeting involved a close look at the mission of AERA; 'to advance knowledge about education, to encourage scholarly enquiry related to education, and to promote the use of research to improve education and serve the public good.' Our mission *is* sound. We have been vigilant in executing the first half of our mission: We hold each other to high standards, we review critically each other's scholarship, and we invest significant time and energy in an effort to publish only the best educational research. But many of our education constituencies are much less aware of how we, as educational researchers and as an organization, go about promoting *'the use of research to improve education and serve the public good.'*
>
> Ball and Tyson 2012: 3, emphasis in original

We know much about procedures and principles in action research (Noffke 2009), and how people can influence the evolution of good social orders: the examples in this book are testament. You use your knowledge to help others find ways of contributing. You contribute to the education of your social formation or community of practice, intellectually, professionally and spiritually. You encourage them to believe in their own capacities. These social groupings influence the education of wider communities in different disciplines. The influence spreads; the Academy itself is influenced. Your capacity for communicative action enables them to develop the same capacity.

Your collective influence in the learning of global communities: you and the environmental order

Communities taking communicative action can contribute to good order in the world by raising awareness of the symbiotic relationship between humans and nature (Sinclair 2012). Human intervention is not necessary for maintaining the environmental order, but it is when that order is under threat through human greed and self-centredness. Unless this intervention is forthcoming, the planet itself will re-assert its rights for survival, as is happening now. You can do something about it through your action research, to show how personal and social practices are intertwined with the environment.

A case study from Julia O'Brien illustrates how a personal order can influence a social order: her story has the potential to influence others.

Case study: Julia O'Brien, UK

Following illness during my early years, and my subsequent success in publishing poetry, I completed an MA in Creative Writing and Personal Development. As part of this course I trained to facilitate creative writing groups within health and social care settings. I was also recommended to take at least a year's counselling training to support the facilitation of such groups.

One of my projects was to devise a creative writing workshop for people with vitiligo, a chronic depigmentation disorder of the skin, currently incurable. Sufferers develop expanding patches of strikingly white pigment-free skin often on the most visible and most sensitive areas of the body (face, hands, genitals). I read that the most devastating aspect of the disease was not the disfigurement itself but its potentially damaging quality-of-life consequences.

I developed vitiligo in my late teens. While planning the workshop, I wrote poems exploring my feelings around my experience of vitiligo. It felt good and also challenging to look at my emotions in this way, including my fears for my children.

I then focused on my studies and was surprised to discover a change in the attitudes I had adapted to my vitiligo over the years. Instead of covering up from head to toe (long-sleeved, high-necked shirts, trousers, wide-brimmed hat), hiding inside or under shady trees, I bought a silver UV golf umbrella for protection and began to wear sleeveless summer dresses. At our regular campsite I sat on the side of the pool in my bikini with bare legs paddling in the water, shaded by my umbrella.

Since completing my Master's I have published more poems and facilitated workshops in schools but have remained baffled at the quality-of-life improvements relating to my skin disorder. I now wish to explore the issue with other vitiligo sufferers as a possible doctoral research programme.

My supervisor lent me some books about research. One was on qualitative research, which introduced me to the language and rigour of the research world and its methodologies. I found it enlightening but felt no particular connection with the ideas. I moved onto *Action Research: Principles and Practice* and the possibilities of action research opened up. Jean's words struck a chord. I had been starting to feel overwhelmed by how little I know about academic research, and now I began to understand, particularly as a mature student, how much tacit knowledge I have and how I might learn to access and share that knowledge by contributing to the knowledge base of linking creative writing and chronic illness. I was particularly struck by the holistic and humane philosophy of this type of research.

What processes take place for different individuals when they express feelings about vitiligo in poetic form, and why? Through the facilitation of shared cycles of convening a group, writing and reflection, I can also explore and refine my actions as a facilitator to contribute to improving the quality-of-life outcomes for participants. This is an exciting and life-enhancing concept.

Orders and history

Stories like Julia's contribute to a body of knowledge that constitutes a people's history of action research. A people's history is emergent, transformational and interconnected, thus reflecting the nature of the natural order. In the traditions of an imperialist order, one person tells other people's stories on their behalf, from their own interpretations. The external narrator is sanitised from daily contact with life, like Roseanne Clear's 1920s Irish priest, 'sacrosanct, pristine, separate, as if separate from the history of Ireland itself' (Barry 2008: 56). Those stories can be misleading. When I was at school in England, my history books told about the Irish rebels who refused to accept British colonisation. When I went to work and live in Ireland, I could not find any rebels. Instead I found people who wanted to be free of colonisation; and I also was one of them.

Because people's stories tell the history of a place and people, they are bound to be contested. Columbus did not 'discover' America as official history books say. It was already there, populated with a rich culture, which the colonisers systematically destroyed, setting in motion an irremediable set of events leading to misery, disease and death (see also Zinn 2005a). Such experts who write history books take over people's lives, slyly and without consent.

I like the idea of a people's history of action research, a dialogical approach that lends itself to people's living accounts. Action research is about real people living together, in diverse places with their own cultures. People on the streets do action research, as I experienced through working in South Africa. Work with the teachers took me to the streets of Khayelitsha, so I took the university to the streets. When the teachers came to a teachers' centre for other studies, they brought their streets into the university. This is as it should be. Bayat (2009) speaks about streets as the sites for a politics of practice, where people he calls 'noncollective actors' sell their wares on pavements. I see this in Dubai, Delhi and Cape Town, and saw it in 1990s Dublin where women pushed old-fashioned sprung perambulators from which they sold illegally acquired cigarettes, and vanished when the Gardaí hove into view. Also, 'a large number of people acting in common has the effect of normalizing and legitimizing those acts that are otherwise deemed illegitimate' (Bayat 2009: 20). They have perfected 'the art of presence', taking 'direct actions in the very zones of exclusion' (p. 5). This is why I encourage people to celebrate their life stories. People living and working together form networks that mirror the natural order; their stories unfold and link with other stories to form a body of knowledge with transformational influence. Here is a story that contributes to this body of knowledge, by Mark Aldrich, who works in a prison.

Case study: Mark Aldrich

The rehabilitation potential of applied theatre

I have been the librarian at the Garner Correctional Institution, a maximum-security facility in Newtown, Connecticut, for the past 16 years, and have been helping inmates produce, direct, and write plays since 2009. I have also co-taught a writing class with Chris Belden, a poet and novelist. Inmates read and perform their plays for a small audience that includes the staff of *The Newtowner* Magazine, a local literary publication. Various prison and school officials, businessmen, and interested parties also attend. At one point, Lonnie Athens, a noted criminal sociologist, came to one of our performances: his interest in my work brought me to the John Jay International Conference on Criminal Justice, where I presented a version of this essay.

This past year, I enrolled in the Master's Program in Applied Theatre at the City University of New York (CUNY), School of Professional Studies, and have been bringing fellow students to the prison to help lead our theatre group, 'The Garner Players', in new and exciting directions.

The idea for the playwriting and performance group arose from discussions in the writing class. One inmate, an aspiring screenwriter (now released and making a documentary about a park in his community), began writing screenplays, and encouraged others to write plays. The men and I wrote short pieces on topics including a discussion between a father and son who had been estranged while the father was incarcerated, a job interview of a recently released inmate by a recovering alcoholic, and a disagreement between two friends who are writing the book of Genesis.

Rehearsals, as with any theatre production, were sometimes stormy and plagued by unforeseen developments, including the lockdown of a block when one of our stars got into a fight on the night before a performance. But things are changing: for about two years we did straight performances with little training – lots of hard work with talented men, but with little cohesion or group commitment. Then came applied theatre. Since the fall of 2012 and my part-time enrolment in the CUNY program, my commute from Connecticut has allowed me a space in which to think about strategies for presenting techniques I have acquired in class. I am able to try out ideas as soon as I have learned them, allowing me to experience, with exhilarating immediacy, the interpenetration of new theory and practice.

Applied theatre is outside mainstream theatre, and is usually performed in small community settings for marginalized populations, such as AIDS patients, the elderly, victims of abuse, the homeless, mentally ill people, and prisoners. Trained practitioners use techniques developed by Augusto Boal, who used theatre exercises and games to teach illiterate peasants to read. Applied theatre is different from drama therapy, although the results may be similar, and drama therapists – who are also licensed psychotherapists – address trauma in patients. Such trained professionals work in our prison.

My studies have introduced me to asset mapping, which concentrates on a way of engaging individuals and organizations as allies. This form of community organizing has helped me to gather people I already know in dialog about recidivism reduction. A businessman, John Santa, director of the Malta Prison Volunteers of Connecticut, is a frequent guest at our performances. He aggressively advocates for the employment of ex-offenders, and speaks frequently at business gatherings. He has introduced me to others engaged in similar community work. Kenny Jackson, an ex-felon from Bridgeport, Connecticut, who was a major drug dealer and spent 14 years behind bars, now heads the agency Family ReEntry. Vivien Blackford is, at the time of writing, chair of the Connecticut Coalition for Criminal Justice Reform and a member of the Connecticut Sentencing Commission. Both hope to attend future performances and support some of the men who will soon be on the street.

I want to bring influential people together to talk about combating recidivism with political activism. John Santa is open to gathering business associates, politicians, and people from the community to view video-recordings of our plays. This could help change public perceptions that inmates are the bloodthirsty, savage monsters on MSNBC's *Lockup*. Inmates' families may also be more favorably inclined towards them after viewing the work. Men report conversations with family members who are surprised at their progress. They also show concern for issues of relevance to their neighborhoods, and see ways of using their coping and problem-solving skills to address community issues.

Readings in class have included McNiff and Whitehead (2011), which suggests that practitioners investigate their own practice, and let their intuitive knowledge and values give direction to their work. This for me is action research. If my values include personal responsibility for allowing myself to be human, my teaching will reflect that; and my students will respond. Two applied theatre graduates, Wil and Michael, presented a two-day seminar to my students on what it means to be a man in prison. The students redefined the issue into the question, 'How can I be human in prison?' They eventually based plays on the tableaux and scene constructions from this class. Their process was remarkable for showing respect for others and recognising their own capacity for vulnerability and error. It is not easy to do this in a prison. They created knowledge through dialog, experience, and self-reflection, and their stories showed this. McNiff and Whitehead suggest that theorists these days are more in tune with these principles of action research. This is certainly true of the Applied Theatre Department at CUNY. My practice begins when I hop off the train in Connecticut, excited about ideas and theories that I then introduce to my students.

I am not proposing a plan magically to reduce recidivism, but I am suggesting that a start may be found in a consistent, steady commitment to a physically and emotionally safe place with institutional support in which individuals are treated fairly and with respect, with opportunities to participate in their own education. The men in my classes are excited about their potentials for effecting change in their community. One man, who will be released in nine years and regards that as being 'just around the corner', has just read a biography of Boal, and is looking forward to learning to teach forum theatre to young people. He observes:

> You know, when we were coming up, people used to talk to us, lecture us. Kids don't listen to that. If I'd had theatre at that young age, I can see myself as not winding up the way I did. I want to get to those kids who have nobody and give them their own voice through applied theatre. We can change things.
>
> Indeed, we can.

In July 2012, Mark wrote:

> One of the inmates who helped form my playwriting group is now an award-winning documentary filmmaker and is being honored in two weeks by the mayor of Hartford. He makes films about local heroes, such as 'Joe the Barber', who gives free haircuts and soup to homeless people. He also provides them with soup. If you go to www.JVHfilms.com, and to movie trailers, you can see an excerpt.

Action research stories for a new history for a natural order

I am speaking about developing a people's history, but ask whether I am actually contributing to one. Kiberd (1996) says that a country's literatures help shape its identity. I agree, but I am also aware how bodies of literature can help one community to colonise another, leading to new forms of cultural hegemony.

I am saying this because I have only fleetingly referred to cultures outside my own, in spite of having worked in their countries. I have reproduced their stories here without acknowledging the intellectual and cultural heritages from which the stories were born. I began to reflect on whether I have demonstrated cultural blindness while involved in the development of professional education programmes in those countries, and have also become alarmed at the outrageous arrogance of companies who seek to export their knowledge and knowledge systems to others who do not ask for or want them. This has made me wonder whether I am not doing the same thing. So I intend immediately to remedy my educational failings by engaging systematically with literatures outside my own culture, beginning with forthcoming return visits to those same countries.

One thing I do take seriously, however, is not to write about only unproblematic stories. MacLure (1996) cautions against representing research as only about 'victory stories' without also acknowledging 'stories of ruin'. I encounter many stories of ruin, when action research studies do not go smoothly, meet institutional obstacles, or are conducted in troublesome and often violent settings. Perhaps the most uplifting, for me, are those that show how people can learn with others to turn disaster into hope, and do things for themselves; this is what I also try to do. These are stories where the transformational capacity of action research is evident, when one person passes on their knowledge to others, who use it for the benefit of all.

Odd Edvardsen, with whom I work at the University of Tromsø, tells stories like this; the case study here is adapted from his Master's dissertation. Odd works with Tromsø Mine Victim Resource Center, which is connected with the University Hospital of Tromsø. Here Norwegian doctors cooperate with health personnel in mine-infested areas all over the world in training and developing health services. Since 1998, the programme in North Iraq has been led by a local doctor, Mudhafar Murad, who is in charge of both the training and the administration of the project. The case study is an example of embedded stories, showing also the transformational relationships between the storytellers and their stories.

Case study: Odd Edvardsen, Norway

After the 1980–8 Iraq–Iran war, the border area in Kurdish North Iraq was one of the world's worst landmine areas. Villagers evacuated by force returned to a mined battlefield, resulting in large numbers of dead and injured, with long journeys to the closest medical help service. In 1996 the Norwegian help organisation Trauma Care Foundation (see www.traumacare.no/) started an action research-based training programme for local first aid workers, in what became known as the Village University, to form a chain of survival from the minefields to surgery services in the city. Village-based first aid workers would learn how to deal with injuries to increase the chances of survival of landmine victims.

As a member of the Foundation, I needed to evaluate whether the programme was working for local people. My findings show that the project has gone far beyond expectations.

Kurdish co-workers and I conducted group interviews with first aid workers from a selection of Kurdish villages in the Suleimaniah province. This has given us increased access to the Kurdish world, and consolidated a network of actors in the local context. The survival chain has thus moved into local health institutions. Future challenges will be to implement the model within the public trauma care system in the province.

Here is a story by Hikmat, a local first aid worker who participated in the programme.

I am Hikmat, a medic from Tawela, a village located at the Iraqi border. It is in the Halabja district, a mountainous area, about 200 kilometers east of Suleimaniah City. This village has been occupied by the Iranians many times, and then again by the Iraqis. It became a battlefield between the two armies, and mines were planted everywhere. Some have been removed but many remain undetected.

After the Uprising in 1991, the villagers started to go back to their villages, including the people from Tawela, because life in the city was hard. The embargo was on, and villagers wanted to rebuild their houses and start farming, hoping for some income from limited trading between the Iranians and the Iraqis. Consequently, many people were killed or injured by the still-present mines.

At that time I was working as a nurse at our small two-roomed health centre. We had virtually no medicines or equipment – no gauze, IV fluids or IV cannulas, almost nothing. We had no idea how to deal with mine injuries. If anyone was injured by a mine, we would put on a tourniquet and immediately take the patient, still bleeding and in pain, along the rough mountainous roads to the hospital 200 kilometres away. Any help the mine victims got was the wrong kind. This was a daily problem for me, as the nurse in the health centre.

After the Trauma Care Foundation started their work in Kurdistan, in 1996, coordinators Hans Husum and Torben Wisborg visited my village and registered me on their first 15-day training course. It was 100 very hard hours of training. Day and night we learned. On completing the course, we got our certificates and backpack, or Burma-pack as we call it, and went back to our villages. We were confident and felt we could now treat the more serious cases.

We started implementing the Village University programme in our village, teaching local people basic first aid and life support. Our helpers would let us know of accidents in or around the village. We advised drivers that from now on they should not take patients directly to the hospital, or without a nurse or medic; we would treat them first and go with them to the hospital. We showed the Burma-pack to the villagers, assuring them that we had all the necessary medical equipment for any emergency. We also advised them that from now on we would go to the site of the accident to treat victims rather than have them brought to the health centre.

Here is a story about Abdul, one of the patients I treated.

It was a very cold winter's night, snowing hard, and most of the villagers were inside, sleeping or talking around wood stoves, mainly about how they and their families would survive. They could not work by day because of the embargo in Iraq, and going to the other side of the border in daylight to get food was forbidden. The only thing was to go to the Iranian side by night to try to get food for the next day.

Abdul was of one of those people, a young man, 20 years old. He lived with his parents in small rooms. His father had psychological problems, brought on when his village was destroyed by chemical bombs, and never left the house.

This incident happened one winter's night, in 1999, around midnight in the high mountains between Iran and Iraq. Abdul and his friend Massoud were carrying some kilos of flour about one hour from the village, from the Iranian side. Heavy snow covered the ground so it was impossible to see where the road was, and Abdul stepped on a mine. It was a Valmara, a fragmentation mine.

Fortunately Massoud had participated in our first training programme in the village. He turned Abdul upside down to stop the bleeding, and ran to the village to find me. I took my backpack and ran back with him to the site of the accident, accompanied by most of the villagers who had also participated in the village training programme. It was dark, but I had a headlight in the backpack. It took an hour and a half to get there. I found Abdul, whose legs had been bilaterally amputated, with severe injuries to the upper limbs and fragment injuries in the lower limbs. He was unconscious, but responded to pain stimuli. One of the villagers had brought warm water. Three of them compressed the femoral artery and the brachial arteries. Some helped to prepare the IV fluids and packing for the wounds.

I recalled everything I had learned from Doctors Hans [Husum] and Torben [Wisborg; two of Odd's colleagues] in the Village University, and all the necessary procedures. I put two big IV cannulas into the patient and gave him analgesics and warm IV fluids. I packed the wounds with gauze and put the elastic bandage in a cross pattern from the injured end of the patient's limbs to the groin and to the shoulders. We put plastic bottles of warm water over his chest and on the central parts of his body, covered him with four blankets, took him to the village, got a car, and from there went to the hospital. We used analgesics three or four times during the journey, and more IV fluids. The road was bad because of the ongoing war, and we had to pass between many army checkpoints. Abdul's family were frantic with worry, but when they knew that I was going with him and treating him they were somewhat reassured. I told them he wouldn't die; he would survive. The next morning we arrived at the hospital in Suleimaniah and took him to the emergency room. They carried out a bilateral amputation over the knee and he survived.

Abdul still lives in Tawela village, and makes local Kurdish shoes for his small business in the Tawela market. His father died, unfortunately, so he now supports his mother. He got married just a few months ago. Abdul and I are close friends; he knows I helped save his life.

Abdul was just one of the patients treated by the medics, using the knowledge learned at the Village University. It is known in the village that I can manage emergency cases, and I have confidence in the villagers' trust.

And that's my story.

When you do action research, you move into the business of saving lives. In the case of people like Odd Edvardsen and colleagues, you save lives in a direct and immediately visible way. In the case of people like Mark Aldrich, you save lives by helping people find themselves again. In the case of people like Julia O'Brien, you save lives by helping people to cope with an often hostile world and their own internal dilemmas. Here is the generative transformational power of action research, where what you do transforms into how you are and can be, and does the same for others.

I am making the point, I hope, that the natural order is generative and emergent. You are part of this natural order. You grow, and help others to do so. You contribute to life. In this, you justify your life through your influence in helping others do the same.

What stories do we tell of how we learn about our practices and use our knowledge for other people's benefit? Each person has their place on earth and is privileged to be alive. We contribute to new understandings, practices and histories that show what it means to be alive. We stay open to the world and life; we focus on the practice of being ourselves in company with others. The world turns as it does, and so do we. I think of Friedman's lovely story, of Rabbi Zusya who said:

> 'In the coming world, they will not ask me: "Why were you not Moses?" They will ask me: "Why were you not Zusya?"'
>
> Friedman 2002: 20

Perhaps this is the most stringent validity test of all: you show that you know who you are, and use your knowledge to contribute to saving lives, either literally or by helping people give meaning to their lives. In this, you and the world are truly blessed.

We now turn to a consideration of the relevance of these ideas for potential new directions in action research. As in our dealings with the planet, action research is being misused, through a misguided focus on technical interests. Emancipatory interests in many instances appear to have flown into space. The question is, should we attempt to retrieve them, or develop new orders, as is established tradition in human enquiry. See what you think.

Part V

Hopes and prospects

This Part contains one short chapter that asks: Whither action research?

Chapter 13

Whither action research?

This is inevitably a short chapter because it is still being written, and not only by me. What happens in the world of action research depends on the community of action researchers and our commitments to what we know and how we use this knowledge, as well as what we do not know and whether we need to know it. I have ideas, and set them out here. This requires a return to the idea of order, and how we see ourselves in relation to different orders.

I said earlier that 'order' and 'orders' can mean different things. Here are examples of what I mean by them.

When I was working in Northern Ireland, I often heard people say, 'That's the way things are because that's the way things are'. It took a long time to understand that they were not speaking about the things themselves, but the way things were. They were not speaking about living in a divided community, but the fact that it was natural to live in a divided community. That was the nature of their social order in the community. Many people disagreed with this way, and changed it.

Now look at what Mary Gauthier sings:

Fish swim
Birds fly
Daddies yell
Mamas cry
Old men
Sit and think
I drink

This is an example of a personal order. It is the way it is for the character Mary represents. She could do something about it, but she chooses not to. I know alcoholism and what it means. You can stop if you want to.

Here is an example of an environmental order. In my garden, I see this: mice run, birds fly, flowers grow, flowers die, old trees wither away, foxes play. This is the way it is in my garden. I can change this too if I wish. I could put down pesticides and kill the birds, foxes and flowers. I could stop them playing. These matters are all in my control.

What is not in my control is that the sun came up this morning. This is the natural order, the way things are in the universe. The grass will grow again when I am gone. The sun does not need me to rise; I need it to stay alive.

As humans, we live in embedded orders. There is a personal order (how we live as individuals) within a social order (how we live as groups) within an environmental order (how the natural context we live in lives). These orders are interrelated and transformational. Each level moves further and further away from individual control, but influence can permeate the entire system. We can influence how we live as persons and as groups. We have a certain amount of influence over our environments – we desalinate water to help us live in deserts, and create artificial wind tunnels to help us learn to live in the Arctic. We can exercise influence in the furthest reaches, although we may not see it over time and space. As our technological expertise grows, so we have greater powers of influence.

We have no influence over the natural order. No one can stop hurricanes or the tides. The natural order controls us. Perhaps we need to change our thinking about how we can exercise our agency as humans living on a host planet, not by choice but by invitation.

In *The Legend of Bagger Vance* (Pressfield 2001), Bagger Vance says that the game of golf can act as an analogy for life. He says that everyone has an Authentic Swing, which represents their Authentic Self. You cannot create this Swing. You can work at it with discipline and application, but the Swing is in you. You do not learn it; you remember it. You cannot find it; it finds you. 'It has no objective reality of its own, no existence at all save when our bodies create it, and yet who can deny that it exists, independently of our bodies, as if on another plane of reality' (p. 59). The Swing is not in our control: 'We cannot overcome golf by force of will' (p. 61). The natural order is outside, and inside. It invites us. We are part of it, whether we want to be or not.

Now let me return to Bohm and Peat (2000). They say that the natural order is one of growth and coherence; growth happens of itself. This is empirical fact. The difficulties set in when people begin to create theories about how the world works, and use only forms of thinking that analyse things into categories. They imagine that they can split reality up, when in fact reality cannot be split up: 'we increasingly ignore the wider context that gives things their unity' (p. 11). Analytical forms of thinking then turn into a reality themselves, a 'tacit infrastructure of knowledge and skills'. This tacit infrastructure becomes normative, a model; it becomes 'inseparably interwoven into the whole fabric of science as well as into its institutions, on which depends the professional security of each scientist' (p. 22). They become part of a fragmented institutional epistemology that tries to fragment phenomena and experiences, so it justifies itself by reproducing itself. Scientists and philosophers protect their ways of thinking because this means protecting themselves: 'the mind's strong tendency to cling to what it finds familiar and to defend itself against what threatens seriously to disturb its overall balance and equilibrium' (p. 22). So we impose our view of division onto a natural order that is itself undivided. This gets us into trouble. How to get out of trouble is to change our way of thinking and perceiving, how we think about how we think; this is in our control.

We can control and change the way we think about action research. Many people approach action research using a logic of control; they see it as a means of imposing order on people and on public perceptions of action research; it becomes codified, another classification. Action research is condemned to death; it loses its power for self-renewal, because renewal is in the act of renewal, not in the mind of another person.

I see action research as a form of thinking and practice that enables people to realise their capacities for growth, at personal and social levels. These capacities are in us; we do not learn them, we remember them. We remember that they are as they are, not because we make them so.

Social practices in Northern Ireland changed because people challenged the way things were; this first meant challenging how they thought by thinking anew. They changed their practices by changing their thinking. They kept records and consulted the records to help them remember the past so they could move forward; they did collective action research. They drew on MacDara Woods' (2001) idea of knowledge in the blood. They listened and remembered. They passed on their knowledge as teachers, to us. Their public is us: look at this conversation:

> Sir Thomas More: Why not be a teacher? You'd be a fine teacher; perhaps a great one.
>
> Richard Rich: If I was who would know it?
>
> Sir Thomas More: You, your pupils, your friends, God. Not a bad public, that …
>
> Bolt 1960: 4

We test the validity of our lives through the way we live and how other people experience us. Action research is a methodology of change. We can change our personal order and our social order, and to a certain extent we can change our environmental order. We can change understandings of action research and how it will develop in the future; perhaps it needs to be seen more as a paradigmatic attitude than a methodology. But we cannot change the natural order. Instead, we need to give ourselves up to it, and change our perceptions of its relationship with us.

Case study: Iris Stokes, Mexico

Love stories in action research

After completing a bachelor's degree in Spanish and working for six years in language instruction, translation and social work in the US, Spain, Costa Rica, Taiwan and Mexico, I accepted an offer to volunteer for a small non-profit organisation, being founded in a town in Yucatán, Mexico, primarily of Mayan descent. I found myself, accompanied by two friends, among the official founding members: a vibrant anthropologist from the Universidad de Guadalajara; the local shop owner *el genio*; the secondary teacher *el maestro chocomilk*; and *el psicólogo*. We soon signed into existence *La Casa de los Niños de Yucatán*.

We dreamed big. We wanted children to have a place for creative expression, to build a cultural center that revitalised traditional Mayan architecture and agriculture. I fell in love. I had to figure out how to stay once my visa ran out, so I decided to study. With the help of the Professor of Anthropology, I was accepted onto the Master's in Educational Research at the Universidad Autónoma de Yucatán.

I thought about what I wanted to do and found 'intercultural education', and I fell in love again. It was perfect, what I'd dreamt of. I wanted to develop an after-school programme based on the principles of intercultural education as recognised by UNESCO and based on the experiences of similar projects in other communities around Mexico and the world. My thesis advisor was another anthropologist, a native *yucateco* with years of experience working in other Mayan communities of the region. He introduced me to participatory action research. I had read Paulo Freire, so it was no surprise that I soon fell in love once more. We discussed how international discourses around intercultural education were flawed. All education is intercultural, but not democratic or equitable. Maybe action research could be a way to develop the right kind of intercultural education.

Now comes my real love story: why I'm really still here in spite of frustrations with the town, the organisation and myself. It's the story of a love that led to these realisations, almost two years on, that is shaping *our* future.

I realised that action research, like love, doesn't always make sense, but something feels right and we like being in it. I began to appreciate what was really keeping me in this community. I had a strong connection with one specific family, without whose support the organisation would not exist. Yet while my love for this new family was important personally, I didn't yet know its significance for my action research practice. That bond of family love was an essential aspect of my love for the community and thus of myself within it. I am a part of the community because I like being here and have a family here. You can't become a part of a community without falling in love with it, and if you can't really become a part of the community, you can't do real action research.

I care about the children and want, as do their parents, for them to have the best opportunities possible. I also like them. I like how they are. I don't want to change everything. I want to offer my solidarity and support in changing things they want to change, in understanding their reality, past, present and future, in relation to mine, and building new positive spaces with them.

I love that three-year-olds go to the corner store to buy candy unattended, sometimes in their underwear; that they (and now we) greet one another just calling out our names while passing by; that young and old alike sit on the sidewalk socialising, enjoying the refreshment of the night's breeze, that I feel comfortable with how they laugh at me when I wear their traditional clothing and know that I can laugh with them.

I was once asked early in my research, aren't you being invasive? Yes I am, I always am and always will be. I am *me*; wherever I go I will be imposing *me* on *them*. The differences between *me* and *them* will differ but I have to be *me* somewhere. The colour of my skin is a symbol that relates me directly to a dominant global culture; I cannot escape that. Even if I were not from where I'm from, people see me and assume that I am, and everything I do is looked at through that lens.

So I ask: How can I be here for such a selfish reason? What about my cause? Maybe action research works better when it goes beyond a cause. Maybe it's about wanting to be there regardless of the project. It's not about convincing people to join a cause, or act in a different way. It's about discussing life and trying to make things better when some are not convinced with their reality. If you can fall in love with people, it's not about the success or failure of a project or its improvement, it's about living and learning together. You have to let yourself fall in love. If you can't, then maybe you shouldn't be there.

Letting myself be loved

I am considering the other side of this love and its possible implications for my practice. I have often felt I have to hide parts of who I am to the community, but I am just as often proven wrong, and astounded by their ability to accept new perspectives, different behaviors; to laugh and still love me. I still haven't let go of that control. I know I need to be more transparent. They are capable of accepting me and working with me, for or despite who I am. Letting them know me completely (and hopefully love me as such) is also essential for my being a real part of the community and thus able to engage in what to me is real action research.

We need to see ourselves as recipients, learners, invited guests. We do not help the world to turn; it turns, and in turning, it looks after us. When we go into the garden, we do so as guests. We do so also when we arrive on the planet. Our job is to be the best we can be with these gifts, and stay true to our human nature, as it reflects the natural order of which it is a part. Thus we fulfil our responsibilities to the planet and ourselves. Zusya becomes Zusya; you stay true to your practice, because your practice is the person you are.

There is little doubt that action research is under attack, from both internal and external forces. Its original impulses were those of freedom and collaboration. This is going out of the hands of practitioners into the hands of intellectual elites, who live by 'the tacit infrastructure of knowledge and skills'; they work hard to insert this infrastructure into the public mind so that it is seen as normative; they turn freedom into their freedom and collaboration into a seller–client relationship. There is nothing wrong in seller–client relationships, but there is everything wrong in seeing knowledge and freedom as for sale. At the moment, many people in the community of action researchers are going along with these views. They are doing a kind of action research that denies the nature of action research, in the same way as when we claim colonial rights over a territory we are claiming ownership of land that is not ours.

Perhaps the most insidious form of subversion comes from many in the action research community itself, who uncritically internalise this tacit infrastructure of knowledge and perpetuate it through insisting on engaging in increasing fragmentation, battles for empire and a place in history. This needs to stop. Action research will not survive with its original commitments to freedom and collaboration intact unless the family of action researchers decide that this is where they wish to go.

You play your part too. Bagger Vance looked at the pathways of spinning balls in the dew, and said:

> 'The grain will shift tomorrow as the blades of grass follow the sun.' His hand traced an arc east-to-west in the sky. 'The same green will break differently in the afternoon than in the morning.'
>
> Pressfield 2001: 53

We can influence our contexts: we water the grass to help it grow. We leave patches of wild flowers for the bees; they need flowers more than we need lawns. We create opportunities for people to create themselves as they wish to be, in company with others who wish to do the same. We can do so too.

For my part, I will continue to run with the foxes. If action research is an attitude, then maybe this is how we should do it: with attitude.

Notes

2 How do we come to know? Linking theory and practice

1 This idea was given to me by Thérèse McPhillips on a plane back from Zambia, where we had been celebrating the end-of-project conference for the Zambia–Ireland Teacher Education Partnership (see p. 69). Thank you, Thérèse!

5 How do we do action research? Planning and doing a project

1 In earlier texts, I used the language of 'What is my concern?' However, I now appreciate that the terminology can be misleading. This was brought home to me strongly in July 2012, when I attended a meeting at the University of Central Lancashire, and colleagues there explained how easy it was to turn the word 'concern' into 'problem'. 'My practice is fine,' said a lecturer, 'although I appreciate that I need to produce evidence to show how this is so.' I have therefore abandoned the word 'concern'. I have in any case always understood it as implying 'something to be investigated' but am now concerned that 'concern' may be too readily seen as 'problem'. I do not see life as a problem, but as something to be engaged in, wondered about, and enjoyed.

References

Abrams, D. (2011) *Becoming Animal: An Earthly Cosmology*. New York, Vintage.

Alexander, R. (ed.) (2009) *Children, their World, their Education: Final Report of the Cambridge Primary Review*. Abingdon, Routledge.

Alford, C. F. (2001) *Whistleblowers: Broken Lives and Organizational Power*. Ithaca, NY, Cornell University Press.

Anderson, G. L. and Herr, K. (1999) 'The new paradigm wars: Is there room for rigorous practitioner knowledge in schools and universities?', *Educational Researcher* 28(5): 12–21.

Antonovsky A. (1979) *Health, Stress and Coping: New Perspectives on Mental and Physical Well-Being*. San Francisco, CA, Jossey-Bass.

Apple, M. (1993) *Official Knowledge: Democratic Education in a Conservative Age*. New York, Routledge.

Arendt, H. (1958) *The Human Condition*. Chicago, University of Chicago Press.

Argyris, C. and Schön, D. (1995) *Organizational Learning: Theory, Method and Practice* (2nd edn). London, Prentice Hall.

Bakhtin, M. (1986) *The Dialogical Imagination* (ed. M. Holquist). Austin, University of Texas Press.

Ball, A. and Tyson, C. (2012) 'Foreword', in *Non Satis Scire: To Know is Not Enough: Programme for the 2012 Annual Meeting of the American Educational Research Association*. Washington, DC, AERA.

Ball, S. (1990) *Foucault and Education: Disciplines and Knowledge*. London, Routledge.

Barenboim, D. and Said, E. (2004) *Parallels and Paradoxes: Explorations in Music and Society*. London, Bloomsbury.

Barrow, J. (1990) *The World within the World*. Oxford, Oxford University Press.

Barry, S. (2008) *The Secret Scripture*. London, Faber & Faber.

Bassey, M. (1992) 'Creating education through research', *British Educational Research Journal* 10(1): 3–16.

Bassey, M. (1999) *Case Study Research in Educational Settings*. Buckingham, Open University Press.

Bateson, G. (1972) *Steps to an Ecology of Mind*. New York, Dutton.

Bateson, M. C. (1994) *Peripheral Visions: Learning along the Way*. New York, HarperCollins.

Bayat, A. (2009) *Life as Politics: How Ordinary People Change the Middle East*. Cairo, American University in Cairo Press.

Bergson, H. (1998) *Creative Evolution*. Mineola, NY, Dover Publications. (Originally published in 1911.)

Berlin, I. (1997) *Against the Current: Essays in the History of Ideas* (ed. H. Hardy). London, Pimlico.

Berlin, I. (2002) *Freedom and its Betrayal*. London, Chatto & Windus.

Berlin, I. (2009) *The Hedgehog and the Fox*. London, Phoenix.

Bernstein, R. (1991) *The New Constellation: The Ethical-Political Horizons and Modernity/Postmodernity*. Cambridge, Polity Press.

Berry, W. (2000) *Life is a Miracle*. Washington, DC, Counterpoint.

Bertoft, H. (1996) *The Wholeness of Nature: Goethe's Way of Science*. New York, Floris.

Biesta, G., Field, J., Hodkinson, P., Macleod, F. and Goodson, I. (2011) *Improving Learning through the Lifecourse: Learning Lives*. London, Routledge.

Bohm, D. (1983) *Wholeness and the Implicate Order*. London, Ark Paperbacks.

Bohm, D. (1996) *On Dialogue*. London, Routledge.

Bohm, D. and Peat, D. (2000) *Science, Order and Creativity* (2nd edn). London, Routledge.

Bolt, R. (1960) *A Man for All Seasons*. London, Heinemann Educational.

Bourdieu, P. (1990) *The Logic of Practice*. Cambridge, Polity Press.

Boyer, E. (1990) *Scholarship Reconsidered: Priorities of the Professoriate*. New Jersey, Carnegie Foundation for the Advancement of Teaching.

Brown, J. S. and Duguid, P. (2000) *The Social Life of Information*. Boston, Harvard Business School Press.

Browning, C. (2001) *Ordinary Men*. London, Penguin Books.

Bruce Ferguson, P. (1999) 'Developing a research culture in a polytechnic: an action research case study.' Unpublished PhD thesis, University of Waikato, Hamilton, New Zealand. Available from http://fergs.org/wp-content/uploads/2012/01/PipPhD.pdf.

Bruce Ferguson, P. (2012) 'Viruses without vaccines, or valuing indigenous research? The tensions of introducing Western research assessment practices into an indigenous university.' Paper presented at the Value and Virtue in Practice-Based Research conference, York St John University, UK, July 11–12.

Buber, M. (1937) *I and Thou* (trans. R. G. Smith). Edinburgh, Clark.

Buber, M. (2002) *Between Man and Man*. London, Routledge.

Butler, J. (1999) *Gender Trouble*. London, Routledge.

Byron (2006) *The Prisoner of Chillon, with Other Poems*. Charleston, SC, BiblioLife.

Calderisi, R. (2007) *The Trouble with Africa: Why Foreign Aid isn't Working*. New Haven, Yale University Press.

Capone, D. M. (2011) *Uncle Al Capone*. New York, Recap Publishing.

Capra, F. (1996) *The Web of Life: A New Synthesis of Mind and Matter*. London, HarperCollins.

Capra, F., Steindl-Rast, D. and Matus, T. (1992) *Belonging to the Universe: New Thinking about God and Nature*. London, Penguin.

Carr, W. and Kemmis, S. (1986) *Becoming Critical: Education, Knowledge and Action Research*. London, Falmer.

Carr, W. and Kemmis, S. (2005) 'Staying critical', *Educational Action Research* 13(3): 321–7.

Chomksy, N. (1965) *Aspects of the Theory of Syntax*. Cambridge, MA, MIT Press.

Chomsky, N. (1986) *Knowledge of Language: Its Origins, Nature and Use*. New York, Praeger.

Chomsky, N. (1996a) 'The responsibility of intellectuals', reprinted in N. Chomsky (1988) *The Chomsky Reader* (ed. J. Peck). London, Serpent's Tail.

Chomsky, N. (1996b) *Powers and Prospects: Reflections on Human Nature and the Social Order*. London, Pluto.

Chomsky, N. (2000a) *Chomsky on MisEducation*. Lanham, Rowman & Littlefield.

Chomsky, N. (2000b) *New Horizons in the Study of Language and Mind*. Cambridge, Cambridge University Press.

Chomsky, N. (2010) *Hopes and Prospects*. London, Hamish Hamilton.

Chomsky, N. and Foucault, M. (2006) *The Chomsky-Foucault Debate: On Human Nature*. New York, New Press.

Clydesdale, T. (2009) 'Wake up and smell the new epistemology', *Chronicle of Higher Education* 55(20): B7. Available at http://chronicle.com/weekly/v55/i20/20b00701. htm?utm_source=at&utm_medium=en.

Coetzee, J. M. (2004) *Elizabeth Costello: Eight Lessons*. London, Vintage.

Coffey, T. M. (2008) *The Long Thirst: Prohibition in America 1920–1933*. New York, W.W. Norton & Co.

Collier, J. (1945) 'United States Indian administration as a laboratory of ethnic relations', *Social Research* 12: 265–303.

Collingwood, R. G. (1939) *An Autobiography*. Oxford, Oxford University Press.

Collins, J. (2010) *Bring on the Books for Everybody: How Literary Culture Became Popular Culture*. Durham, NC, Duke University Press.

Corey, S. (1953) *Action Research to Improve School Practices*. New York, Teachers College Press.

Cresswell, J. (2007) *Qualitative Inquiry and Research Design: Choosing Among Five Approaches*. Thousand Oaks, CA, Sage.

Crichton, M. (2006) *Jurassic Park*. London, Arrow.

Crichton, M. and Preston, R. (2012) *Micro*. London, Harper.

Cyrulnik, B. (2009) *Resilience: How to Gain Strength from Childhood Adversity*. London, Penguin.

Dadds, M. (1995) *Passionate Enquiry and School Development: A Story about Teacher Action Research*. London, Falmer.

Dadds, M. and Hart, S. (2001) *Doing Practitioner Research Differently*. Abingdon, Routledge.

Davies, P. (1992) 'Is the universe a machine?', in N. Hall (ed.) *The New Scientist Guide to Chaos*. London, Penguin.

Dawkins, R. (2006) *The God Delusion*. London, Transworld Publishers.

Deleuze, G. (1988) *Spinoza: Practical Philosophy* (trans. R. Hurley). San Francisco, CA, City Lights Books.

Department of Education and Skills Ireland and Ministry of Education Zambia (2012) *Learning through Interaction: Experiences of Collaboration in Teacher Education*. Dublin, Zambia–Ireland Teacher Education Partnership,

Department for Further Education and Skills (UK) (2012) *The Lingfield Report: Professionalism in Further Education: Interim Report*. London, DFES.

Derrida, J. (1997) *Of Grammatology*. Baltimore, Johns Hopkins University Press.

Dewey, J. (1916) *Democracy and Education*. New York, Free Press.

Dewey, J. (1938) *Logic: The Theory of Inquiry*. New York, Henry Holt.

Donn, G. and Al Manthri, Y. (2010) *Globalisation and Higher Education in the Arab Gulf States*. Oxford, Symposium Books.

Ebbutt, D. and Elliott, J. (eds) (1985) *Issues in Teaching for Understanding*. London, Longman/Schools Curriculum Council.

Educational Action Research (2010) Special Issue: A celebration of Bridget Somekh's contribution. *Educational Action Research*, 18(1).

Eisner, E. (1997) 'The promise and perils of alternative forms of representation', *Educational Researcher* 26(6): 4–10.

Elliott, J. (1976–77) 'Developing hypotheses about classrooms from teachers' practical constructs: An account of the Ford Teaching Project', *Interchange* 7(2): 1–22.

Elliott, J. (1991) *Action Research for Educational Change*. Buckingham, Open University Press.

Elliott, J. (1998) *The Curriculum Experiment: Meeting the Challenge of Social Change*. Buckingham, Open University Press.

Elliott, J. (2007) *Reflecting Where the Action Is: The Selected Works of John Elliott*. Abdingon, Routledge.

Everett, D. (2009) *Don't Sleep, There are Snakes: Life and Language in the Amazonian Jungle*. London, Profile Books.

Everett, D. (2012) *Language: The Cultural Tool*. London, Profile Books.

Ferguson, B. and Ferguson, P. (2010) 'Can the goldfish see the water? A critical analysis of good intentions in cross-cultural practice.' Paper presented at the 8th World Congress, Participatory Action Research and Action Learning, Melbourne, Australia, September 6–9. Available from http://wc2010.alara.net.au/Formatted%20Papers/1.3.2.EDU.2.pdf.

Ferguson, P. (1991) 'Liberation theology and its relevance to the Kiwi Christian.' Unpublished Master's thesis, University of Waikato, Hamilton, New Zealand.

Feynman, R. (1992) *The Character of Physical Law*. London, Penguin.

Feynman, R. (1999) *The Meaning of It All*. London, Penguin.

Feynman, R. (2001) *The Pleasure of Finding Things Out*. London, Penguin.

Foucault, M. (1980) *Power/Knowledge: Selected Interviews and Other Writings: 1972–1977* (ed. C. Gordon). New York: Pantheon Books.

Foucault, M. (1991) *Discipline and Punish: Birth of the Prison* (2nd edn). London, Vintage.

Foucault, M. (2001) *Fearless Speech*. Los Angeles, Semiotext(e).

Francis, B. (2010) 'Impact in education – or not? A challenge for BERA', *Research Intelligence* 111: 25–6.

Frankl, V. (1984) *Man's Search for Meaning*. New York, Pocket Books.

Freire, P. (1970) *Pedagogy of the Oppressed*. New York, Continuum.

Freire, P. (1972) *Pedagogy of the Oppressed*. Harmondsworth, Penguin Books.

Frenk, J., Chen, L. and Associates (2010) The Lancet Commissions: 'Health professionals for a new century: transforming education to strengthen health systems in an interdependent world', *Lancet* 376: 1923–58.

Friedman, M. (2002) *Martin Buber: The Life of Dialogue* (4th edn). London, Routledge.

Fromm, E. (1976) *To Have or To Be?* New York, Bantam

Fromm, E. (1995) *The Art of Loving* (revised edn). London, HarperCollins.

Fromm, E. (2001) *The Fear of Freedom*. London, Routledge.

Fukuyama, F. (1999) *The Great Disruption: Human Nature and the Reconstitution of Social Order*. London, Profile Books.

Furlong, J. and Oancea, A. (2005) *Assessing Quality in Applied and Practice-Based Educational Research: A Framework for Discussion*. Oxford, Oxford University Department of Educational Studies.

Gardner, H. (1987) *The Mind's New Science: A History of the Cognitive Revolution*. New York, Basic Books.

Gibbons, M., Limoges, C., Nowotny, H., Schwartzman, S., Scott, P. and Trow, M. (1994) *The New Production of Knowledge: The Dynamics of Science and Research in Contemporary Societies*. London, Sage.

Glavey, C. (2008) 'Helping eagles fly: A living theory approach to student and young adult leadership development'. PhD thesis, University of Glamorgan, UK. Available from http://www.jeanmcniff.com/items.asp?id=44.

Goethe, J. W. (1962) *Goethes Werke in Zwei Bänden*. Munich, Knaur.

Goodson, I. (2012) *Developing Narrative Theory: Life Histories and Personal Representation*. London, Routledge.

Goodson, I., Biesta, G.J.J., Tedder, M. and Adair, N. (2010) *Narrative Learning*. London: Routledge.

Gray, J. (1995a) *Berlin*. London, Fontana Press.

Gray, J. (1995b) *Enlightenment's Wake: Politics and Culture and the Close of the Modern Age*. London, Routledge.

Habermas, J. (1972) *Knowledge and Human Interests* (trans. J. J. Shapiro). London, Heinemann.

Habermas, J. (1975) *Legitimation Crisis*. Boston, Beacon Press.

Habermas, J. (1979) *Communication and the Evolution of Society* (trans. T. McCarthy). Boston, Beacon Press.

Habermas, J. (1987) *The Theory of Communicative Action*. Vol. 2. *The Critique of Functionalist Reason*. Oxford, Polity.

Hampshire, S. (2001) *Justice is Conflict*. Princeton, Princeton University Press.

Hargreaves, A. (2003) *Teaching in the Knowledge Society: Education in the Age of Insecurity*. New York, Teachers College Press.

Harland, T. and Pickering, N. (2011) *Values in Higher Education Teaching*. London, Routledge.

Higgins, A. (2000) 'Action research: A means of changing and improving the clinical learning environment', in J. McNiff, G. McNamara and D. Leonard (eds), *Action Research in Ireland*. Dorset, September Books.

Hitchcock, G. and Hughes, D. (1995) *Research and the Teacher: A Qualitative Introduction to School-Based Research* (2nd edn). London, Routledge.

Horton, M. and Freire, P. (1991) *We Make the Road by Walking: Conversations on Education and Social Change*. Philadelphia, Temple University Press.

Hoyle, E. (1974) 'Professionality, professionalism and control in teaching', *London Educational Review* 3(2): 13–19.

Hoyle, E. and John, P. (1995) *Professional Knowledge and Professional Practice*. London, Cassell.

Ignatieff, M. (1998) *Isaiah Berlin: A Life*. London, Chatto & Windus.

Ilyenkov, E. (1977) *Dialectical Logic*. Moscow, Progress.

James, A., Slater, T and Buckman, A. (2012) *Action Research for Business, Nonprofit and Public Administration: A Tool for Complex Times*. Los Angeles, CA, Sage.

James, G. (1991) *Quality of Working Life and Total Quality Management*. Work Research Unit Occasional Paper No. 50. London, ACAS, WRU.

James, M. (2007) *Towards a Living Theory of Theopraxis*. Working Paper. Twickenham, UK, St Mary's University College.

James, M. (2012) 'Developing a theopraxis: How can I legitimately be a Christian teacher-educator?' Draft PhD thesis, York St John University, UK.

Jenkins, H. (1992) *Textual Poachers: Television and Participatory Culture*. New York, Routledge.

Jenkins, R. (1992) *Pierre Bourdieu*. London, Routledge.

Jentoft, R. (2009): 'Facilitating practical knowledge by using ECT', Seminar. net. *International Journal of Media, Technology & Lifelong Learning*. Available from http://seminar.net/index.php/volume–5–issue–1–2009–previousissuesmeny–126/116–facilitating–practical–knowledge–by–using–ect (retrieved 16 February 2012).

Jentoft, R. (2009) 'Facilitating practical knowledge using flexible forms of learning in the education of occupational therapists in Palestine.' Available from http://www.ub.uit. no/munin/bitstream/handle/10037/2294/article.pdf?sequence=1.

Johnson, S. (2001) *Emergence: The Connected Lives of Ants, Brains, Cities and Software.* London, Allen Lane/Penguin Press.

Kauffman, S. (1995) *At Home in the Universe: The Search for Laws of Complexity.* London, Viking.

Kemmis, S. (1993) 'Action research', in M. Hammersley (ed.), *Educational Research: Current Issues.* London, Paul Chapman/Open University.

Kemmis, S. (2009) 'Action research as a practice-based practice'. *Educational Action Research* 17(3): 463–74.

Kemmis, S. and McTaggart, R. (1988) *The Action Research Planner.* Geelong, Deakin University Press.

Kemmis, S. and Smith, T. (2007) *Enabling Praxis: Challenges for Education.* Rotterdam, Sense.

Kiberd, D. (1996) *Inventing Ireland: The Literature of the Modern Nation.* London, Vintage.

Krashen, S. (1981) *Second Language Acquisition and Second Language Learning.* Oxford, Pergamon.

Kristeva, J. (2002) 'Interview', reproduced in J. Lechte and M. Margaroni (eds) *Julia Kristeva: Live Theory.* London, Continuum.

Kuhn, T. (1996) *The Structure of Scientific Revolutions* (3rd edn). London, University of Chicago Press.

Lankshear, C. and Knobel, M. (2011) *Literacies: Social, Cultural and Historical Perspectives.* New York, Peter Lang.

Lave, J. and Wenger, E. (1991) *Situated Learning: Legitimate Peripheral Participation.* Cambridge, Cambridge University Press.

Lawson, A. (ed.) (2009) *Action Research: Making a Difference in Education*, Vol. 1. Slough, NFER.

Lewin, K. (1946) 'Action research and minority problems', *Journal of Social Issues* 2(4): 34–46.

Lewin, M. (1993) *Complexity: Life on the Edge.* London, Phoenix.

Lilla, M. (2001) *The Reckless Mind: Intellectuals in Politics.* New York, New York Review of Books.

Longman Zambia/Ministry of Education (Zambia) (2001) *New Breakthrough to Literacy Teacher's Guide.* Zambian Primary Reading Programme.

Lyons, J. (1970) *Chomsky.* London, Fontana.

Lyotard, J.-F. (1984) *The Postmodern Condition: A Report on Knowledge.* Manchester, Manchester University Press.

MacDonald, A. (1999) *Dead Famous: Al Capone and his Gang.* London, Scholastic.

MacDonald, B. and Walker, R. (1976) 'Reading practice: Essays in dialogue and pedagogical conversation.' Unpublished Working Paper. Treforest, University of Glamorgan.

Macdonald, B. J. (1995) (ed.) *Theory as a Prayerful Act: The Collected Essays of James B. Macdonald.* New York, Peter Lang.

Machiavelli, N. (1998) *The Discourses.* London, Penguin Classics.

MacIntyre, A. (1985) *After Virtue* (2nd edn). London, Duckworth.

Macintyre, C. (2000) *The Art of Action Research in the Classroom.* London, David Fulton.

MacLure M 1996. 'Narratives of becoming an action researcher', *British Educational Research Journal* 22(3): 273–86.

Macmurray, J. (1957) *The Self as Agent*. London, Faber & Faber.

Macmurray, J. (1961) *Persons in Relation*. London, Faber & Faber.

Mahmoud Abu-Mallouh, L. (2010) 'How do I encourage students to speak English in their English lessons?' Available from http://www.jeanmcniff.com/userfiles/file/qatar/Qatar_Action_Research_booklet_email.pdf (retrieved 25 June 2012).

Marx, K. (1987) *The Eighteenth Brumaire of Louis Bonaparte*. New York, International Publishers.

Maslow, A. (1998) *Towards a Psychology of Being* (3rd edn). New York, Wiley.

Mason, J. (2002) *Qualitative Researching* (2nd edn). London, Sage.

McIntosh, E. (2011) *John Macmurray's Religious Philosophy*. London, Ashgate.

McKernan, J. (1991) *Curriculum Action Research: A Handbook of Methods and Resources for the Reflective Practitioner*. London, Routledge.

McKernan, J. (2007) *Curriculum and Imagination: Process Theory, Pedagogy and Action Research*. London, Routledge.

McLaren, P. (1995) *Critical Pedagogy and Predatory Culture*. London, Routledge.

McNiff, J. (1989) 'An explanation for an individual's educational development through the dialectic of action research.' PhD thesis, University of Bath, UK.

McNiff, J. (1993) *Teaching as Learning*. London, Routledge.

McNiff, J. (1994) 'Conversations with action researchers', *Action Researcher*, 1 (Spring): 18–19.

McNiff, J. (2000) *Action Research in Organisations*. London, Routledge.

McNiff, J. (2002) *Action Research: Principles and Practice* (2nd edn). London, RoutledgeFalmer.

McNiff, J. (2010) *Action Research for Professional Development: Concise Advice for New (and Experienced) Action Researchers*. Poole, September.

McNiff, J. (2011) 'New cultures of critical reflection in Qatar', *Educational Action Research* 19(3): 279–96.

McNiff, J. and McCourt, M. (2010) 'Professional education for teachers in Qatar for epistemological transformation in educational knowledge'. Paper presented at the British Educational Research Association annual meeting, University of Warwick, September. Available from http://www.jeanmcniff.com/userfiles/file/Writing/JMMCBERA2010Qatarfinal.pdf (retrieved 28 November 2012).

McNiff, J. and Whitehead, J. (2009) *Doing and Writing Action Research*. London, Sage.

McNiff, J. and Whitehead, J. (2010) *You and Your Action Research Project* (3rd edn). Abingdon, Routledge.

McNiff, J. and Whitehead, J. (2011) *All You Need to Know about Action Research* (2nd edn). London Sage.

Mellor, N. (1998) 'Notes from a method', *Educational Action Research* 6(3): 453–70.

Memmi, A. (2003) *The Colonizer and the Colonized*. London, Earthscan.

Midgley, M. (1991) *Wisdom, Information and Wonder: What is Knowledge for?* London, Routledge.

Miller, R. (2002) *Free Schools, Free People: Education and Democracy after the 1960s*. Albany, NY, State University of New York Press.

Mitroff, I. and Linstone, H. (1995) *The Unbounded Mind: Breaking the Chains of Traditional Business Thinking*. Oxford, Oxford University Press.

Murdoch, I. (1985) *The Sovereignty of Good*. London, Ark Paperbacks.

Naidoo, A. (2011) 'Towards a just world.' Paper presented at the Symposium 'Developing new epistemologies for strengthening the moral bases of academic practice', European Conference on Educational Research, Berlin, 12–13 September.

Nesbo, J. (2006) *The Devil's Star*. London, Vintage.

Newby, M. (1994) 'Living theory or living contradiction?', a review essay of J. McNiff's *Teaching as Learning: An Action Research Approach*, London, Routledge (1993)', *Journal of Philosophy of Education* 28(1): 119–26.

Noffke, S. (1997) 'Themes and tensions in US action research: towards historical analysis', in S. Hollingsworth (ed.), *International Action Research: A Casebook for Educational Reform*. London, Falmer.

Noffke, S. (2009) 'Revisiting the professional, personal and political dimensions of action research' in S. Noffke and B. Somekh (eds) *The Sage Handbook of Educational Action Research*. Sage, London.

Noffke, S. and Somekh, B. (2009) *The Sage Handbook of Educational Action Research*. Sage, London.

Nonaka, I. and Takeuchi, H. (1995) *The Knowledge-Creating Company*. Oxford, NY, Oxford University Press.

O'Reilly, P. (1994) *Writing for the Market*. Dublin, Mercier Press.

Parlett, M. and Hamilton, D. (1976) 'Evaluation as illumination: A new approach to the study of innovatory programmes' in D. A. Tawney (ed.) *Curriculum Evaluation Today: Trends and Implications*. Basingstoke, Macmillan Education.

Patton, M.Q. (2002) *Qualitative Research and Evaluation Methods* (3rd edn). Thousand Oaks, CA, Sage.

Pearson, J. (2011) 'Adapting the boundaries in primary physical education: An account of my learning, my educational influence and improved practice', *Educational Action Research* 19(4): 503–15.

Polanyi, M. (1958) *Personal Knowledge*. London, Routledge & Kegan Paul.

Polanyi, M. (1967) *The Tacit Dimension*. New York, Doubleday.

Popper, K. (2002) *The Poverty of Historicism*. London, Routledge.

Piaget, J. (1932) *The Moral Judgement of the Child*. London, Routledge & Kegan Paul.

Pressfield, S. (2001) *The Legend of Bagger Vance*. Bath, Windsor Selection, Chivers Press.

Pring, R. (2000) *Philosophy of Education*. London, Continuum.

Putnam, R. (2000) *Bowling Alone: The Collapse and Revival of American Community*. New York, Simon & Schuster.

Rawson, M. (2008) 'Was ist Waldorf? Eine Antwort aus Kosovo' [What is Waldorf? An answer from Kosovo]. *Erziehungskunst* 2: 170–2.

Rawson, M. and Richter, T. (eds) (2000) *The Educational Tasks and Content of the Steiner Waldorf Curriculum*. Forest Row, UK, Steiner Waldorf Schools Fellowship Publications.

Rawson, M. and Rose, M. (2003) *Ready to Learn: From Birth to School Readiness*. Stroud, Hawthorn Press.

Reason, P. and Bradbury, H. (eds) (2008) *The Sage Handbook of Action Research* (2nd edn). London, Sage.

Reason, P. and Rowan, J. (1981) *Human Inquiry: A Sourcebook for New Paradigm Research*. London, Wiley.

Riel, M. (2010) The Center for Collaborative Action Research@Pepperdine University, i.e.: inquiry in education: 1(1), Article 1. Available from http://digitalcommons.nl.edu/ie/vol1/iss1/1.

Renowden, J. (2012) 'A living theory of educational accountability: How can I create opportunities for student teachers and myself to learn?' Draft PhD thesis, University of Newcastle, UK.

Ridley, M. (1997) *The Origins of Virtue*. London, Softback Preview.

Rizvi, F. (1989) 'In defence of organizational democracy', in J. Smyth (ed.), *Critical Perspectives on Educational Leadership*. London, Falmer.

Robson, C. (2011) *Real World Research* (3rd edn). London, John Wiley & Sons.

Rorty, R. (1999) *Philosophy and Social Hope*. London, Penguin.

Rorty, R. (2006) (ed. E. Mendicta) *Take Care of Freedom and Truth Will Take Care of Itself: Interviews with Richard Rorty*. Stanford, CA, Stanford University Press.

Rudduck, J. and Hopkins, D. (eds) (1985) *Research as a Basis for Teaching*. London, Heinemann.

Russell, B. (1992) *Education and the Social Order*. London, Routledge.

Rutishauser Ramm, B. (2011) *Frieden Lernen: Friedens- und Notfallpädagogik als Herausforderung in Krisenzeiten* [Learning peace: peace and emergency pedagogy as challenge in times of crisis]. Basel, AAP Verlag.

Ryle, G. (1949) *The Concept of Mind*. Chicago, University of Chicago Press.

Sacks, J. (2007) *The Home We Build Together*. London, Continuum.

SACMEQ (Southern and Eastern Africa Consortium for Monitoring Educational Quality) (2010) *111 Project Results: Pupil Achievement in Reading and Mathematics*. Working document No. 1. SACMEQ.

Said, E. (1991) *The World, the Text and the Critic*. London, Vintage.

Said, E. (1994) *Representations of the Intellectual: The Reith 1993 Lectures*. London, Verso.

Said, E. (1995) *Orientalism*. London, Penguin.

Said, E. (1997) *Beginnings: Intention and Method*. London, Granta.

Said, E. (2002) *The End of the Peace Process* (3rd edn). London, Granta.

Sanford, N. (1970) 'Whatever happened to action research?', *Journal of Social Issues* 26: 3–13. Reprinted in Kemmis *et al.* (eds) *The Action Research Reader* (1983). Geelong, Deakin University Press.

Schön, D. (1983) *The Reflective Practitioner*. New York, Basic Books.

Schön, D. (1995) 'Knowing-in-action: The new scholarship requires a new epistemology', *Change*, November–December: 27–34.

Schwab, J. J. (1969) 'The practical: A language for the curriculum', *School Review* 78: 1–24.

Sen, A. (1999) *Development as Freedom*. Oxford, Oxford University Press.

Senge, P. M. (1990) *The Fifth Discipline: The Art and Practice of the Learning Organization*. New York, Currency Doubleday.

Sennett, R. (2011) *The Foreigner: Two Essays on Exile*. London, Notting Hill Editions.

Sinclair, A. (2012) *Transfer Papers*. University of York St John, York.

Somekh, B. (2006) *Action Research: A Methodology for Change and Development*. Maidenhead, Open University Press.

Somekh, B. and Lewin, C. (2011) *Theory and Methods in Social Research* (2nd edn). London, Sage.

Sontag, S. (2004) *Regarding the Pain of Others*. London, Penguin.

Sowell, T. (1987) *A Conflict of Visions: Ideological Origins of Political Struggles*. New York, William Morrow.

Spinoza, B. de (1996) *Ethics* (trans. E. Curley). London, Penguin.

Stenhouse, L. (1975) *An Introduction to Curriculum Research and Development*. London: Heinemann.

Stenhouse, L. (1983) 'Research is systematic enquiry made public', *British Educational Research Journal* 9(1): 11–20.

Stockdale, T. (1996) *The Life and Times of Al Capone*. Bristol, Paragon.

Stringer, E. (2007) *Action Research* (3rd edn). Thousand Oaks, CA, Sage.

Sun Tzu (2006) *The Art of War*. Stepney, Australia, Axiom.

Tallmadge, J. (1997) *Meeting the Tree of Life: A Teacher's Path*. Salt Lake City, University of Utah Press.

Taylor, P. (2011) *Talking to Terrorists: Face to Face with the Enemy*. London, HarperPress.

Thayer-Bacon, B. (2003) *Relational '(e)pistemologies'*. Oxford, Peter Lang.

Thomas, G. (1998) 'The myth of rational research.' *British Educational Research Journal* 24(2): 141–61.

Vico, G. (1999) *New Science*. London, Penguin.

Von Bertalanffy, L. (1968) *General System Theory: Foundations, Development, Applications*. New York, George Braziller.

Waldrop, M. (1992) *Complexity: The Emerging Science at the Edge of Order and Chaos*. London, Penguin.

Waters, J. (2010) *Feckers: 50 People Who Fecked Up Ireland*. London, Constable.

Watson, T. (2006) *Organising and Managing Work* (2nd edn). London, Financial Times/ Prentice Hall.

Wenger, E. (1999) *Communities of Practice*. Cambridge, Cambridge University Press.

Wheatley, M. (1992) *Leadership and the New Science: Learning about Organization from an Orderly Universe*. San Francisco, CA, Berrett-Koehler.

Whitehead, J. (1989) 'Creating a living educational theory from questions of the kind, "How do I improve my practice?"', *Cambridge Journal of Education* 19 (1): 137–53.

Whitehead, J. (1999) 'How do I improve my practice? Creating a new discipline through educational enquiry.' PhD thesis, University of Bath. Available from http://www. actionresearch.net/jack.shtml (retrieved November 2012).

Whitehead, J. (2010) 'As an educator and educational researcher, how do I improve what I am doing and contribute to educational theories that carry hope for the future of humanity?' *Inquiry in Education* 1(2), Article 2. Available from: http://digitalcommons. nl.edu/ie/vol1/iss2/2) (retrieved November 2012).

Winter, R. (1989) *Learning from Experience*. London; Falmer.

Winter, R. (2002) 'Truth or fiction: Problems of validity and authenticity in narratives of action research.' *Educational Action Research* 10(1): 153–4.

Woods, M. (2001) *Knowledge in the Blood: New and Selected Poems*. Dublin, Daedalus Press.

Yin, R. (2008) *Case Study Research: Design and Methods* (3rd edn). Thousand Oaks, Sage.

Yovel, J. (1992) *Spinoza and Other Heretics: The Adventures of Immanence*. Princeton, NJ, Princeton University Press.

Zinn, H. (2005a) *A People's History of the United States: 1492–Present*. New York, HarperPerennial.

Zinn, H. (with D. Macedo) (2005b) *Howard Zinn on Democratic Education*. Boulder, Paradigm.

Zuber-Skerritt, O. (1996) 'Emancipatory action research for organisational change and management development', in O. Zuber-Skerritt (ed.), *New Directions in Action Research*. London, Falmer.

Zuber-Skerritt, O. (ed.) (2012) *Action Research for Sustainable Development in a Turbulent World*. Bingley, Emerald.

Index